333693

GOTTFRIED BÖHM

EDITED BY SVETLOZAR RAÈV

GOTTFRIED BÖHM

LECTURES BUILDINGS PROJECTS

KARL KRÄMER VERLAG STUTTGART / ZÜRICH

HERAUSGEGEBEN VON SVETLOZAR RAÈV

GOTTFRIED BÖHM

VORTRÄGE BAUTEN PROJEKTE

KARL KRÄMER VERLAG STUTTGART / ZÜRICH

CIP-Titelaufnahme der Deutschen Bibliothek

Böhm, Gottfried:
Vorträge, Bauten, Projekte / Gottfried Böhm. Hrsg. von
Svetlozar Raèv. – Stuttgart; Zürich: Krämer, 1988
 ISBN 3-7828-1604-8

Gestaltung:
Svetlozar Raèv

Übersetzung ins Englische / Translation into English:
Peter Green

© Karl Krämer Verlag Stuttgart 1988
Alle Rechte vorbehalten. All rights reserved
Druck: Heinrich Fink Offsetdruck GmbH + Co., Stuttgart
Printed in Germany

ISBN 3-7828-1604-8

Inhalt

Vorwort	7
Geleitwort	9
Vorträge, Bauten, Projekte	
Wohnungsbau	15
Kirchenbau	69
Rathäuser	119
Theaterbau	141
Öffentliche und öffentlich-private Einrichtungen	185
Verwaltungsbauten	225
Städtebauliche Zusammenhänge	243
Biographie	309
Ortsregister	310
Fotographenverzeichnis	312

Contents

Preface	7
Introduction	9
Lectures, Buildings, Projects	
Housing	15
Churches	69
City Halls	119
Theatres	141
Public and Semi-Public Institutions	185
Administration Buildings	225
Urban Connections	243
Biography	309
Index of place names	310
Index of Photographers	312

Saarbrücken, Schloßplatz — Brunnenhaus

Saarbrücken, Schlossplatz — Well house

Vorwort

Die Veröffentlichung der sieben Vorträge, die Gottfried Böhm zum Abschluß seiner Lehrtätigkeit an der RWTH Aachen vor einer großen Zahl von Studenten und Architekten gehalten hat, stellt erstmals sein bisheriges Gesamtwerk, einschließlich Seminararbeiten, in thematischer Gliederung vor. Die Herausgabe eines Bildbandes »Gottfried Böhm, Bauten und Projekte 1950–1980« war 1982 vorausgegangen. Die daraus übernommene Reihe von Bildern wurde durch Abbildungen der neuesten Bauten und Projekte Böhms weitgehend ergänzt. Außerdem wurden Zeichnungen und Skizzen, die als Vorlage für die Ausführung von Wandmalereien, Mosaiken und Plastiken entstanden sind, hinzugefügt. Die Texte geben die frei gesprochenen Vorträge fast vollständig wieder. Auf eine Übertragung der gesprochenen Sprache in die geschriebene wurde verzichtet mit der Annahme aller Vor- und Nachteile, die sich daraus ergeben. Vor allem vermißt Böhm hier und dort den Einklang zwischen dem spontan Gesagten und dem von ihm selbst Gebauten. Und wenn er sich mit der Veröffentlichung der Vortragsreihe einverstanden erklärt habe, so mit dem Wunschglauben, daß man ihm dies nicht nachtragen möge.

S. R.

Preface

The publication of the seven lectures that Gottfried Böhm held before large audiences of students and architects at the close of his period of teaching at the Technical University of North Rhine-Westphalia in Aachen represents the first thematic review of his oeuvre to date, including seminar projects. It was preceded in 1982 by the illustrated publication »Gottfried Böhm, Bauten und Projekte 1950–1980«. The pictures taken from that volume have been complemented by an extensive selection of illustrations of Böhm's latest buildings and projects. In addition, drawings and sketches that served as models for murals, mosaics and sculptures have also been included. The written material reproduces the impromptu lectures more or less unabridged. The retention of the spoken form has its advantages and disadvantages. Here and there Böhm remarks a certain lack of consonance between his own spontaneous utterances and his own work. In allowing this series of lectures to be published, therefore, he does so with the request and in the hope that the reader will not take this amiss.

S. R.

Geleitwort

Svetlozar Raèv

Gottfried Böhm ist einer der bedeutendsten Vertreter der Nach-Bauhaus-Architektur, und dennoch wäre es falsch, ihn als »postmodern« zu bezeichnen. Sein bisheriges Gesamtwerk ist so komplex, daß es sich jedem schematischen Einordnen entzieht.
Gottfried Böhm erscheint als Einzelgänger, der von Konventionen etablierter Architekturrichtungen abweicht und oft einen Schritt vorausgeht. So war es, als die moderne Architektur der 50er Jahre und der Brutalismus der 60er Jahre die Architekturszene beherrschten, so ist es auch, seit die Postmoderne diese beide Richtungen ablöste. Hatte Böhm damals auf den Gemütswerten der Architektur bestanden, so warnt er heute vor historisierenden Übertreibungen, die zu sinnlosen Nachahmungen vergangener Epochen führen. War er damals gegen Verödung und Brutalisierung der Umgebung, so ist er heute entschieden gegen ihre Belastung durch unnötige Formspielereien. Man spürt, daß Böhm trotz aller Kontroversen zum Bauhaus an einigen Grundprinzipien dieser Schule – wie Strenge, Klarheit und Gegenwartsbezogenheit beim Bauen – weiter festhält.
Sein eigenes Leitprinzip – mit dem Begriff »Zusammenhänge« kurz zusammengefaßt – markiert sein Schaffen von Anfang an bis heute. Damit ist gemeint das komplexe Zusammenwirken von materiellen und immateriellen Komponenten eines Bauwerkes in der jeweiligen natürlichen und kulturellen Situation. »Ich glaube«, sagt er, »die Zukunft für die Architekten liegt nicht so sehr darin, noch immer mehr und weiter die freie Landschaft zu bebauen, sondern die Städte und Dörfer wieder in Ordnung zu bringen, indem man die Zusammenhänge in den Funktionen, Strukturen, Materialien usw. schafft«.
Die »Zusammenhänge« im Sinne Böhms schließen die passive Anpassung an die Umgebung aus. Sie verlangen nach Flexibilität und Variabilität bei der Integration von Altem und Neuem, Geistigem und Materiellem. Daher erklärt sich, daß er im Laufe der Zeit sehr unterschiedlich gebaut hat: einfach und komplex, bescheiden und monumental; mit Be-

Introduction

Svetlozar Raèv

Gottfried Böhm is one of the most important representatives of post-Bauhaus architecture. It would nevertheless be wrong to apply the epithet Post-Modern to his work. His oeuvre to date is of such complexity that it is impossible to place it in any schematic category.
Gottfried Böhm is an individualist who deviates from the conventions of established trends and schools, and who is often enough one step ahead of his time. Examples of this may be found in his work of the 50s and 60s, when the architectural scene was otherwise dominated respectively by post-war Modern Movement architecture and by Brutalism. One can also find an example of it in his work today, now that these two former movements have given way to Post-Modernism. Just as Böhm advocated emotional values in architecture then, so today he warns against historicist excesses that lead to meaningless imitations of periods of the past. Just as he spoke out then against a growing desolation and brutalization of the environment, so today he is a decided opponent of overloading it with unnecessary formal games and allusions. One senses that, in spite of all disagreements with the Bauhaus, Böhm continues to adhere to certain principles of that school, – a concept of rigour, clarity and contemporary relevance in building.
His own guiding principle – which can be summarized in the term creating »connections« – forms an unfailing part of his work, from the very beginning to today. What is implied here is the complex interplay of material and immaterial components of a building within its own natural and cultural context. »I believe,« he once said, »that the future for architects does not lie so much in continuing to consume ever more areas of open countryside with building, but in mending and restoring order to existing towns and villages by creating links between functions, structures, materials and so on.«
The term »links« or »connections« in Böhm's sense of the words excludes mere passive

ton, Ziegelstein, Glas, Metall usw. Wie auch immer seine Bauten aussehen – ob plastisch, expressiv, originell oder in Verwandtschaft mit historischen Vorbildern –, sie sind alle durch eine besondere Zeichenhaftigkeit gekennzeichnet, die manchmal – wie beim Rathaus in Bensberg und bei der Wallfahrtskirche in Neviges – in das Symbolische übergeht und dadurch die Kraft hat, Einzigartiges und Gewöhnliches in einer Zusammenschau zu einem einheitlichen Stadtbild zu verbinden. Die Zeichenfunktion von Architektur war in der Tat für ihn ein zentrales Thema, bevor in den 70er Jahren die öffentliche Diskussion darüber ausbrach.

In eben diesen Jahren interessierte er sich mehr und mehr für die Stadtbereichsplanung. Ein Schwerpunkt seiner Überlegungen war nun die Problematik der Zusammenhänge von privatem, öffentlichem und halböffentlichem Raum sowie die Belebung toter städtischer Zonen durch Einführung neuer Nutzungen und Funktionen, wobei seine besondere Aufmerksamkeit sich auf die Gestaltung von Straßen- und Platzwänden, unter Berücksichtigung des Zusammenspiels mit den Grundrissen der Randbebauung, richtete. Lehrreiche Beispiele dafür sind unter anderem seine Projekte für die Domumgebung und den Heumarktplatz in Köln, den Prager Platz in Berlin, die Schloßumgebung in Saarbrücken, das Lingotto-Viertel in Torino, das Stadtzentrum in Boston. Städtebaulich interessant – in der Doppelfunktion als Markierung und als Verbindungsglied zwischen zwei Stadtteilen – ist auch eines der letzten Bauwerke Böhms, das Züblin-Haus in Stuttgart. Darüber hinaus zeigt die große verglaste Halle dieses Gebäudes, wie man schöpferisch mit historischen Vorbildern umgehen kann, ohne in bloße Nachahmung zu verfallen.

Die Erkenntnisse, die sich aus der Koordination von städtischer Architektur und Städtebau ergeben, führen manchmal Böhm dazu, Bestandteile aus dem einen Bereich in den anderen zu übertragen. »Plätze«, »Gassen«, »Rampen« und »Brücken« erscheinen im Innern und/oder im Äußeren seiner Bauten und umgekehrt anheimelnde Elemente in seinen städtischen Strukturen. Solche ungewöhnlichen Konzepte verleihen der Architektur und ihren Benutzern eine unverwechselbare Identität, dem öffentlichen Raum eine besondere Intimität.

conformity to an existing order. It calls for flexibility and variability in the integration of old and new, spiritual and material qualities. That explains why, over the years, he has created buildings quite different in nature from each other, – some simple, some complex; some modest, others monumental; and in concrete, brick, glass, metal, etc. Whatever appearance his buildings may have, whether sculpturally articulated, expressive, highly original, or related to historic models, they are all endowed with a particular signification, which often merges with the symbolic, as for example in Bensberg Town Hall or the Pilgrimage Church in Neviges, and thus has the power to fuse unique and everyday elements into a cohesive urban image. The communicative component of architecture was indeed a central preoccupation for him long before it became the subject of public debate in the 1970s.

It was at this time that Böhm became more and more interested in aspects of urban planning. A focus of his thinking in this respect was the question of the links between private, public and semi-public spaces and the revival of defunct urban zones through the introduction of new uses and functions. In this context he was particularly concerned with the design of street faces and the enclosing walls of squares and other open spaces, seen in conjunction with the layout plans of the peripheral building developments. Instructive examples of this can be found in his projects for the redevelopment of the cathedral precinct and the Heumarkt in Cologne, the Prager Platz scheme in Berlin, or the proposals for the area round Saarbrücken Palace, for the Lingotto district in Turin, or for Boston city centre. Also of interest in an urban planning context – in its dual function as a development marking a boundary, and forming a link between two urban districts –, is one of Böhm's latest works, the Züblin Building in Stuttgart. Furthermore, the spacious glazed hall of this structure serves to show how one can creatively handle historic models without resorting to mere imitation.

The insights gained from co-ordinating city architecture and urban planning sometimes lead Böhm to transpose elements from one realm into the other. Squares, alleyways,

Das sind kurz dargestellt die Grundzüge des Böhmschen Werkes. Seine Persönlichkeit läßt sich, genauso wie seine Bauten und Projekte, in ein Schema nicht pressen. Auffallend ist sein undogmatisches Verhalten. »Wer die Kraft zum Sündigen nicht hat (...), der wird deshalb noch lange nicht zum Heiligen oder zum guten Architekten, sondern ist eher nur ein Langweiler«, sagt er in einem seiner Vorträge. Auffallend ist auch die Art und Weise, wie er denkt. Böhm – der Architekt, Bildhauer und Grafiker in einem – ist selbstverständlich ein Mensch des anschaulichen Denkens. Auf das Bildhafte greift er immer wieder wie auf eine unerläßliche Stütze zurück. Wenn er sich darauf einläßt, sich über Grundsätze der Architektur und Städtebau zu äußern, spricht er schlicht und vorsichtig, oft mit Unterbrechungen, die als der Versuch erscheinen, sich im Stillen dem, was richtig ist, anzunähern.

Es empfiehlt sich, die vorliegenden Vorträge in Kenntnis dieser besonderen Wesenszüge Böhms zu lesen. Sie alle sind gekennzeichnet durch eine zwar knappe, aber aufschlußreiche Darlegung der wesentlichen Probleme, die heute beim Planen und Bauen auftreten, wie auch durch die Erläuterung der Lösungen, die Böhm für sie erarbeitet hat.
Böhm untermauert seine Ansichten zum Teil mit historischen Beispielen, die bis zur jüngsten Zeit reichen. Mit allem Respekt, den er vor Mies van der Rohe hat, legt er das Prinzip »weniger ist mehr« neu aus. Anschließend plädiert er, im Hinblick auf die Ausdruckskraft von Architektur und Städtebau, für eine angemessene Betonung der Verbindungen von kleinen wie großen, elementaren wie komplexen Baubestandteilen. Sein Appell zur Wiederherstellung der Zusammenhänge von Strukturen richtet sich eindeutig gegen die »freie Planung« der vorangegangenen Jahrzehnte. Er selbst hat nie davon Gebrauch gemacht. Wie aus dem Bildmaterial zu entnehmen ist, hat er immer für klare Orientierungsverhältnisse durch Anwendung symmetrischer und asymmetrischer Ordnungen gesorgt. Darüber hinaus enthüllt das Bildmaterial andere Aspekte des ästhetischen Wollens und Wirkens Böhms, worüber er sich nur sehr zurückhaltend äußert, wenn überhaupt.

lanes, ramps and bridges, for example, may appear in one form or another on the inside and/or outside of his buildings. Conversely familiar-looking domestic elements reappear in his urban structures. Unusual concepts of this kind afford his architecture and its users a feeling of unique identity and lend the public realm a particular sense of intimacy.
In summary form, these are the basic features of Böhm's architecture. His personality can just as little be pressed into a preconceived mould as his buildings and projects. What is striking about him is his undogmatic behaviour. »Anyone who does not have the strength to sin will not necessarily be a saint or a good architect, – more likely a bore«, he said in one of his lectures. What is striking is his mode of thought. Böhm, architect, sculptor and graphic artist in one, is of course a man of clear and vivid thinking, who uses visual images as a indispensable prop. On those occasions when he allows himself to voice an opinion on the basic principles of architecture and urban planning, he speaks in a simple, cautious, straightforward manner, with frequent pauses, as if he were attempting silently to come closer to the truth.
It is worthwhile reading the following lectures with an awareness of these special characteristics of Böhm's nature. The papers contain a brief, informative exposition of the main problems confronting the architect in planning and building today and a description of the solutions Böhm found.
Böhm supports his views in part with historic examples that extend down to modern times. Despite the great esteem in which he holds Mies van der Rohe, he provides a new interpretation of Mies's adage »less is more«. Finally, in view of the expressive power inherent to architecture and urban planning, he pleads for an appropriate emphasis to be placed on the connections between the smaller and larger, elementary and complex components of buildings. His appeal for a restoration of the links between structures is clearly directed against the »free planning« concept of previous decades, – something he himself has never employed. As one may see from the illustrations, he has always tried to achieve clear orientation, using both symmetrical and asymmetrical ordering systems. The pictures also serve to reveal other aspects of Böhm's aesthetic will and influence, a subject on which Böhm himself has hitherto spoken with great reticence, if at all.

VORTRÄGE

BAUTEN

PROJEKTE

LECTURES

BUILDINGS

PROJECTS

Wohnungsbau

Seeg	Wohnhaus, 1946
Köln	Wohnhaus, 1955
München	Wohnhaus, 1969, mit Manfred Jäger
Porz-Zündorf	Wohnquartier, 1. Bauabschnitt 1973, 2. Bauabschnitt 1984, mit Hans Linder, Klaus Burk, Franz Kilian, Bernd Hellriegel
Bensberg	Kinderdorf, 1965, mit Wilhelm Jungherz, Hans Schmalscheidt, Franz Kilian, Manfred Jäger
Köln-Chorweiler	Sozialer Wohnungsbau, 1963, mit Werner Finke, Stefan Conrad, Konrad Schalhorn, Manfred Jäger
Düsseldorf-Garath	Altenwohnheim, 1962, mit Hans Linder, Hans Schmalscheidt, Franz Kilian
Berlin	Hasenheide, Wohnbebauung, Projekt 1980, mit Gudrun Wurlitzer
Saarbrücken	Talstraße, Wohnbaukomplex mit Läden und Parkhaus, 1978, mit Stefan Conrad, Stefan Abelen, Monika Adolphi, Reinhard Angelis, Simon Häußler, Markku Kari, Bruno Kauhsen, Stefan Schmitz, Federico Valda
Berlin	Fasanenplatz, Wohnblock, 1980, mit Hans Linder, Harald Thomä, Franz Kilian
Berlin	Prager Platz, Gesamtprojekt 1977, mit Harald Thomä, Georg F. Adolphi, Fritz Steinigeweg, Hermann Neuerburg
Turin-Lingotto	Fiat-Baukomplex, Gutachten, 1983, in Zusammenarbeit mit Stefan Böhm, mit Stefan Schmitz, Maria Mocanu
Salzburg-Aigen	Altenwohnheim mit Krankenhaus, Wettbewerb, 1986, in Zusammenarbeit mit Peter Böhm, Fritz Steinigeweg

Kurz nach Ende des Krieges habe ich zusammen mit meiner Frau das Seeger Haus gebaut, ein Haus, an dem eigentlich nichts Besonderes dran ist, aber ich wäre froh, wenn mir später alle anderen Bauten ebenso selbstverständlich gelungen wären. Das Haus steht im Allgäu am Rande eines Dorfes. Seine Mauern sind zum Teil aus Lehmstein errichtet, weil man damals gebrannte Steine schwer bekommen konnte. Dadurch sind die Wände dick und warm. Das Haus ist 10 m lang und 5 m breit. Es hat einen Küchenteil mit einem Erker von 1,55 m Breite. Das geht gerade noch als Größe und ist sehr gemütlich zum Brotzeit machen und Skatspielen usw. Vorne an der Südseite liegt das Wohnzimmer mit Kachelofen, dazwischen die Diele mit der gewendelten Treppe zu den Schlafzimmern im Dachgeschoß. Vor der Diele ist eine offene Nische, die gegen den Wind schützt, und bei Sonne ist sie sogar im Winter manchmal als Sitzplatz nutzbar.

Das Haus, ganz freistehend, ist ohne Bezug zu einer Straße, nur über Fußwege vom Ort aus erreichbar. Wie die Bauernhöfe der Umgebung steht es selbständig in der Landschaft, eine Zelle, die in sich selbst geschlossen ist und die in der Form

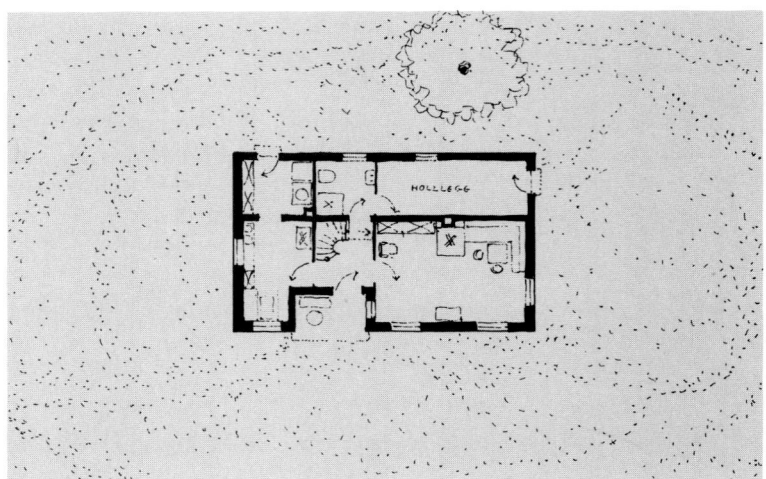

Shortly after the war I built the Seeger House together with my wife. It stands at the edge of a village in the Allgäu in southern Germany. The walls were built partly of air-dried bricks, because at the time it was difficult to obtain kiln-burnt bricks. As a result of this, however, the walls are thick and warm. The house is 10 m long and 5 m wide. There is a kitchen area with a recess 1.55 m wide. The size is just adequate, and it is quite a cosy corner for small meals, for playing cards, etc. At the front, on the south side, is the living room with a tiled stove; and between these two areas is a hall with a spiral staircase leading to the bedrooms in the attic storey. An open recess in front of the hall affords protection against the wind, and, if the sun is shining, it can be used as an outdoor sitting area even in winter.

The house is detached. It stands quite on its own and is not related to a street situation. From the local village it can only be reached by footpath. Like the farmhouses in the surrounding area, it stands independently in the landscape, a self-contained cell that establishes its own particular relationship to the environment and to nature through the form of habitation

des Wohnens ihr besonderes Verhältnis zur Umgebung und zur Natur findet. Noch deutlicher ist dieses Verhältnis vom Haus zur Natur bei den sehr einfachen Häusern, die ich einmal in Nepal gesehen habe. Dort gibt es viele einzeln stehende Bauernhäuser, rundherum die Natur, vor der man sich schützt mit der Öffnung nur zu der wetterabgewandten Seite. Die meisten dieser Häuser sind oval oder rund: der Urtyp einer Wohnzelle. Nicht weit von der Stelle entfernt, wo ich eines davon aufgenommen habe, steht eine Gruppe von Häusern, gleich groß, im gleichen Material wie die Einzelhäuser. Aber da auf einmal haben sie nicht mehr die runde, eigenständige Form; sie sind rechteckig und ermöglichen damit den Bezug zueinander, es bildet sich Nachbarschaft und schon so eine Art Straßenraum. Bei einer weiteren Häusergruppe ganz in der Nähe davon empfindet man dann ganz deutlich, daß der Straßenraum sich zu einem geschlossenen gemeinsamen Lebensraum für die Bewohner entwickelt hat. Die Öffnungen der Häuser – Türen, Fenster, Nischen – schauen zum Straßenraum hin, und dadurch entsteht wie von selbst ein mit öffentlichem Leben erfüllter Raum.

it accommodates. This relationship between house and nature is even more apparent in the case of the simple dwellings I once saw in Nepal. There one finds a lot of farm houses standing completely isolated, surrounded only by nature, from which the house is protected by restricting the openings to the side sheltered from the weather. The majority of these houses are oval or circular on plan: the primitive form of a habitable cell. Not far from the place where I took one of the photographs is a group of houses of the same size, and built of the same materials as the isolated examples. These, however, do not have the same round, independent form. They are rectangular on plan, which facilitates the establishment of relationships between the units, the creation of neighbourhoods and a kind of street space. In another group of houses not far away one can see quite clearly how the street space has developed into a self-contained communal habitat for the inhabitants. The openings in the flanking buildings – doors, windows, niches – overlook the street space, and this seems to give rise almost automatically to a realm filled with public life.

Das Wohnhaus in Köln-Weiss habe ich 1955 gebaut. Es hat eine andere Art der Beziehung zur Umgebung. Das Gebäude steht in einem Gartenbezirk, ist Teil dieses Bezirkes. Vom Eingang an einem kleinen Zufahrtsweg führt ein geradliniger »Korridor« durch den Gartenteil, den Vorhof, durch das Haus am inneren Hof entlang, durch den Wohnteil hindurch und wieder zu einem Gartenraum, der sich zum Rhein und zur dortigen Landschaft hin öffnet. Dem Gedanken dieses Hausbezirkes, von dem das Gebäude nur einen Teil einnimmt, entspricht auch der niedrige, durch offene Räume gegliederte Bau. Die Rankgerüste über dem inneren Hof und entlang der langen Glaswand verbinden das Haus noch stärker mit den

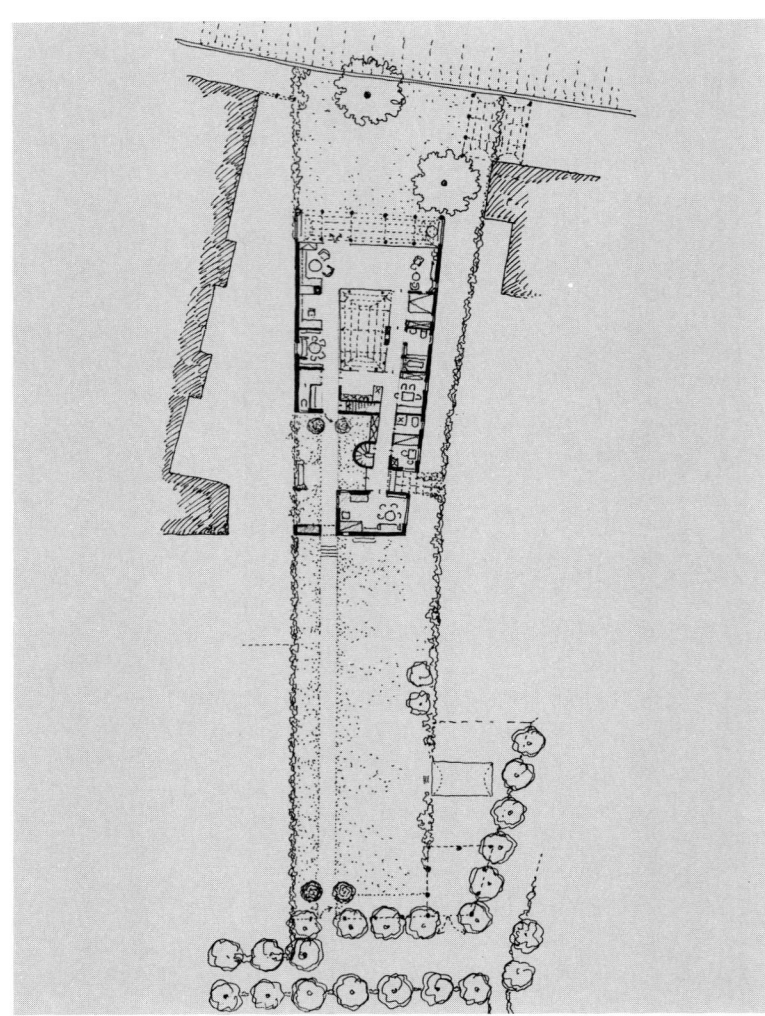

I built the house in Weiss, Cologne, in 1955. It has a different kind of relationship to its surroundings. The building is located in a park-like garden district. The entrance is reached via a small access drive. From here a straight »corridor« leads through the garden, the forecourt, through the house, along the interior courtyard, through the living area and into a further garden space beyond, which opens out on to the landscape and overlooks the Rhine. This low-rise building, articulated into a series of open, interflowing spaces, reflects the underlying concept of the residential district in which it is situated. The trellis-work over the internal courtyard and along the long glazed wall helps to integrate the house even more firmly

Außenräumen und dem Garten.
Die Räume rings um den inneren Hof sind nur 3,5 m breit, dafür ist der Wohnraum ziemlich lang. Und das ist gut, daß man irgendwo in einem Haus Platz hat, wo man auch ab und zu seinen Ärger ausrennen kann. Wir haben nachträglich Decken und Wände mit Architekturen farbig so bemalt, daß der Kontrast von Geschlossenheit und Öffnungen stärker und vielfältiger in Erscheinung tritt. Dadurch wird der gebaute Teil des Hauses noch mehr zu einem komplexen Gebilde, das im Gegensatz zu den Öffnungen steht.

with the garden and external spaces.
The rooms about the courtyard are only 3.5 m wide. The living room is, however, quite long, and that has its positive aspects, for it is necessary to have one place in the house to run off a bit of steam on occasion. We subsequently had the walls and ceilings painted with coloured trompe l'oeil architecture, in order that the opposition between enclosure and opening would be brought out more strongly and in a greater variety of ways. As a result of this, the built structure of the house assumes an even more complex form, and is contrasted with the openings.

Haus in Köln-Weiss

House in Weiss, Cologne

Haus in Köln-Weiss

House in Weiss, Cologne

Haus in München, 1969

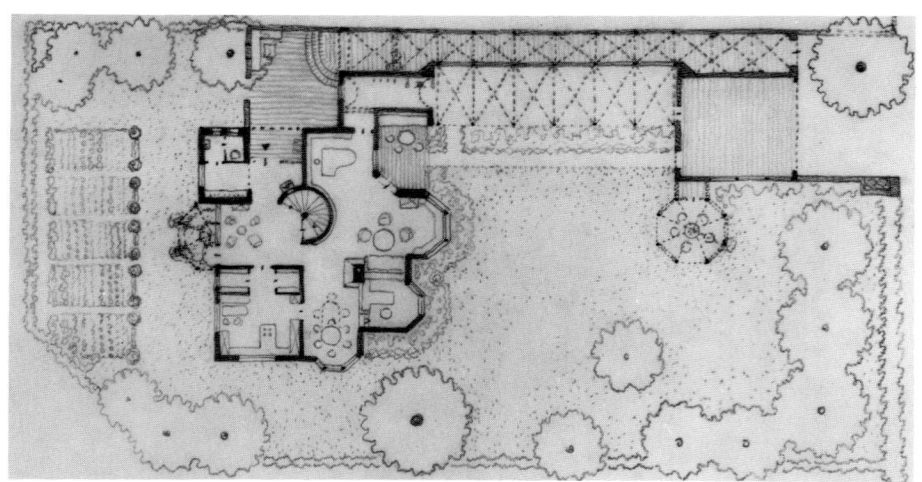

24 House in Munich, 1969

Haus in München

House in Munich

Porz-Zündorf ist ein kleiner alter Ort in der Nähe von Köln, am Rhein gelegen. Auch hier sind die alten Wohnhäuser meist Teil eines Wohnbezirkes, bestehend aus Haus, Hof und Garten. Hierbei ist der Hof – meist seitlich des Gebäudes gelegen, durch eine hohe Mauer gefaßt und mit einem Tor versehen – die eigentliche Anknüpfung zur Straße. Die Häuser wenden, im Gegensatz zum Haus in Köln, ihr Gesicht zur Straße hin und geben zusammen mit dem Hofraum und den Toren der

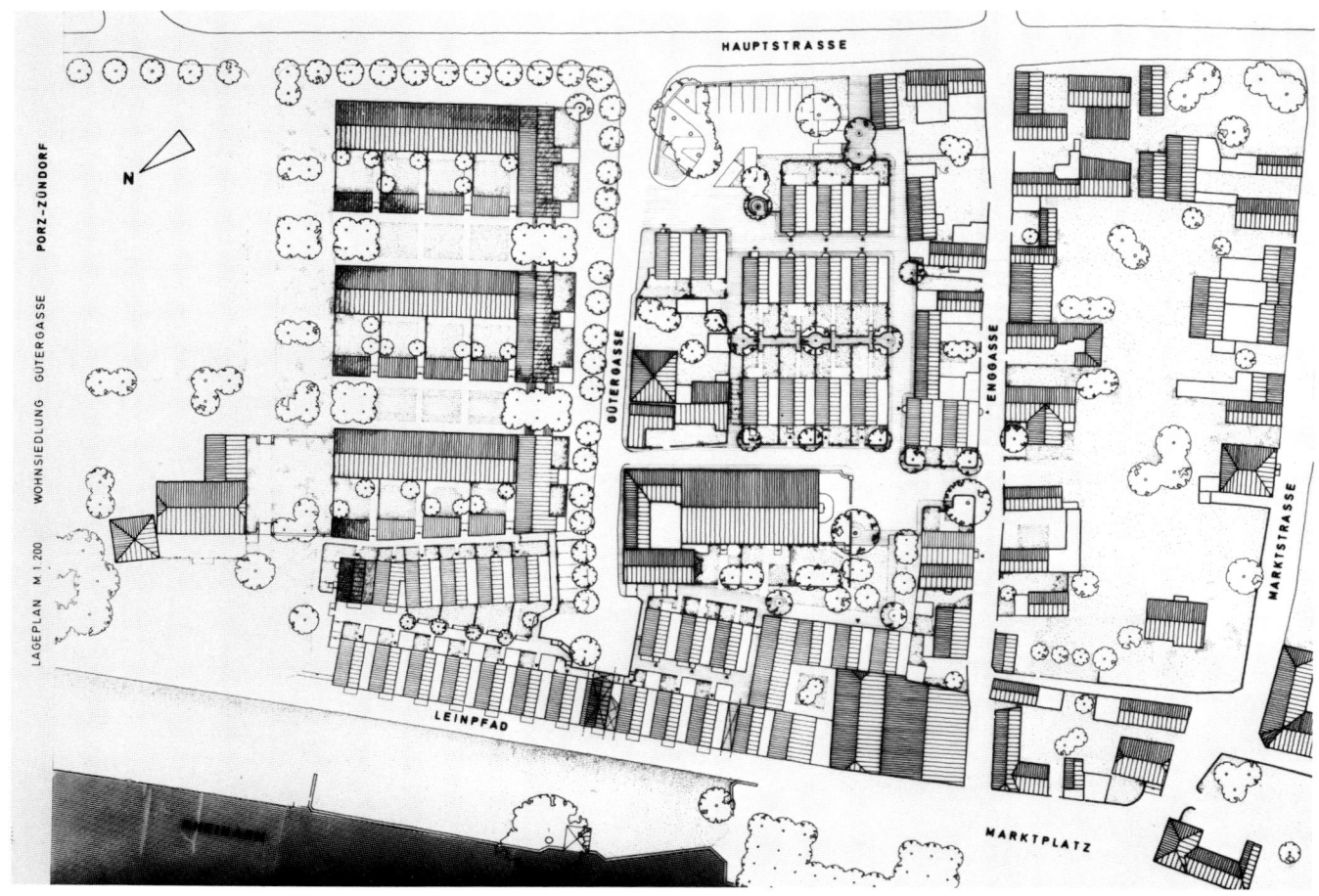

Porz-Zündorf is a small old town on the Rhine not far from Cologne. Here too most of the older houses form part of a residential district with a structure that consists of house, courtyard and garden. The courtyards, which form the actual link to the street, are usually situated to one side of the building. They are enclosed by a high wall, and access to them is via a gate. In contrast to the house in Cologne, these buildings face on to the street and thus, in conjunction with courtyard space

Straße das Gepräge. Wir wollten dieses Verhältnis von Straße, Vorhof mit Mauer und Haus in den neuen Gebäuden aufnehmen, obwohl sie mit einer stärkeren Flächennutzung viel enger gebaut werden mußten. Während des Bauens aber bekamen wir etwas Bedenken, ob dieser Vorhof von den neuen Bewohnern, die ja meist Städter sind, so verwendet wird wie es die alten Dorfbewohner noch tun, eben mit eingebauten Schuppen für Geräte und Werkstätten, mit kleinen Hasen- oder

and gateways, give the street its own special character. It was our intention to adopt this relationship between street, forecourt with wall, and house into the new development, even though the need for a more intense exploitation of the site meant that the units had to be built to a much tighter layout. In the course of construction, however, we had second thoughts, whether the forecourts would be used by the new residents – who were mostly town people – in the same way as by the

Hühnerställen und so fort. Wir haben die Höfe deshalb nur halbhoch geschlossen. Es zeigt sich auch, daß anstatt Hofnutzung mit Ställen und Schuppen nun eine Art Vorgartennutzung entstand mit vielfach immergrünen Gewächsen, wie das der deutsche Vorgarten jetzt so an sich hat.

In einer engen Gasse sind die Häuser ohne Vorhöfe aneinander gereiht. Die vorgelagerten Eingangsstufen zusammen mit der seitlichen Sitzbank betonen die Verbindung vom Haus zur Gasse. Sie sorgen außerdem dafür, daß die Passanten nicht allzu nah an den Fenstern vorbeigehen. Diese engen Gassen sind für den Ort sehr charakteristisch. Sie sind ja auch, weil sie das Räumliche so betonen, besonders beliebt. Baurechtlich waren sie nur sehr schwer durchzusetzen.

older villagers, who had inserted their own small structures, workshops, tool sheds, rabbit hutches, chicken pens and the like in this space. We therefore decided to leave the courtyard half open. It has indeed proved to be the case that, instead of erecting stalls or sheds in this area, the new residents treat it as a kind of typical front garden area with many evergreen plants.

The houses without forecourts are built in continuous terraced form along a narrow lane. The projecting entrance steps, together with a sitting place with bench to one side, emphasize this link between house and lane. They also ensure that passers-by do not come too close to the windows. The narrow lanes are a typical feature of this place. They are also very popular, as a result of the way they bring out the spatial quality. In terms of building regulations, however, it was no easy matter to realize them in this form.

Kinderdorf in Bensberg. Das war natürlich in den 60er Jahren für mich eine großartige Aufgabe, ein ganzes Dorf planen zu dürfen. Der Bauplatz war eine abseits in einem Wald gelegene Lichtung. Die Anbindung an eine städtische Situation war nicht gegeben. Es entstand daher eine in sich geschlossene Ortschaft. Die kleine Zufahrtsstraße haben wir ringförmig durch das Dorf weitergeführt. An dieser Ringstraße liegen die Häuser für jeweils zwölf Kinder, eine Mutter und eine Helferin. Jede Hausgemeinschaft ist in gewissem Sinn autark, mit eigenem Einkommen, mit dem sie wirtschaften muß. Das ist meiner Ansicht nach eine ideale Sache. An einem inneren Platz liegen außerdem Läden, Poststelle, Wirtschaftsräume, Bibliothek und Verwaltung. In der Mitte des Platzes steht eine kleine Kirche verbunden mit einem Kloster. Bei den Wohnhäu-

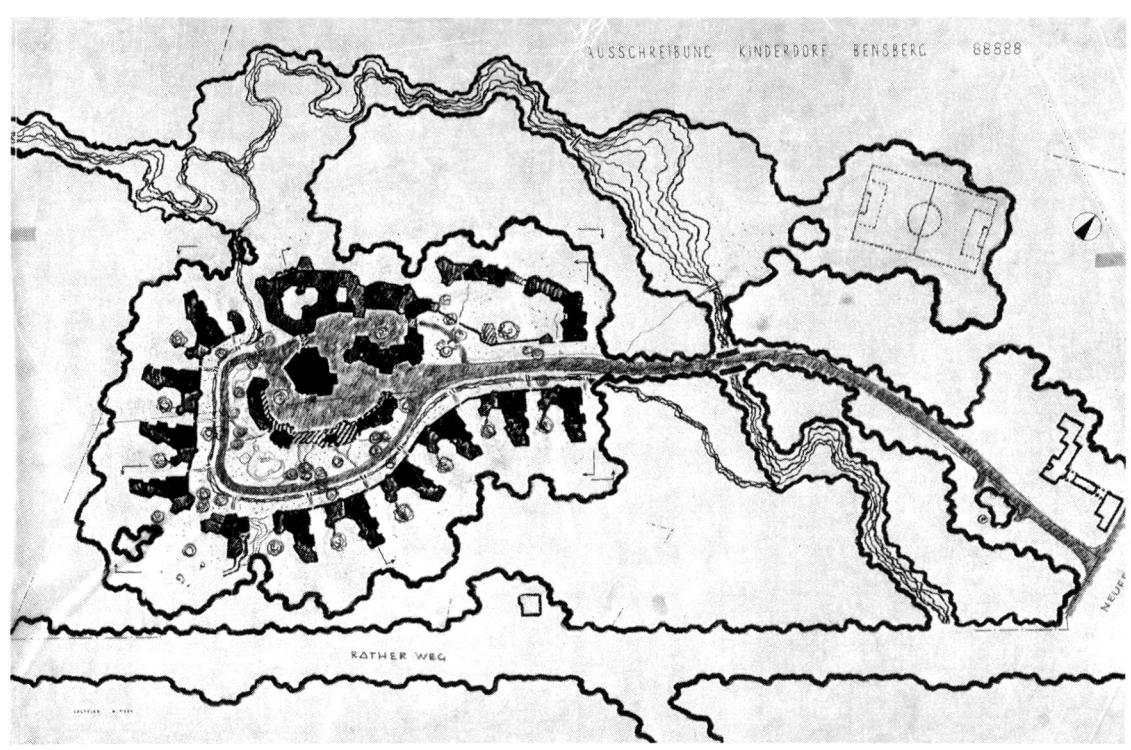

Children's Village in Bensberg. In the 1960s the opportunity to design an entire village represented a marvellous commission for me. The site was an out-of-the-way clearing in a forest. No links existed to any urban context to which one might orientate one's planning. The design therefore proposed a self-contained locality. We continued the small access road leading to the site through the village in the form of a ring. The individual houses, each accommodating twelve children, a home mother and an assistant, were laid out along this ring road. Each household is self-sufficient in a certain sense. It has its own income and has to manage on this. To my mind that is an ideal situation. In addition shops, a post office, utility rooms and working spaces, a library and the administration are located about an open space at the centre of the site. In the mid-

sern ist der Straßenbezug über einem seitlich angeordneten Hof mit hoher Mauer sehr viel markanter dargestellt. Der Hof wird hier auch meist als Werkhof mit Abstellschuppen und kleinen Stallungen angenommen. Das Tor in der Hofwand, mit einer Leuchte betont, stellt zusammen mit der kleinen Brücke über den Bach den Bezug zur Straße bzw. zum Dorfanger her. Das Wasser sollte von einem Bach hergeleitet werden, der am Ort vorbeiführt. Das ist aber nicht genehmigt worden. So haben die Kinder halt ihren Spaß mit Schiffchen fahren, Dammbau usw. nur dann, wenn es viel regnet und die Wasserspeier das Rinnsal füllen.

dle of this open space is a small church attached to a convent. The link with the street is much more boldly articulated in the case of the residential buildings, where it is in the form of a side courtyard enclosed by a high wall. Here too the courtyard has in the main been put to use as a working area with storage sheds and small pens. The gateway in the enclosing wall is emphasized by a light-fitting. Together with the little bridge over the channel, it forms the point of contact between house and street or village green. We had intended to divert water for this channel from a stream that flows past the village. Permission was not granted for this, however. The children can therefore only sail their boats, build dams, etc., when there is a lot of rain and the gargoyles fill this channel with water.

Bensberg, Kinderdorf — Ansicht mit der Kapelle

Bensberg, Children's Village — View with chapel

Bensberg, Kinderdorf   Kapellenfenster

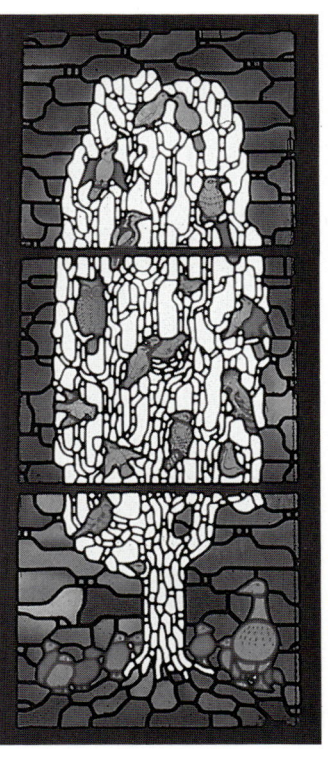

Bensberg, Children's Village   Chapel windows

Köln-Chorweiler — Wohnquartier

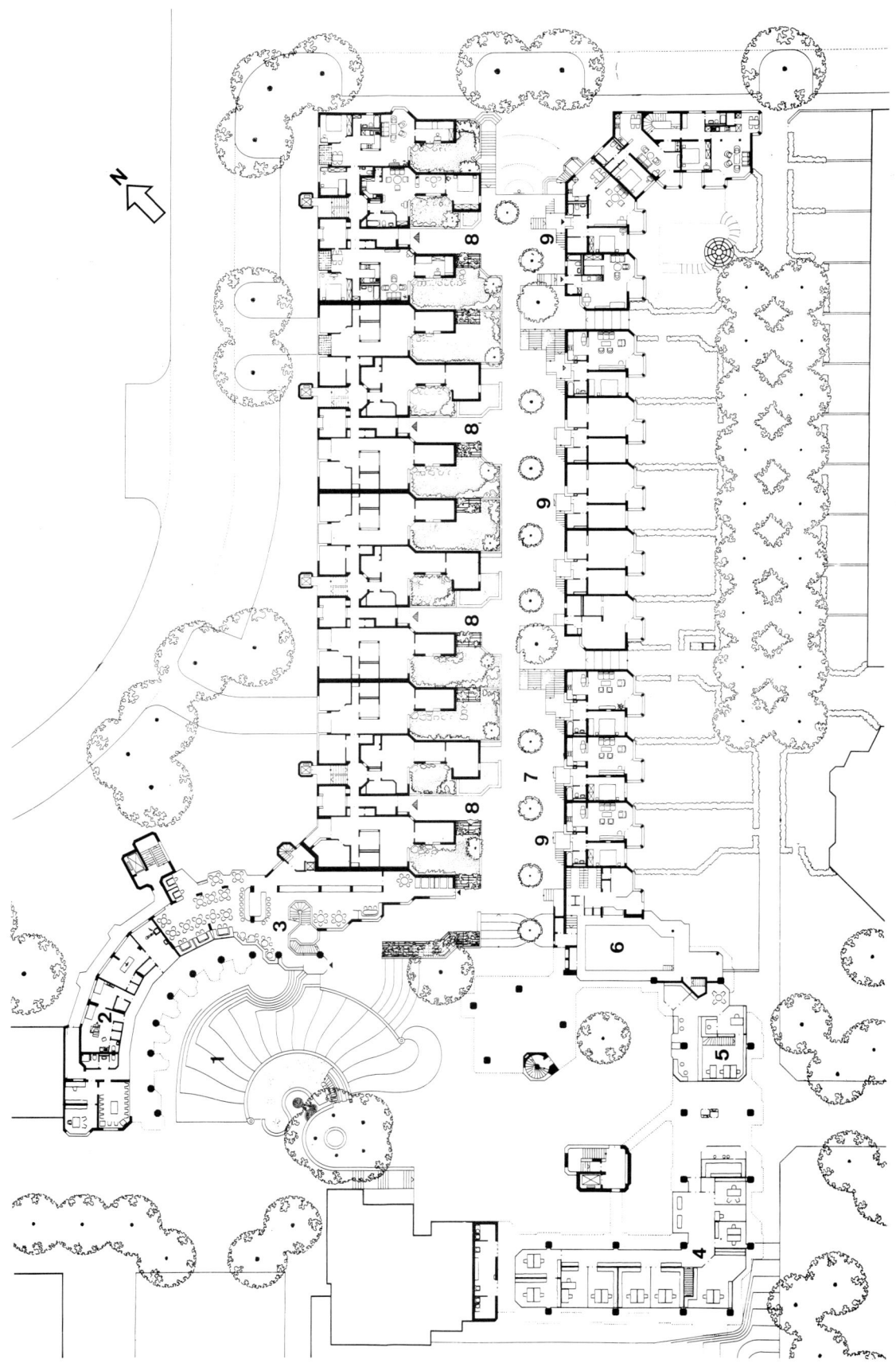

Chorweiler, Cologne — Residential area

Während der siebziger Jahre haben wir in der Satellitenstadt Köln-Chorweiler ein Wohnquartier mit einer kleinen Ladenzone geplant und zum Teil durchgeführt. In dem vorgegebenen städtebaulichen Grobkonzept waren ein Straßennetz für den Autoverkehr und eine Fußgängerwegeverbindung festgelegt.

Eine solche Anlage bringt mit sich, daß die Häuser nicht mehr eine eindeutige Straßen- oder Vorderfront bzw. eine eindeutige Hof- oder Gartenseite haben. Das Haus hat folglich beiderseits einen fast gleichwertigen Öffentlichkeitsbezug. Diesem Umstand entsprechend haben wir die Erschließung der Wohngruppen so angelegt, daß sie von beiden Seiten erfolgt. Wir haben jedoch die Zugänge an der Straßenseite mit dem Autoverkehr besonders betont.

Die Fußgängerseite hat den Wert einer vielfältig verbundenen Hofzone. Nach unserer Planung sollten diese blockinneren Verbindungen und deren bauliche Fassung auch über die Querstraße hinweg bis zum Grünbereich fortgesetzt werden.

Der Zugang von der Straße zum Treppenhaus ist nicht, wie üblich, nur ein kleiner Windfang, sondern ein größerer allge-

In the 1970s we designed and realized in part a residential district with a small shopping zone in Chorweiler, a satellite town outside Cologne. The brief called for a road network for vehicular traffic and a connecting pedestrian route. With developments of this kind the street front and rear garden or courtyard aspects of the blocks are usually not clearly defined and differentiated, with the result that such buildings often have a relationship to the public realm of virtually equal intensity on both sides. With this in mind, we allowed access to the various groups of housing from both sides, but gave special emphasis to the entrances on the street face with vehicular traffic.

The pedestrian side has the quality of a varied courtyard zone with a multiplicity of links and cross-relationships. Our scheme proposed the continuation of these internal links and their structural articulation beyond the lateral streets and out to the countryside around.

mein nutzbarer Raum, in dem man auch mal den Kinderwagen abstellen kann, sein Fahrrad richtet oder Verschiedenes bastelt, in dem die Kinder auch bei Regenwetter spielen können und so fort. Leider ist die Erschließungsstraße kein richtiger Straßenraum geworden, da die andere Straßenseite nicht als Straßenwand gebaut wurde. Dadurch wirkt unsere Straßenrandbebauung wie die Hinterseite des Gebäudekomplexes, obschon wir uns durch die Grundrißbildung der Wohnungen mit den Loggien, durch die Bebauung der Hauseingänge und mit Vorschlägen für eine Begrünung mit Straßenbäumen Mühe gegeben haben, der Straße ein ihr gebührendes Gesicht zu geben. Eine Straße sollte eben nicht nur Anlieferstraße sein, wie bei der Rückseite eines Kaufhauses. Sie sollte schon gar nicht Trennlinie sein zwischen unterschiedlichen Wohnbereichen, wie sie sich jetzt dort darstellt, sondern sollte wichtiger öffentlicher Lebensraum sein.

Am Kopf der Anlage ist ein kleiner Arkadenplatz mit einigen Läden, einer Kneipe und einem Restaurant mit einer Terrasse angelegt. Eine breite Rampe führt in die Gasse, die über dem Garagentrakt liegt. Von hier aus sind einerseits die zweigeschossigen Altenwohnungen, andererseits auch der Eingangsbereich des Wohntraktes zugänglich. Zu den Erdgeschoßwohnungen gehört immer ein kleiner Gartenhof, dazwischen gibt es kleine Spielplätze für Kleinkinder. Ansonsten sind alle Hof- und Wegebereiche so angelegt, daß die Kinder dort spielen können und in Kontakt mit den Erwachsenen bleiben. Unser besonderes Anliegen war, eine enge Verbindung älterer Menschen mit jungen Familien herzustellen.

Von der Wohngasse führen Treppen in das Garagengeschoß. Sie haben größere begrünte Zwischenpodeste, durch die die Garage natürliches Licht bekommt. Eine Garage ist ja auch ein Lebensraum. Die Frau mit dem Kind an der Hand sollte sich nicht fürchten müssen, wenn sie zum Auto geht.

Bei den Grundrissen der Wohnungen war uns sehr viel daran gelegen, sie durchgängig zu machen, das heißt sie nach zwei entgegengesetzten Himmelsrichtungen auszurichten. Es bereichert das Leben, wenn man in einer Wohnung den Tagesrhythmus des Lichtes erfährt. Wir haben auch auf beiden Seiten Terrassen und Loggien vorsehen können, wobei es nicht einfach war, beim Bauherrn die Loggien an der Straßenseite durchzusetzen. Wie sich gezeigt hat, werden aber gerade die Freiplätze im Westen zur Straße hin sehr viel benutzt, weil eben die meisten Menschen nach dem Arbeitstag erst Zeit haben und die Abendsonne genießen können. Viele Leute sehen auch gerne dem Verkehr auf der Straße zu und zudem hat das einen belebenden Effekt für den Straßenraum.

Die Küche liegt als verglaster Raum in der Mitte des durchgehenden Wohnraums. Die Küchenarbeit braucht dadurch nicht irgendwo abseits gemacht zu werden, und man hat dabei die Kinder im Blickfeld. Das Kochen wird ja heute wieder wichtig genommen und macht auch den Männern Spaß. Es verlangt als Raum wieder einen wichtigen Platz in der Wohnung. Die Schlafzimmer haben wir nach Möglichkeit an den Wohnraum angeschlossen, den man auf Wunsch dadurch erweitern

Access from the street to the staircases is not, as it usually is, through a tiny wind lobby, but via a larger space that can be used for a variety of communal activities; where, for example, it would be possible to leave a pram occasionally, or repair one's bicycle, or do various odd jobs, or where children could play when it is raining outside, etc. Unfortunately this access route never acquired the characteristics of a true street space, since the opposite face was not constructed as a closing wall to the street. As a result the edge of our development facing on to the road looks more like the back of a building complex, even though we made every effort to give the street a fitting face; – i.e. in the layouts of the dwellings and the loggias, in the design if the entrances, and in the form of our proposals for the landscaping of this space with trees, etc. A street should not simply be a delivery route, as one finds at the back of department stores. Nor should it represent a dividing line between different housing zones, as it is here. It should be a major open space for public life.

At one end of the development are a small arcaded open space and a number of shops, a bar and a restaurant with a terrace. A broad ramp leads up to a lane above the garage tract. From here one has access on the one hand to the two-storey old-people's dwellings and on the other to the entrance area to the general housing. Adjoining each of the ground floor dwellings is a modest garden or patio with small play areas for young children in between. All courtyard areas and footpaths are laid out in such a way that children can play there and remain in contact with adults. One of our special aims was to create close ties between older persons and young families.

The stairs leading from the residential lane to the garage level have enlarged, planted landing areas that permit natural lighting to enter the garages.

In designing the layouts of the dwellings we were very much concerned with ensuring that they extended the full depth of the building; in other words, that they should have two diametrically opposed aspects. It represents an enrichment of life to be able to experience the daily rhythm of changing light in a dwelling. It also proved possible to create terraces and loggias on both faces, although it was not easy to persuade the client to accept the loggias on the street front. The west-facing open-air spaces overlooking the street have proved to be very popular and are frequently used, for most people have time only after work to enjoy the evening sun in summer. A lot of people also like watching the traffic in the road below, and this has a further enlivening effect on the street space itself.

The kitchen is designed as a glazed room set in the middle of a continuous living area. Work in the kitchen need not therefore take place removed from other activities; and it is possible to keep an eye on children at the same time.

Bedrooms were, where possible, situated next to living areas and can be used to extend the latter, if required. A sick person confined to bed is sometimes pleased to be able to participate in the life of the family through an open door. In the case of

kann. Ein Kranker, der bettlägerig ist, ist auch manchmal froh, durch die offene Tür am Familienleben teilnehmen zu können. Bei den Altenwohnungen konnten wir sogar durchsetzen, eine Fenstertürverbindung einzubauen, was uns in dem Fall besonders wichtig erschien. Die Wohnungseingänge gleichen Hauseingängen, das heißt die Straße fängt schon ein bißchen im Treppenhaus an. Wir haben den Platz vor dem Eingang so ausgeweitet, daß man sich da auch einmal treffen und aufhalten kann. Ein kleines Fenster schaut auf diesen Eingangsvorplatz. Das alles sind Versuche im Rahmen der Vorschriften und der Mittel, dem Treppenhaus den Miethauscharakter zu nehmen.

Es wurde in Ortbeton ausgeführt. Er war damals relativ billig herzustellen. In Chorweiler haben wir mit 190 DM pro m^3 gebaut. Außerdem war nach dem Krieg das Bedürfnis, sehr »echt« und »wahrhaftig« zu bauen, besonders ausgeprägt. Und das war eigentlich das Ausschlaggebende. In Chorweiler ist die tragende Konstruktion, die wirkliche Mauer sichtbar, so wie wir altes Mauerwerk mit seinen klar ablesbaren konstruktiven Funktionen kennen. Die Wärmedämmung liegt innen, eine heute bauphysikalisch unzulässige Sache.

the old-people's dwellings we even managed to create a link in the form of a glazed door, which seemed of particular importance to us in these circumstances. The entrances of the dwellings resemble house entrances. In other words the street already begins to some extent in the staircase. We extended the area in front of the entrance, so that it would be possible to meet people there and stay for a chat on occasion. A small window overlooks this entrance zone. All these details represent a modest attempt, within the constraints imposed by building regulations and the funds available, to avoid the character of mass housing in these staircase areas.

I designed the Chorweiler development in insitu concrete. There were valid reasons for doing so at the time. Insitu concrete was relatively cheap. We built Chorweiler to a price of DM 190 per m^3. What is more, after the war the need for »honesty«, for »truth« in building was very strongly felt; and that was really a decisive aspect. The load-bearing structure and the actual structural walls in Chorweiler are made evident, much in the same way as one can recognize old brickwork and the clearly legible structural functions it expresses. The thermal insulation is on the inside, – something that would not be al-

Heute würde man außen wärmedämmen und mit einer harten Kunststoffschicht, die nach Verputz aussieht, abdecken: ein uns damals ganz unmöglicher Gedanke. Ich würde heute manches an Chorweiler anders machen wollen, aber das liegt mehr an einigen Details, zum Beispiel der Art und Größe mancher Fenster, der Verschlossenheit der Loggien und Balkonbrüstungen. Es wäre auch eine eindeutigere Zuwendung der Erschließung zur Straße wünschenswert. Aber es dürfte mir sehr schwer fallen, das »Gebaute« ebenso echt darzustellen. Heute wage ich kaum mehr, den Beton ganz in seinem natürlichen grauen Farbton zu belassen. In der Talstraße in Saarbrücken und beim Züblin-Bau sind die Beton-Fertigbauteile rötlich gefärbt. Das sieht dann etwa wie Sandstein aus. Ein Eindruck, den ich in den ersten Nachkriegsjahrzehnten niemals gewollt hätte, weil er eben nicht mehr ganz »echt« ist. Wir haben uns früher auf andere Art sehr viel Mühe gegeben, dem Beton durch besondere Bearbeitung ein gutes Aussehen zu geben. Vielfach haben wir ihn gestockt. Wir waren beim Gießen des Betons dabei und haben aufgepaßt, daß der Guß und die damit verbundene Schichtung in der Fläche interessant erscheint. Heute ist das schon deshalb nicht mehr möglich, weil man als Architekt im allgemeinen kaum mehr Zugang zu diesen Arbeitsgängen hat. Das war allerdings auch damals in Chorweiler schon schwierig. Daher wurden die Fenster- und Türrahmen zusätzlich bemalt. Um das durchzusetzen, haben wir heimlich am Wochenende manches selbst gemacht. Einige Loggien wurden zum Teil mit Schablonen farbig behandelt, um die Bewohner anzuregen, selbst etwas zu tun, zumindest damit sie wissen, daß sie zur Verschönerung ihres Bereiches beitragen dürfen. Das wird nur sehr zaghaft angenommen.

lowed today, since it is seen as contravening the principles of sound building construction. Nowadays one would place the thermal insulation on the outside and cover it with a hard plastic coating that looks like rendering. At the time Chorweiler was built that would have been an inconceivable notion. Today, I would certainly do some things differently, but the differences would relate more to the details than to the basic idea; for example, the size and the type of windows or the degree of openness or closedness of the balustrades to the loggias and balconies. A clearer orientation of the lines of access to the street would also be desirable. But it would probably be extremely difficult for me to express the same sense of »honesty« in the building as I felt I did then. Nowadays I scarcely venture to leave concrete in its natural grey colour. In the Talstrasse scheme in Saarbrücken and in the Züblin project the precast concrete elements were given a reddish tinge. It bears a certain resemblance to sandstone, an impression I would never have wished to create in the first decades after the war, because it would not have been quite »authentic«. In the past we also took a great deal of trouble to obtain a good appearance with concrete, but in quite different ways. In many cases we had it bush-hammered, or we were present during the pouring of the concrete and saw to it that this process and the stratification connected with it produced an interesting surface appearance. That is no longer possible today, because, as an architect, one has scarcely any access to or any say in these working processes any more. At that time in Chorweiler it was already difficult. That is why we had the window and door frames painted additionally; and in order to achieve this, we did a lot of things ourselves, working secretly over the weekend. Some of the loggias were given colour treatments with templet forms, so as to stimulate the inhabitants to do things themselves; or at least so that they would know they were permitted to embellish and improve their own realm. People are faint-hearted at accepting things like that.

Köln-Chorweiler — Teilansicht

Chorweiler, Cologne — Partial view

Die städtebauliche Einbindung von Wohnanlagen für alte und kranke Menschen ist von besonderer Bedeutung, da Alter und Krankheit – ob man es will oder nicht – ein wesentlicher Bestandteil unseres Lebens sind, den man nicht irgendwie pflegeleicht wegschieben sollte. Es ist oft nicht ganz einfach, solche großen Anlagen, vor allem Krankenhäuser mit all ihren technischen Einrichtungen, in ein normales städtisches Wohngefüge einzuordnen, und so stehen sie auch meist irgendwo draußen in ihrer eigenen Welt. Versuchen sollte man eine Eingliederung dennoch immer wieder. Vor allem scheint es mir im Bereich des Altenwohnen und der Altenpflege notwendig und möglich. So hatten wir ursprünglich für den Kern des neuen Stadtteils Düsseldorf-Garath eine größere Wohnanlage geplant, in die das Altenheim städtebaulich und architektonisch mit einbezogen war.

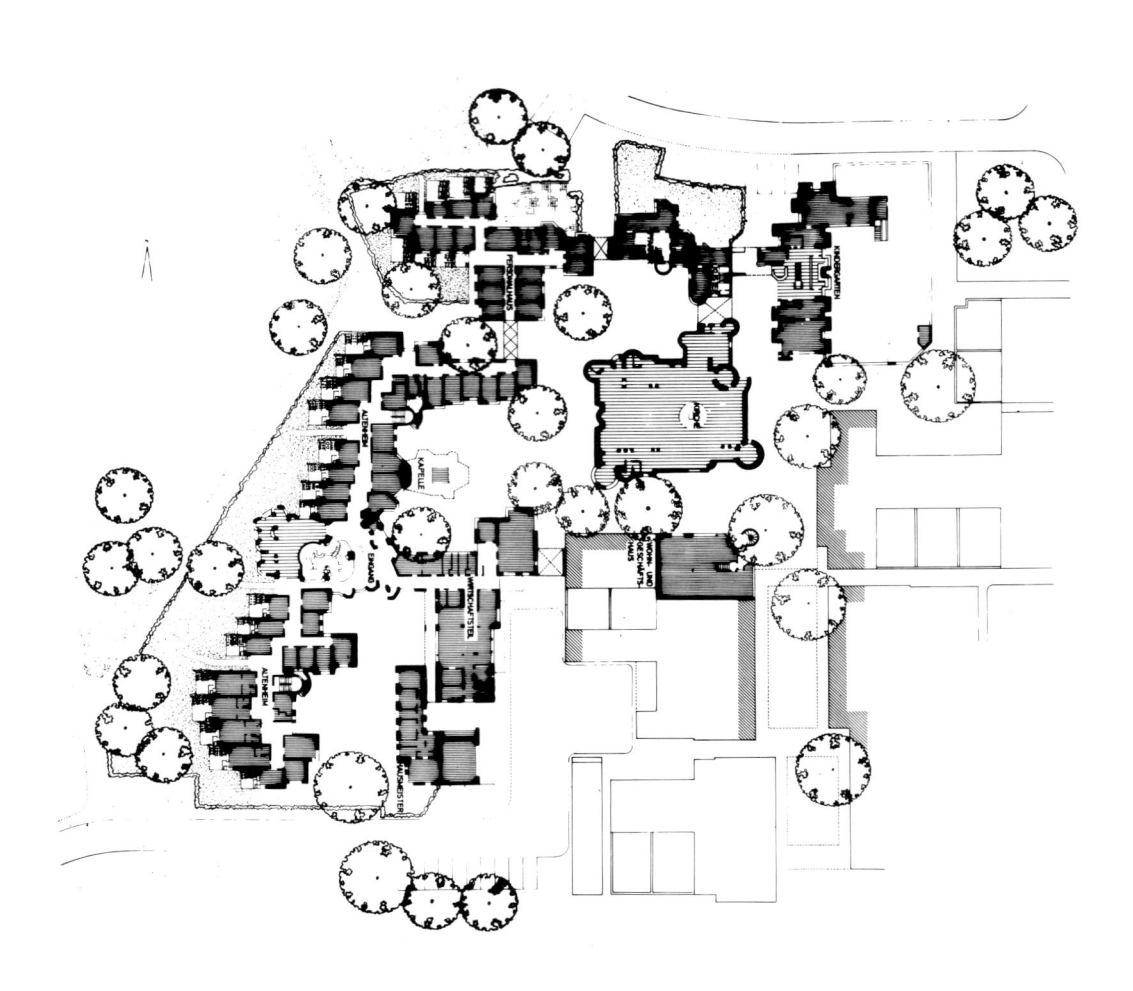

The integration of housing developments for the sick and aged into the urban environment is of the utmost importance. Whether one likes it or not, age and infirmity are major aspects in our lives, and they should not be pushed aside in some easy-care manner. It is not simple to integrate developments of this size – and in particular hospital complexes with all their technical facilities – into the normal urban housing fabric. That is why they usually stand somewhere outside towns in their own environment. Any attempt to integrate them is, however, worthwhile. This seems to me particularly important and indeed feasible in the realm of care and housing for the aged. That is why, in our original plans for the heart of the new city district of Garath in Düsseldorf, we proposed an extensive housing development, with an old-people's home incorporated into the overall architectural and urban planning. These proposals were realized only in part. A sense of identity with

Dies wurde nur teilweise verwirklicht. Weil uns die Zusammengehörigkeit mit einer weiteren Bebauung wichtig erschien, damit unser Baukomplex in die Nachbarschaft eingreift und sich verknüpft, haben wir ein Eckhaus mit Wohnung und Laden selbst gebaut. Leider hat die weitere Entwicklung keine Rücksicht darauf genommen.

Unsere eigene Planung hat die Altenwohnanlage so gegliedert, daß kleine Gassen und Plätze entstehen, die sich in das Innere fortsetzen. Den einzelnen Zimmern haben wir Fenster auch zu den Wohngassen hin gegeben, damit jeder Bewohner das Gefühl hat, in sein eigenes kleines Haus zu gehen. Die »Gassen« im Erd- und Obergeschoß sind durch einen großen Rampenplatz verbunden.

a further proposed development seemed important to us as well, and in order to ensure that our building complex would grow into and tie up with it, we erected a continuation ourselves in the form of a corner building with a dwelling unit and shop. The subsequent development unfortunately chose to ignore this gesture.

In our own planning, the complex for the old people was laid out in such a way that small lanes and open spaces were created that continue on the inside of the building. The individual rooms have windows overlooking these residential lanes, so that every inhabitant may have the feeling of living in his own small house. The »lanes« on the ground and first floors are linked by a large open rampway.

Düsseldorf-Garath — Rampe im Innenbereich der Wohnanlage

Garath, Düsseldorf — Ramp in interior of residential development

Düsseldorf-Garath — Teilansicht mit der Kirche

Garath, Düsseldorf — Partial view with church

Bei dem Projekt in Berlin-Hasenheide – das leider nicht realisiert wurde – ist der Bezug Wohnung-Straße-Platz wesentlich eindeutiger als in Chorweiler. Wir haben für jede Wohnung eine direkte und, wie ich glaube, auch schöne Verbindung zu dem Halbrund der Straße hergestellt. Die offene, gerade durchlaufende Treppe führt durch das ganze Haus und erschließt die Geschosse über offene kleine Vorplätze auf den verschiedenen Ebenen. Das heißt, daß man von jeder Wohnung, die man verläßt – auch in den oberen Geschossen schon –, einen direkten Bezug zur Straße, also zur weiterreichen-

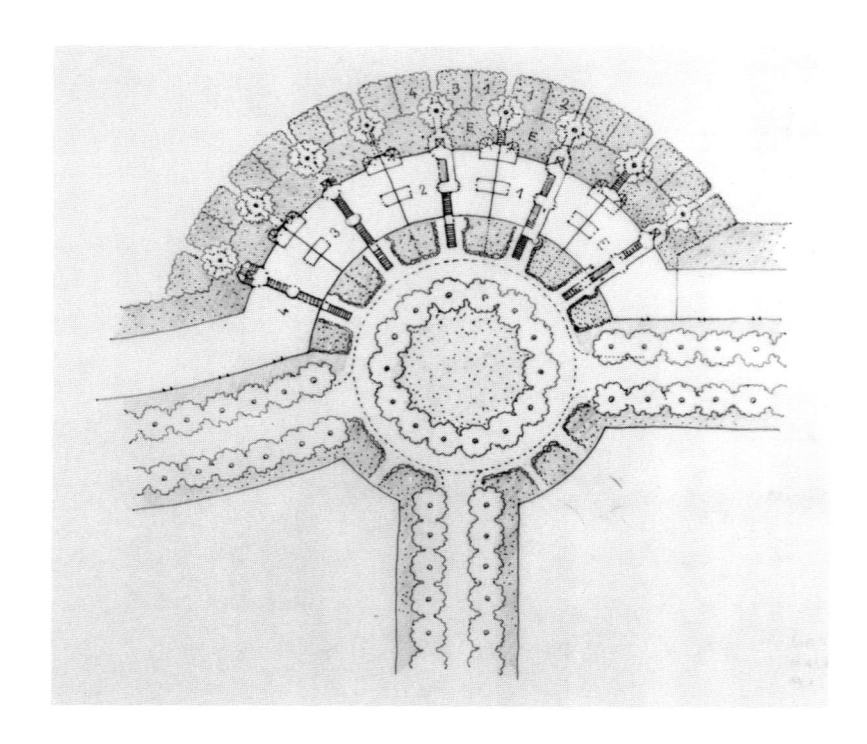

In the Hasenheide Project, Berlin, – which was unfortunately not realized – the sequence of relationships between dwelling, street and open space is much clearer than in Chorweiler. For each dwelling we designed a direct and, to my mind, beautiful link to the semicircle of the street. A continuous open staircase leads up through the entire building, providing access to every storey via small lobbies. In other words, on leaving any dwelling, even those on the upper floors, one has a

den Ordnung hin hat.
Es geht immer wieder um die Frage: Wie kann ich eine Ordnung bauen, die sich in eine nächsthöhere Ordnung einbindet. Natürlich auch umgekehrt: Wie kann ich ein Ordnungssystem herstellen, das für kleinere Ordnungen geradezu einen Anreiz bildet, sich einzunisten.

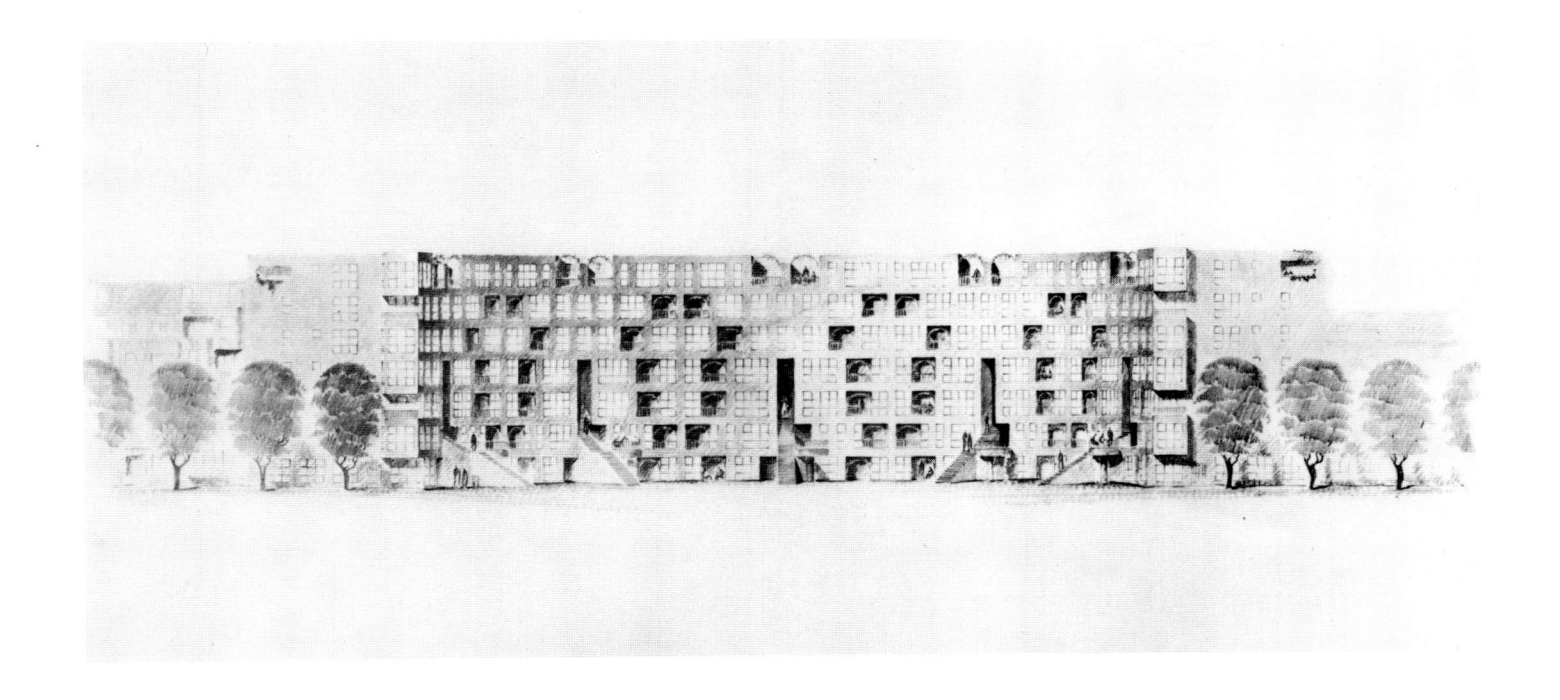

direct relationship to the street, and thus to an element further up the scale of this ordering system.
The recurring question is, indeed, how one can construct an ordering system that ties in with the next higher system; and vice-versa, of course: how one can create an ordering system that encourages systems further down the scale to fit in with the same scheme of things.

Die Talstraße in Saarbrücken besteht aus einer im allgemeinen geschlossenen Straßenfront mit zum Teil recht schönen städtischen Wohnhäusern. Für unser Projekt war ein Garagenhaus, zwei Geschosse unter Straßenniveau, zwei Geschosse darüber, bereits in der Planung festgelegt. Dieser Komplex, der mit seiner Rückseite an einen Steilhang grenzt, sollte mit Wohnungen und Büros überbaut werden. Es erschien uns wichtig, in Form und Nutzung die Straßenwandlücke wieder zu schließen, um den vorhandenen städtischen Charakter der Straße zu bewahren.

Bei dem vorgegebenen Garagenbau gab es nur wenig Platz für einen Ladenbereich an der Straße, in dem das Gebäude in Nutzung und Gestalt eine Verbindung mit der Straße eingehen kann. Es schien auch eine Erweiterung des neuen Fußgängerbereichs unbedingt erforderlich, weshalb uns die Ausführung einer Arkade sehr wichtig war, obschon die verbleibende

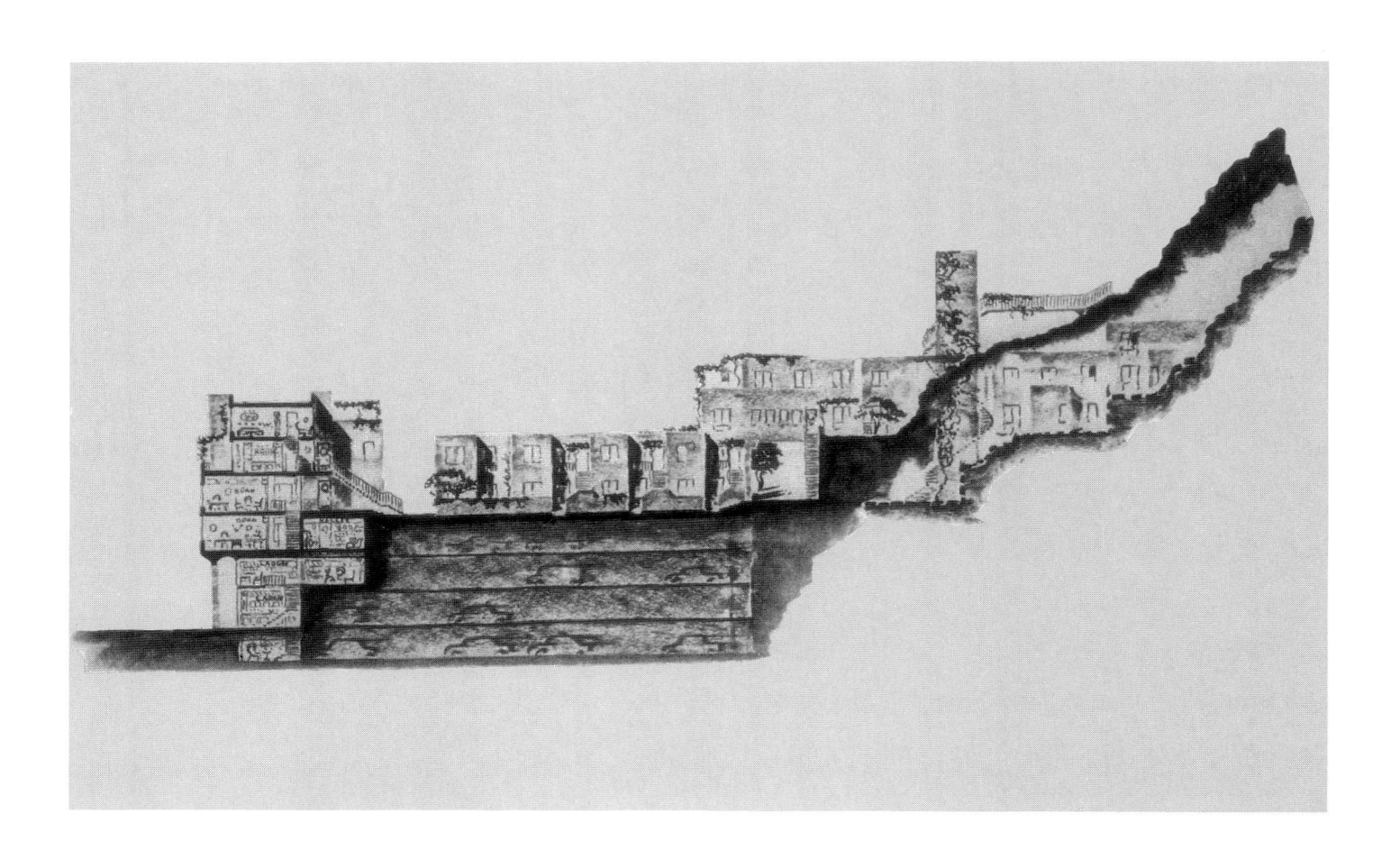

Talstrasse in Saarbrücken consists of a more or less continuous, closed street front and comprises a number of very attractive urban housing blocks. Our planning brief was for a parking block with two storeys below street level and two above, backing on to a steep slope. On top of this structure we were to set a housing and office development. It seemed important to us to find an appropriate form and appropriate functions to close the gap in the street face, so as to maintain the existing urban character of this road.

The garage structure did not leave much space for a street level shopping area that would have integrated the building into the existing street in terms of form and function. Nevertheless an extension of the new pedestrian zone seemed essential, and for that reason we deemed it necessary to create an arcade on the ground floor, even though the area remaining for

Fläche für die Läden gering war. Ein Zwischengeschoß erweitert diese Ladenzone.
Die Überbauung des Garagentraktes mit Wohnungen und Maisonettes zwischen Straßenzeile und Steilhang ist ein selbständiger Kernbereich mit inneren Wegen, Vorgärten und Vorhöfen. Die Zugänge liegen auf der Ebene über dem Garagenblock. Diese Wohnungen und ihre Grünzonen verbinden sich mit dem begrünten Steilhang und der darüber liegenden Einfamilienhausbebauung. Die Baufront in der Talstraße besteht im Arkadenbereich aus rötlichem mit Eisenoxydzusatz gefärbtem Ortbeton, ähnlich der Farbe des angrenzenden Felsenhanges. Die oberen Geschosse sind in Fertigbeton-Sandwich-Konstruktion errichtet.

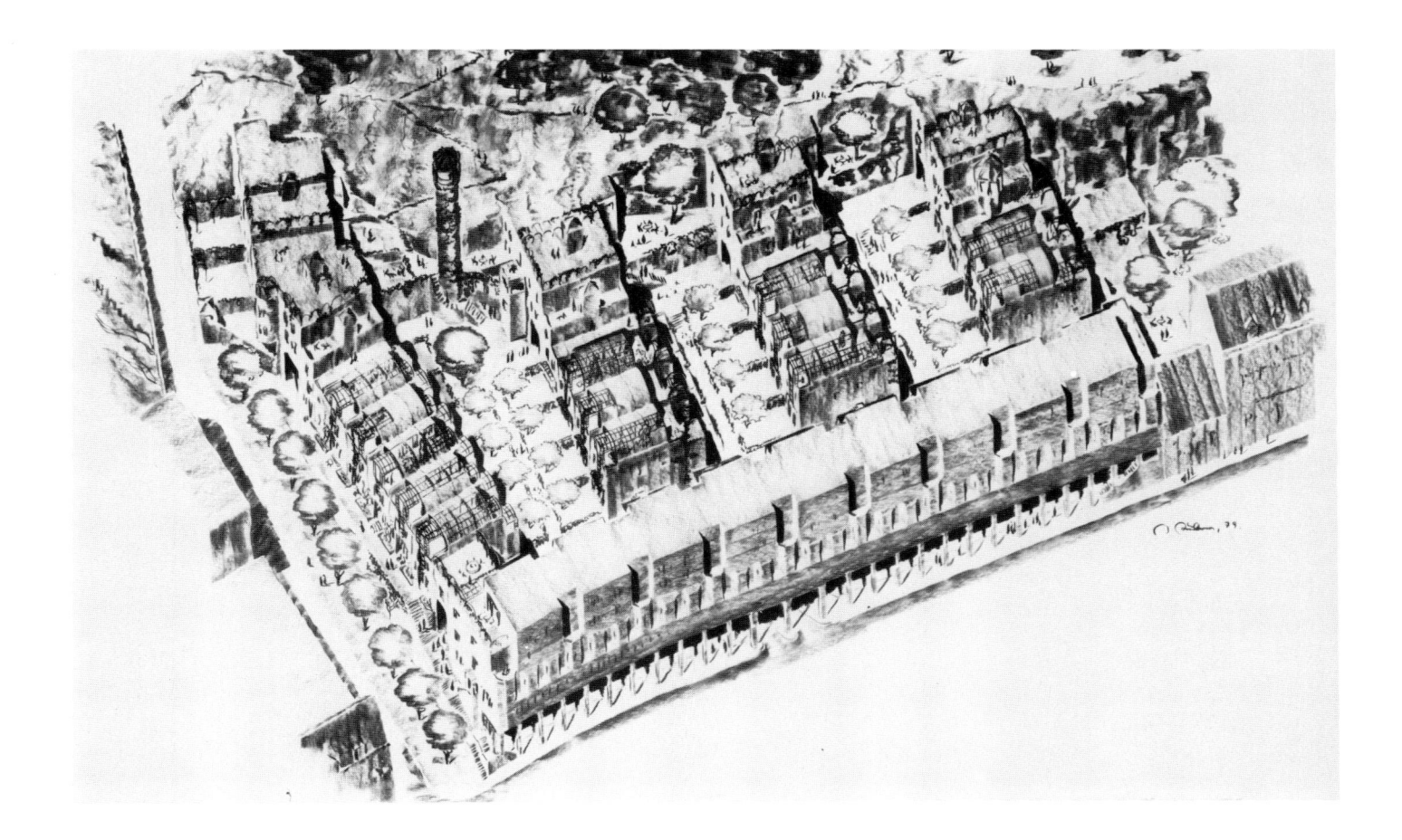

shops was then quite small. It proved possible, however, to enlarge the shop space by introducing a mezzanine level.
The complex to the rear, built above the garage tract between the strip of terraced housing along the road and the hill at the back, contains further flats and maisonettes. It is in the form of an independent core area with its own internal system of paths, front gardens and forecourts. Access is at the level of the deck above the garages. These dwellings and their planted garden areas link up with the landscaped slope to the rear and the single-family housing higher up. The elevation facing on to Talstrasse at arcade level is in insitu concrete coloured red with an iron oxide additive, similar in colour to the adjoining outcrop of rock. The upper storeys are of precast concrete sandwich construction.

Saarbrücken   Talstraße

Saarbrücken — Talstraße

Am Fasanenplatz in Berlin entstand eine Eckbebauung mit Wohnungen. Ursprünglich sollten im Erdgeschoß Läden untergebracht werden, was mir lieber gewesen wäre, da das Gebäude in einem sehr städtischen Bezirk liegt. Es sind auch hier vorläufig in zwei Geschossen Wohnungen eingebaut.

Der Bau ist um einen achteckigen, zum Teil glasüberdachten Innenhof angeordnet. Alle Wohnungen sind von dort über Laubengänge zugänglich. Jede Wohnung hat einen fast dachgartengroßen Balkon. Von Wohnraum und Küche entstehen

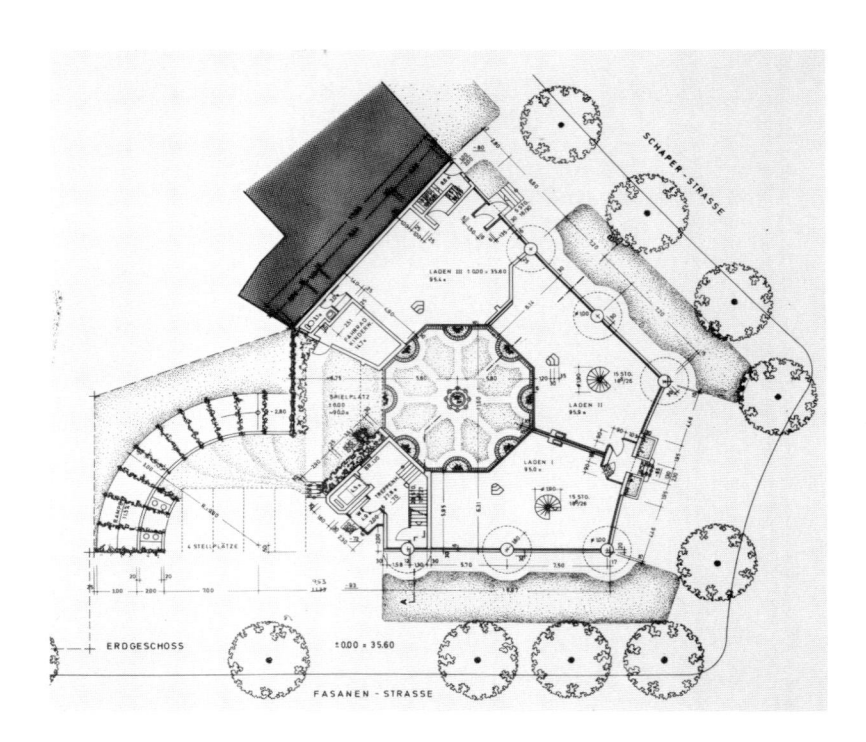

At Fasanenplatz in Berlin we designed a corner block development with housing. Originally it was planned to accommodate shops at ground floor level, and I would have preferred this, since the building is situated in a highly urban district. But for the time being at least further dwellings were incorporated over two storeys at this level.

The building is laid out about an octagonal courtyard, covered in part with glass. All dwellings are reached from this courtyard via access balconies. Every dwelling has a balcony or loggia very nearly the size of a roof garden. From the living room and kitchen one also has a view into the central hall. Seen in conjunction with the access balconies, the entrances to

Durchblicke auch in die Halle. So wirkt die Halle mit den Laubengängen, die wiederum mit den Wohnungseingängen und den Fenstern schon etwas Straßencharakter haben, wie eine Zwischenzone zur Straße. Die Bewohner erhalten dadurch das Gefühl einer eigenständigen Behausung. Ursprünglich wollten wir auch die Wintergärten zur Halle hin öffnen, damit man durch das Gebäude zum Straßenraum schauen kann. So hätte der gesamte Komplex noch transparenter erscheinen können.

the dwellings, and the windows, which suggest the character of a street, this courtyard hall functions as a kind of intermediate zone between the dwellings and the road. Residents thus enjoy a feeling of occupying their own independent houses. Originally we wanted to situate the conservatories so that they would open on to this hall as well, thus affording a glimpse through the entire building to the street beyond. The complex would then have had a much more transparent appearance.

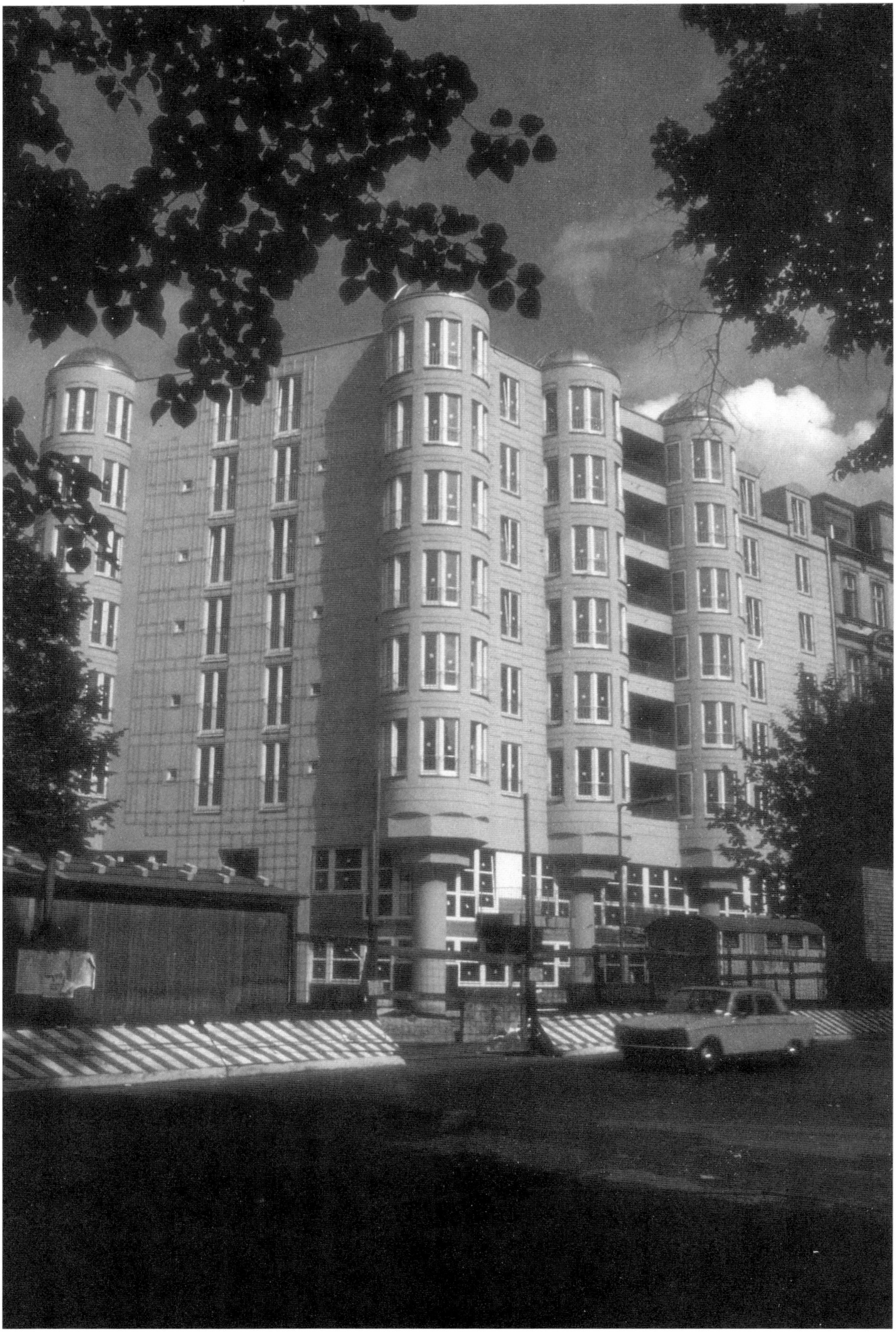

52 Berlin Fasanenplatz

Berlin   Fasanenplatz

Der Prager Platz gehört wie der Fasanenplatz auch zu einem Kranz von fünf einander ähnlichen Plätzen, die von aufeinander zulaufenden Straßen gebildet sind. Vor allem durch die Betonung der Kopfbauten erhielten sie ihren Platzcharakter. Es gibt eine Reihe von Überlegungen zu diesem Platz. Rob Krier hat zum Beispiel eine geschlossene Ringbebauung vorgeschlagen. Ich meine aber, es bringt hier keinen Vorteil, die alte Situation umzustrukturieren. Vor allem bringt die Geschlossenheit eines Ringes mit sich, daß Straßenanschlüsse den Charakter der Rückseiten erhalten. Nach dem ursprünglichen

Prager Platz, like Fasanenplatz, is one of a ring of five public open spaces in Berlin all bearing a certain resemblance to each other and all formed by the intersection of concentrically radiating roads. The character of a public open space that they manifest is created above all by the emphasis placed on the corner buildings. A number of schemes have been put forward relating to this public open space. Rob Krier, for example, suggested a closed ring development. To my mind, however, there is no advantage to be gained in restructuring the existing situation here. Furthermore, a closed ring would mean that the street junctions would have the character of a rear elevation. According to the original brief, in addition to housing

Programm sollten hier neben Wohnungen und Läden ein Freizeitbad und eine Volkshochschule mit Bibliothek entstehen. Eine große Öffnung in der Mitte und ein Arkadengang stellten eine sehr betonte Verbindung des Platzes mit diesen öffentlichen Einrichtungen her. Anstelle der Volkshochschule sind im heutigen Programm, außer Freizeitbad und Bibliothek, überwiegend Wohnungen vorgesehen. Diese Wohnungen haben mit der oberen Arkade einen Erschließungsweg am Platz in einer zweiten Ebene. Der Platzraum erhält damit den Charakter einer Halle mit zwei Erschließungsebenen.

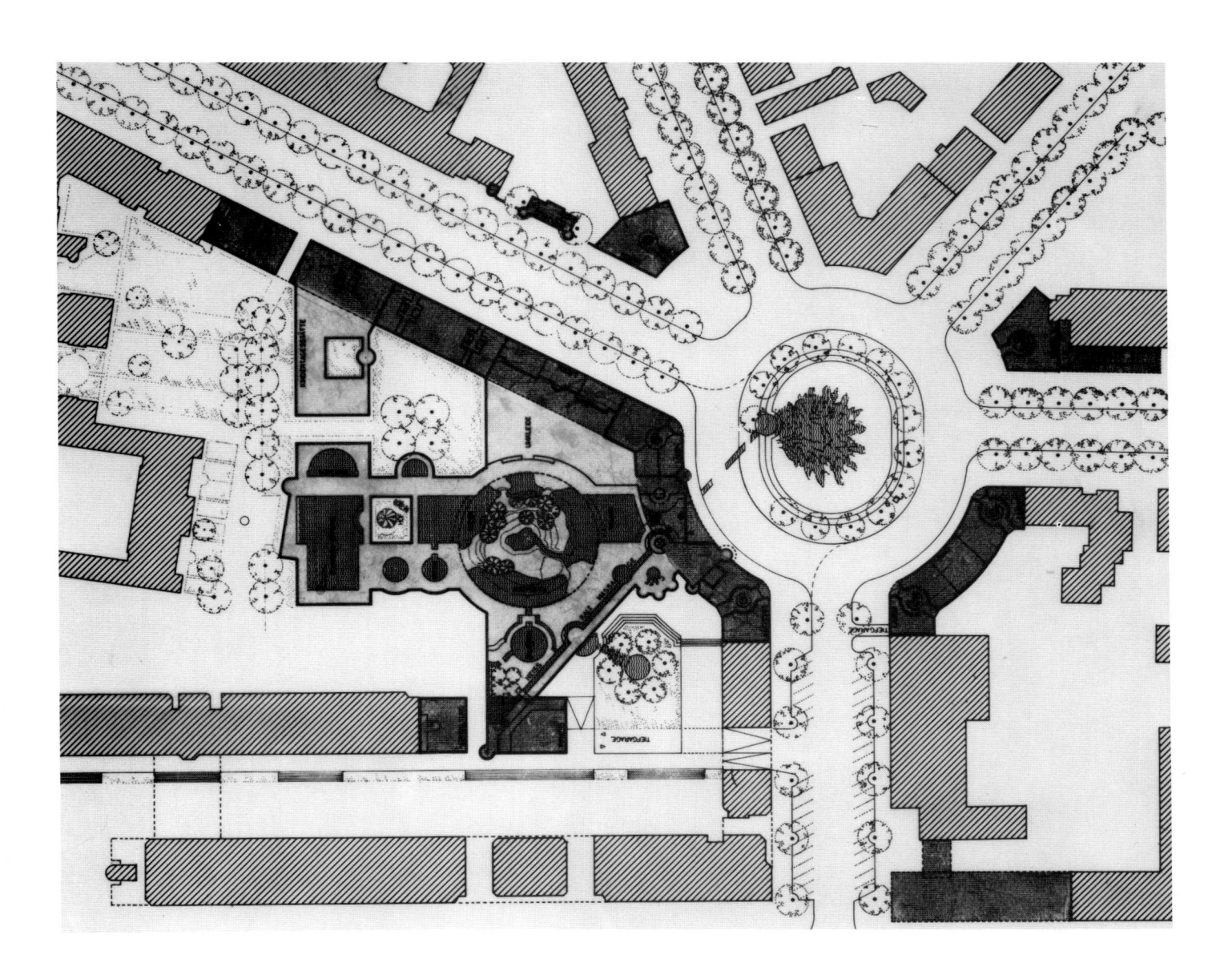

and shops, public baths with recreational facilities and an adult education institute with a library were to be located here. A large opening in the middle and a broad pedestrian arcade create a strong link between the open space and these public facilities. In place of the adult education institute the present programme includes further housing, as well as the public baths and library. The upper floor of the arcade leading to these dwellings also represents a second level of access to the public open space, thus lending it the character of a two-storey hall.

Berlin, Prager Platz

56 Berlin, Prager Platz

Gesamtprojekt

Overall project

Berlin

Prager Platz

Zum Thema Wohnungsbau gehört auch das Gutachten, das ich zusammen mit meinem Sohn Stefan für Lingotto in Turin gemacht habe. Es handelt sich um das alte Fabrikgebäude von Fiat, das ja vor allem wegen seiner Autostraße auf dem Dach weltberühmt geworden ist. Auf dieser Dachstraße wurden die Autos eingefahren, die in den darunter liegenden Hallen hergestellt worden waren.

Es ist architektonisch ein großartiger Bau aus den frühen dreißiger Jahren mit sehr schönen Stahlbetonkonstruktionen in den gewendelten Rampen, die an den Gebäudeenden zur Dachebene führen. Der Bau steht jetzt leer, und die Gutachter sollten Entwürfe mit eigenen Nutzungsvorschlägen vorlegen. Wir haben uns überlegt, daß hier Wohnungsbau, vielleicht für Werksangehörige, sinnvoll sein könnte, vor allem, wenn man die jetzt überflüssigen Gleiszonen in der Nachbarschaft

Under the heading of housing one should also mention the study I made with my son Stefan for Lingotto in Turin. The building in question is the old Fiat plant, which was famous throughout the world above all for the test track built on the roof. The cars that were produced in the workshops below were run in and tested on this rooftop road. Architecturally it is a marvellous building dating from the early 1930s, with some extremely fine reinforced concrete structures in the form of the spiral ramps leading up to the roof at the ends. Today the building stands empty. As consultants, we were called upon to submit our own designs and proposals for its use. We thought that housing, perhaps for employees of the works, would be an appropriate function here, particularly if the disused railway area nearby were landscaped and turned into a park. In order to relate the existing isolated building to the typical urban block structure of Turin, we proposed the erection of a

als Park anlegt.
Damit der jetzt isoliert dastehende Baukörper einen Zusammenhang mit der städtebaulichen Blockstruktur bekommt, die für Turin typisch ist, haben wir an den Längsseiten U-förmige Baukörper angefügt. Der jetzige Zustand des ganzen Stadtteils ist eine typische Stadtrandsituation. Es fehlen Läden, kommunale Einrichtungen, Einrichtungen auch für die nahe Universität, Räume für Büros, Verwaltung usw. Dafür haben wir das Sockelgeschoß der gesamten Anlage vorgesehen und an das städtische Straßennetz angeschlossen.
In den oberen Bereichen, als Überlagerung dieses Sockels, haben wir eine Wohnstadt geplant, die so vielgestaltig ist, daß sie, mit eigenen kleinen Versorgungseinrichtungen, zu einer kleinen Stadt in sich wird. So sind hier über den Dächern alle

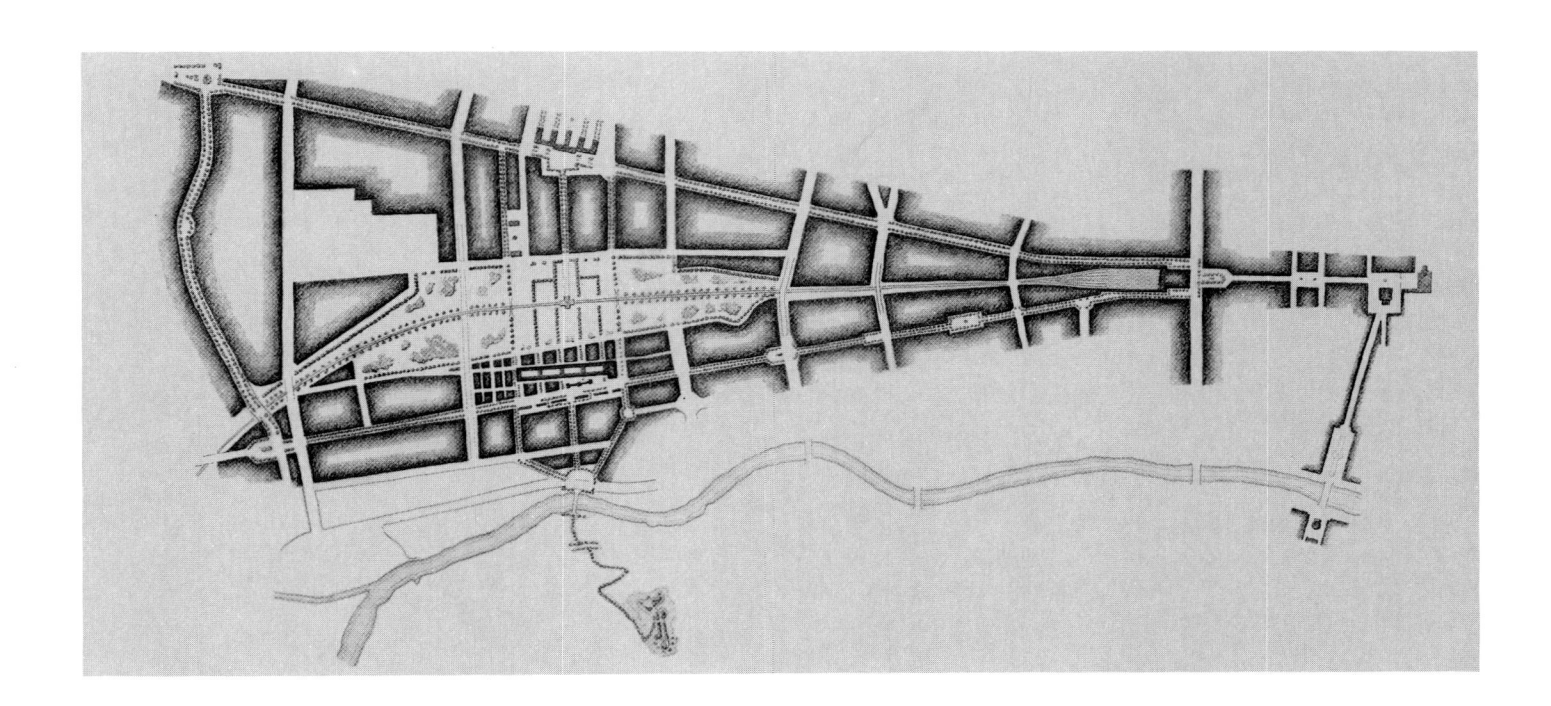

series of U-shaped blocks along the two linear faces of the building.
The present state of this whole area is typical of many peripheral urban situations. There is a lack of shops, communal facilities, amenities for the nearby university, office, administrative and other space. We therefore proposed reserving the plinth storey of the entire complex for such purposes and linking them up with the urban road network. On the levels above the plinth base we proposed a residential urban unit that would be so manifold in nature that, equipped with its own service facilities, would become a little town in itself. Here at rooftop level, therefore, all manner of special amenties were to be provided: a small open-air theatre, bars, an open-air swimming pool, sitting areas and paths for walking and cycling. I can imagine strolling about the entire area, through its alleyways, courtyards and squares, over bridges and ramps, catch-

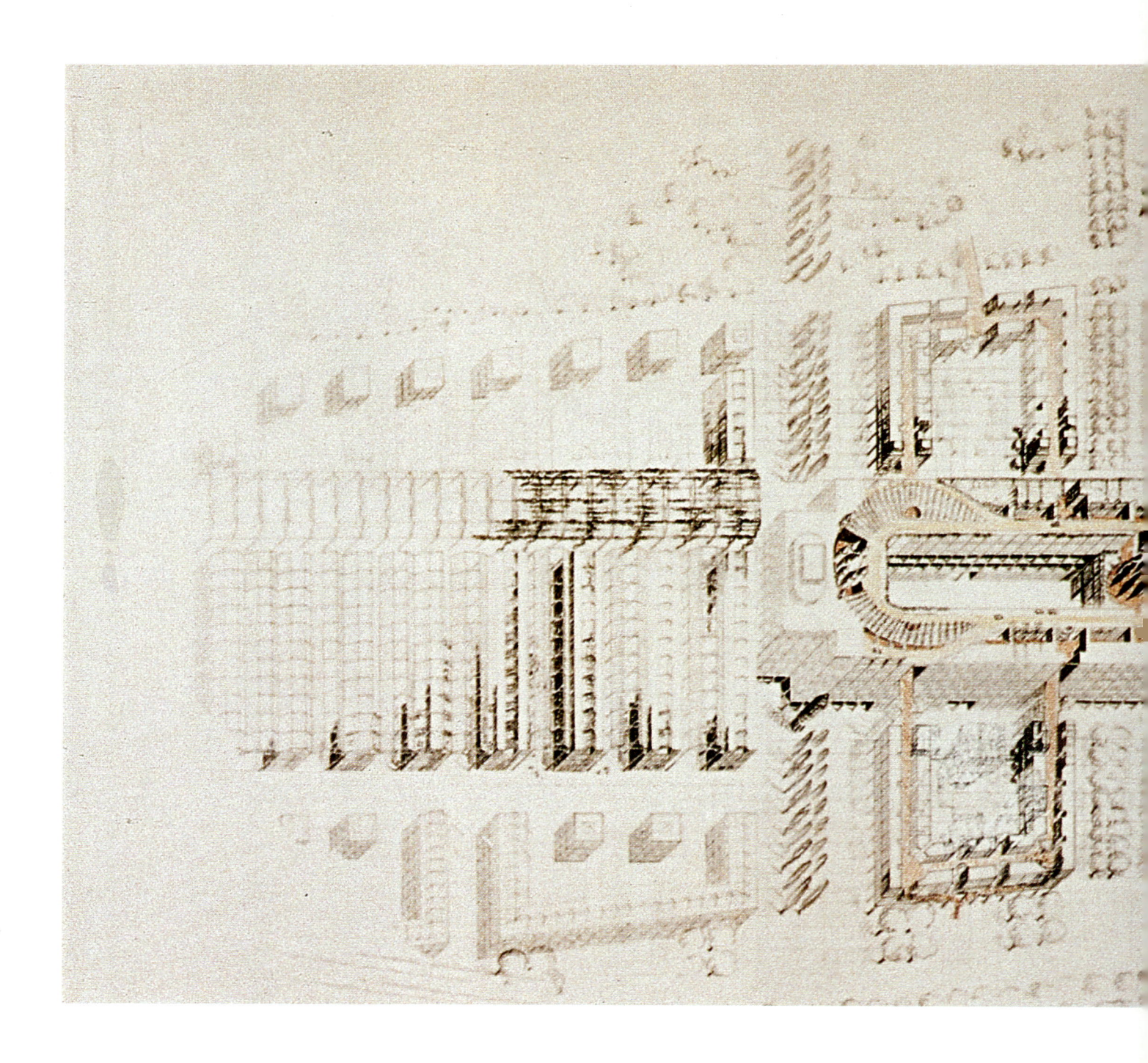

Turin, Fiatwerke — in Zusammenarbeit mit Stefan Böhm

Turin, Fiat Plant — in collaboration with Stefan Böhm

Vorschlag für das Lingottogebäude

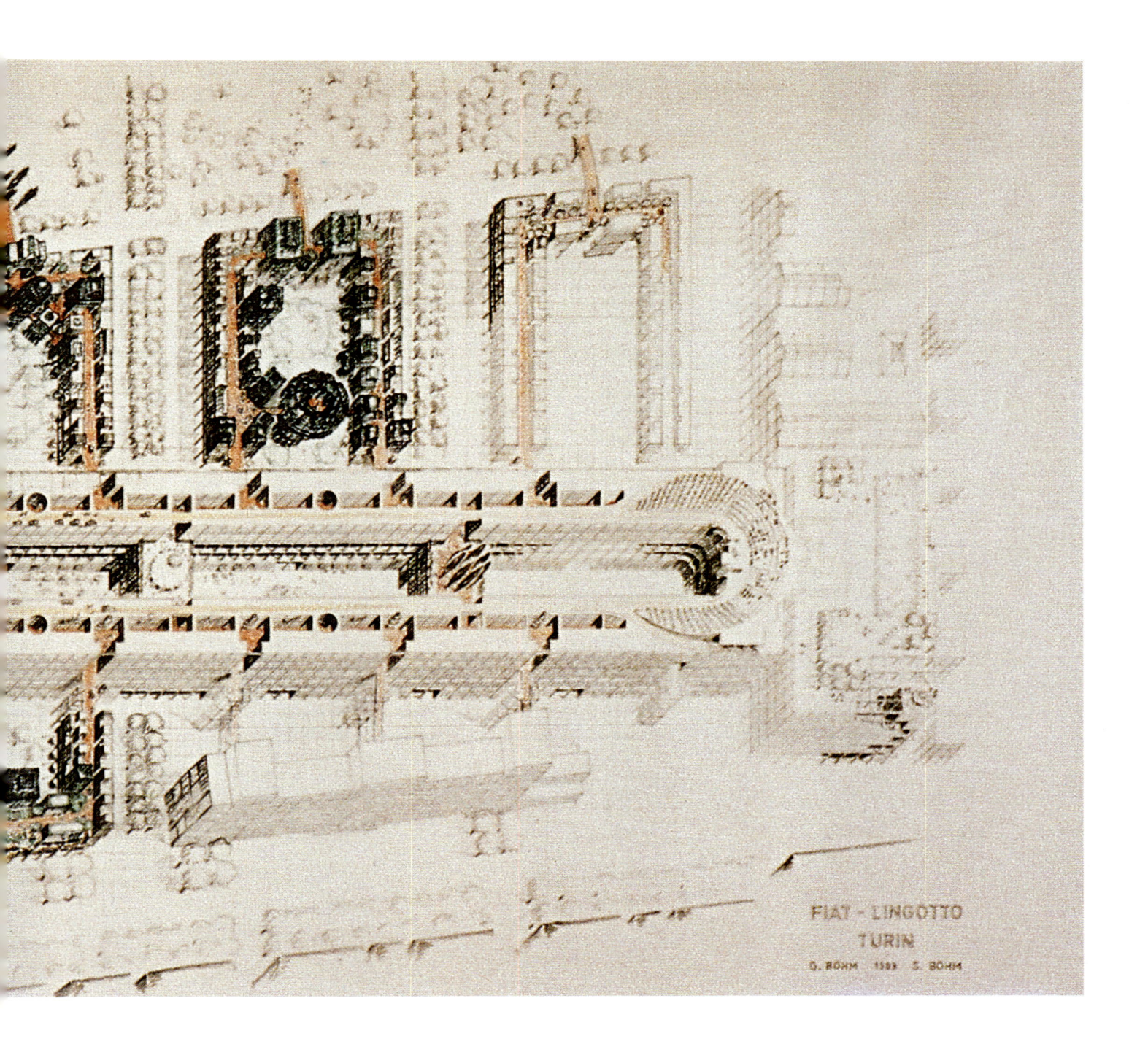

Proposals for Lingotto Building

möglichen Sondereinrichtungen vorgesehen: ein kleines Freilichttheater, Kneipen, ein Freibad, Plätze zum Sitzen, Wege zum Gehen und Radfahren. Ich stelle mir eine Wanderung durch das ganze Gelände mit all den Gassen, Höfen, Plätzen, Brücken, Rampen, mit den vielen Durchblicken, mit Leben und Betrieb wie in einem italienischen Bergstädtchen vor. Zu einer Stadt gehört heute aber auch das Auto. Wir haben nun die Idee der befahrbaren Dachzone weitergesponnen. Die alte Straße wird zum Teil als Autostraße belassen und auch durch die Neubaugebiete geführt, so daß die Anwohner zu ihren Dachgärten und zu ihren Wohnungen und Maisonettes fahren können, die in den Geschossen darunter liegen. Das ergäbe nur geringen Zielverkehr, so daß die Straßen auch für den Fußgänger gemütlich zu begehen sind, daß man verweilen oder vor seiner Wohnung auf der Bank sitzen mag.

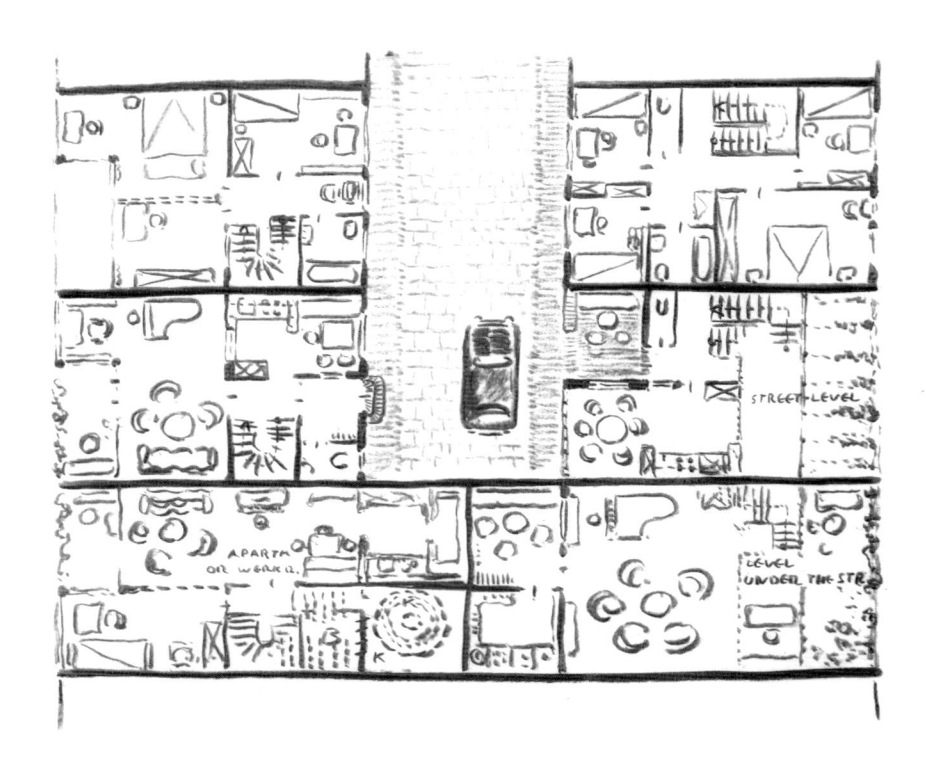

ing glimpses of different perspectives, enjoying changing vistas, the whole organism pulsing with native life and activity, rather like an Italian hill town. Today, of course, the car is an inseparable part of urban life, and we extrapolated the idea of a roof zone accessible to vehicular traffic. The old road would be left in part as a highway and drawn through the new development, so that residents would be able to drive to their gardens and to the flats and maisonettes on the floors below. This would give rise to a relatively low level of local traffic, and the streets would remain spaces in which pedestrians could walk at leisure, where one could stroll about or sit on a bench outside one's own dwelling.
The streets would lead across bridges to the new flanking blocks, where they would expand at certain points to form

Die Straßen führen über Brücken auch in die angebundenen neuen Blocks. Da weiten sie sich manchmal zu Plätzen, da gibt es auch eigenständige Baukörper mit verschiedener Nutzung wie es in einer Stadt normalerweise üblich ist. Diese Straßen und der Dachweg sind den Straßen in der Erdgeschoßebene über Rampen angeschlossen und damit auch Teil des städtischen Straßennetzes.

Diese Überlagerung der zwei Städte – eine eigenständige Wohnstadt mit befahrbaren Straßen und Plätzen und allem, was zu dem Leben dort dazu gehört, über der Geschäftsstadt mit dem Verkehr und Lärm und allem, was auch hier dazu gehört – ergibt sicher eine ideale Wohnsituation.

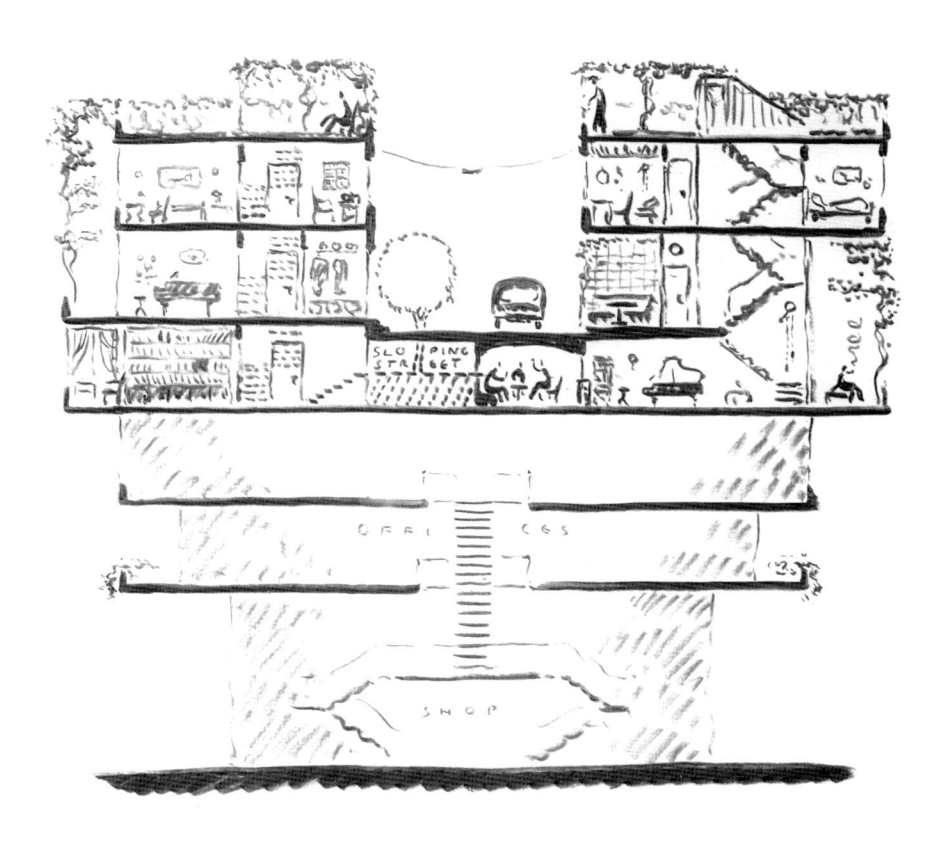

squares. There would be free-standing structures with different uses, as one would normally find in towns. These streets and the rooftop road would be linked to the streets at ground level by ramps and thus form an integral part of the overall urban street network.

The superimposition of two towns like this, – an independent residential urban unit with vehicular roads and open spaces and all the other things that belong to life in such an environment, set above a commercial city with traffic and noise and all those things one associates with this form of urban structure, – this juxtaposition would certainly create an ideal habitat.

Salzburg-Aigen — Altenwohnheim mit Krankenhaus

Old people's home with hospital

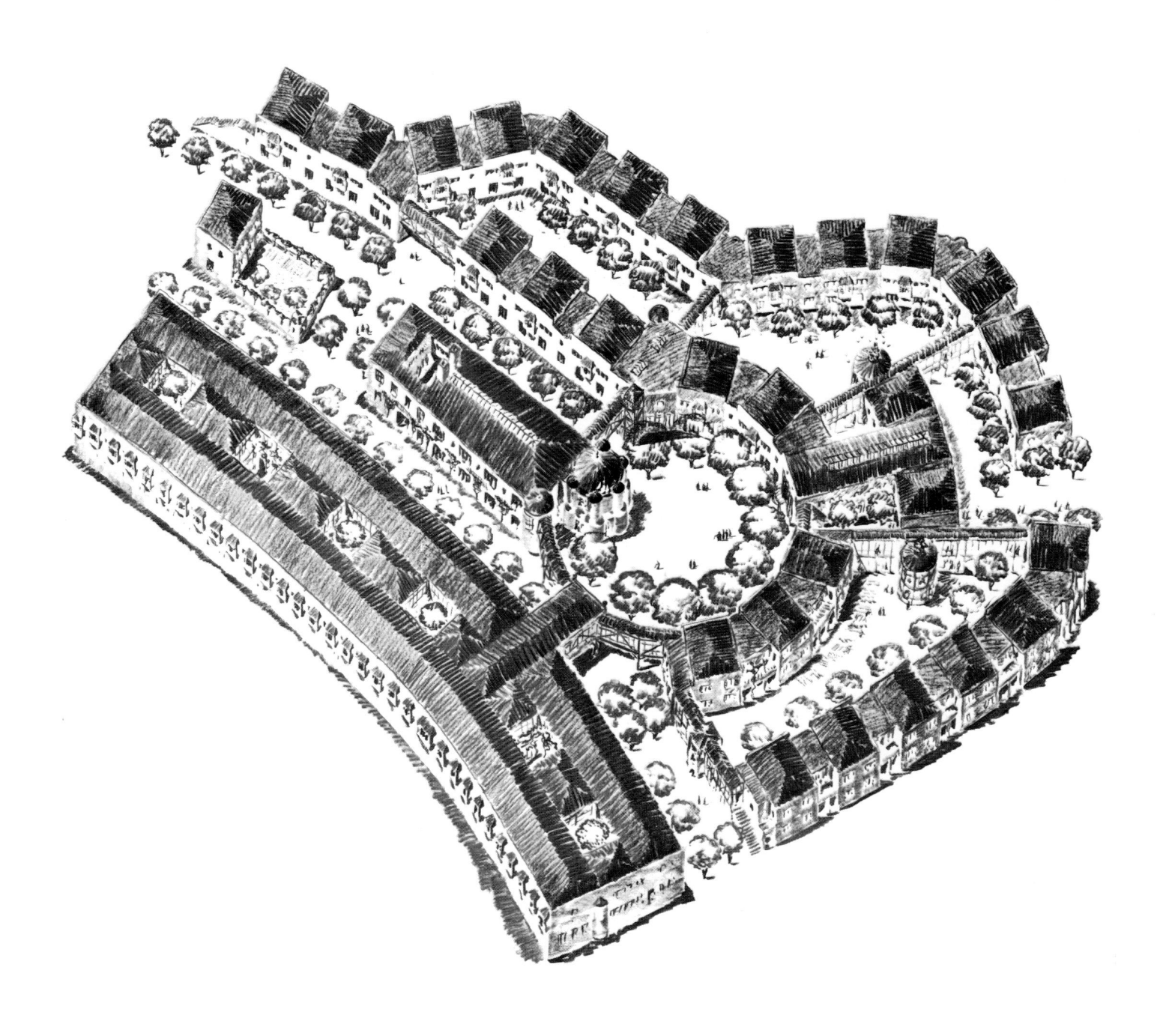

in Zusammenarbeit mit Peter Böhm und Fritz Steinigeweg

Wettbewerb, 1986

in collaboration with Peter Böhm and Fritz Steinigeweg

Competition, 1986

69

Kirchenbau

Köln	St. Columba, 1949
Saarbrücken	St. Albert, 1951
Blumenau, Brasilien	Kirche, 1954
Brusque, Brasilien	Kirche, 1955
Kalscheuren	Kirche, 1958
Tubarao, Brasilien	Kathedrale, Projekt, 1957
Schildgen	Pfarrkirche, 1958, mit Reinhard Stapper, Günter Kaintoch
Ching-Liau, Taiwan	Missionsstation, 1960
Oldenburg	St. Christophorus, 1958, mit H. Schwab
Kassel-Wilhelmshöhe	Pfarrkirche, 1978, mit Hartmut Unger, H. Schwab
Köln	Krefelder Straße, Pfarrzentrum, 1961, mit Hans Schmalscheidt, Wilfried Euskirchen, Klaus Micheel
Neviges	Wallfahrtskirche, 1964, mit Dieter Basilius, Hans Schmalscheidt, F. Wittkopp, Franz Kilian
Köln-Melaten	Kirche mit Jugendheim, 1970, mit Wilhelm Jungherz, Klaus Micheel
Kettwig	Gemeindezentrum: Katholischer Teil, 1977 – Evangelischer Teil, 1983, mit Franz Kilian, Harald Thomä, Günter Kaintoch
Wigratzbad	Wallfahrtskirche, 1976, mit Michael Eberlein
Trier	Restaurierung des Domes, 1969–75, in Zusammenarbeit mit Nikolaus Rosiny, mit Wilhelm Jungherz, Stefan Abelen

Ich finde es sehr schön, daß wir über den Kirchenbau gerade vor dem Weihnachtsfest sprechen, ist doch der Bau der Kirche das sichtbar gewordene Verlangen der Menschen, Gott vom Himmel herunterzuholen und in ihre Welt zu verwurzeln. Unabhängig von Gläubigkeit oder Zweifeln oder Andersdenken war das Errichten einer Kirche für eine Stadt immer ein besonderes Ereignis.

Beim Kirchenbau ist meine Arbeit natürlich in besonderem Maße dem Werk meines Vaters verbunden, und deshalb möchte ich kurz die Hauptstationen seines Schaffens aufzeigen.

Seine erste Kirche baute er 1919, also kurz nach dem Krieg. Das war die Notkirche in Offenbach, im typischen Stil der frühen zwanziger Jahre, in Holz ausgeführt. Es muß ein einfacher, aber ergreifender Bau gewesen sein, wunderbar ausge-

Dominikus Böhm, Kirchen in: Offenbach

Dominikus Böhm, Churches in Offenbach

I always find it a fitting occasion to talk about church building in the pre-Christmas period. The construction of churches is a visible manifestation of the desire in man to bring God down from heaven and make Him part of man's world. Regardless whether one was a believer, a doubter or a dissenter, the erection of a church was always a very special event for a town. My church building work is of course deeply indebted to that of my father. For that reason I should like to outline the main stages of his creative life.

He built his first church in 1919, shortly after World War I. This was the provisional church structure in Offenbach, a timber construction built in the style typical of the early 20s. Simple it may have been, but it must also have been a most moving building, wonderfully decorated on the inside with the paintings of Heiner Holz, who was in my opinion an exceptional ar-

malt von dem Maler Heiner Holz, für meine Begriffe ein ganz außergewöhnlich guter Maler aus dieser Zeit, der Anfang der zwanziger Jahre leider sehr früh gestorben ist. Die Kirche ist in den fünfziger Jahren abgerissen worden, man hat nicht einmal die Bretter mit der Malerei erhalten.

Ebenfalls aus den zwanziger Jahren stammen die Kirche in Neu-Ulm und die Kapelle in Vaals. Beide, wie viele seiner anderen Kirchen in dieser Zeit, haben Gewölbe, die in Rabbiz ausgeführt sind. Hierbei wurde ein Staussziegelgewebe gespannt, das dann mit Betonmörtel verputzt wurde, so daß die entstandene Schale sowohl hängend als auch tragend war. Auch die Kapelle in Vaals ist übrigens aus unverständlichen Gründen abgerissen worden. In der Zeit nach dem Krieg gab es ein heute schwer zu verstehendes Verlangen, alles, was nur ein wenig zerstört oder beschädigt war, ganz zu vernichten

Neu Ulm

Vaals

Frielingsdorf

tist of his generation. He died young, unfortunately, at the beginning of the 1920s. The church was demolished in the 1950s. Not even the timber boards with the paintings were preserved.

The church in Neu-Ulm and the chapel in Vaals also date from the 1920s. In both of these structures, as in many other churches built by my father at this time, he employed a vaulting technique using a wire mesh construction. Stauss clay lathing was fixed in place and coated with cement mortar. The resulting shell construction was both suspended and load-bearing in nature. The chapel in Vaals was also demolished for some inexplicable reason. In the period after the Second World War there was a curious compulsion – difficult to understand today – to pull down and clear away anything that had been even partially destroyed or damaged; a need to forget.

und wegzuräumen: zu vergessen.

Mich haben diese Bauten meines Vaters schon als Student ganz besonders begeistert. Es interessierte mich, wie reich man mit gewebeartigen Konstruktionen Räume gestalten kann.

Aus den dreißiger Jahren ist zum Beispiel die Kirche in Köln-Riehl zu nennen, ein Zentralbau, der wegen seiner neuartigen Raumauffassung wie auch wegen seiner Betonkonstruktion höchstes Aufsehen erregte. Ferner zeige ich Ihnen die Kirche

Dominikus Böhm Köln-Riehl

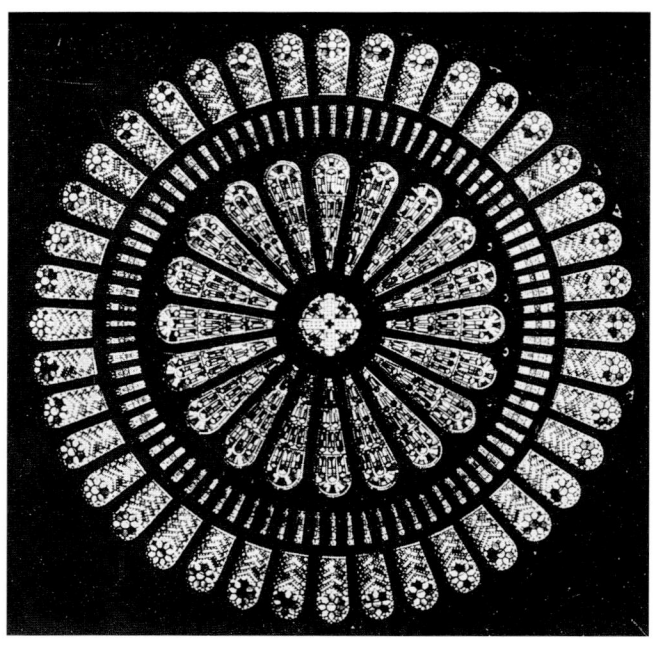

Dominikus Böhm Fensterrose
Rose window

Even as a student I was very enthusiastic about these buildings of my father's. What fascinated me was how richly one could articulate space with web-like constructions.

The church in Riehl, Cologne, for example, with its centralized form, dates from the 1930s. Its spatial concepts, which were modern for the time, and its concrete structure were something of a sensation then. I should also like to mention the church in Hindenburg, which has a markedly directional space. It dates from a period in my father's creative life that was very

in Hindenburg, ein stark gerichteter Raum aus seiner Schaffensperiode, die vom romanischen Raumgedanken geprägt war. Ende der dreißiger Jahre baute er die Kirche in Regensburg mit den großen Fensterrosen, die die gewaltigen Wände sehr reich durchbrechen und auflösen. Von den vielen Fensterrosen, die er gebaut hat, ist wohl diejenige in Dülmen die schönste, bei der das Durchbrechen und Schließen der Wand ganz besonders geglückt ist.

Dominikus Böhm — Kirche in Hindenburg

Dominikus Böhm — Church in Hindenburg

much influenced by Romanesque spatial ideas. At the end of the 1930s he built the church in Regensburg with the great rose windows richly perforating and dissolving the mighty walls. Of the many rose windows he designed, the most beautiful, to my mind, however, is that in Dülmen, in which the piercing and closing of the wall were realized in a particularly fine manner.

Meine eigene erste Bauaufgabe war kurz nach dem Krieg die Kolumba-Kapelle in Köln. Die alte frühgotische Kolumbakirche war sehr stark zerstört und es sah sehr beeindruckend und großartig aus, daß in diesen Trümmern eine Madonnenfigur an ihrem Pfeiler erhalten war. Diese Tatsache wurde in der Öffentlichkeit als besonderes Zeichen des Himmels gesehen und es sollte daher eine Kapelle gebaut werden. Wir haben dazu die Reste des Turms mitverwendet. Ein sehr schönes Glasfenster von Thorn-Prikker, das ausgelagert war, konnten wir hier wieder einsetzen.

Für die Kolumba-Kapelle habe ich meine erste Hängedecke ausgeführt in Anlehnung an die Rabbizgewölbekonstruktion meines Vaters. Dem Wesen eines Gewebes entsprechend habe ich eine hängende Form gewählt. Es wurde über die Mitte

My own first building commission was the St. Columban Chapel in Cologne shortly after the Second World War. The old early Gothic Church of St. Columban had suffered heavy damage. The figure of a Madonna that had survived and still stood on its column amidst the ruins was therefore an impressive and magnificent sight. This circumstance was regarded by the population as a special sign of heaven. It was therefore decided to built a chapel. We incorporated the remains of the old tower in the new structure. It also proved possible to use a particularly beautiful glass window by Thorn-Prikker that had been removed to storage in time.

In the St. Columban Chapel I executed my first suspended ceiling, inspired by the wire mesh vaulted constructions of my

des Raumes ein Stahlträger gelegt, ein Stahlnetzwerk daran gehängt und von oben mit Beton belegt. Durch das Gewicht des Betons ergab sich dann die gewünschte hängende Form. Aus den Trümmern von den Graten der Gewölbe haben wir den Gesimskranz gebildet und ebenfalls aus Trümmerteilen den Fußboden gelegt. Die sehr schönen Fenster von Ludwig Gies kamen später hinzu.
Als Wasserspeier habe ich damals eine Plastik gemacht. Einen Bären, der – wie die Legende sagt – die Heilige Kolumba in Gefahr geschützt hat.
Später gab es noch zwei Planungen mit der Überlegung, wie man die Kapelle in eine Erweiterung der Kirche integrieren

father. I chose to use a suspended form, however, as something more in accordance with the nature of a mesh or web-like structure. A steel beam was laid across the middle of the space and steel netting hung from it. Concrete was poured in top, the weight of the concrete creating the hanging form we desired. We built the cornice ring using rubble from the groins of the old vaulting and used other stone rubble for the floor. The particularly fine windows by Ludwig Gies were a later addition.
For the gargoyles I created a sculpture of my own, – a bear, which, as legend has it, protected St. Columban in time of danger. Two further schemes were subsequently drawn up examining ways of integrating the chapel into an extension of

könnte. Im ersten Projekt stände die Kapelle in einer großen gleichmäßigen Halle, die ebenfalls mit einer Hängedecke versehen werden sollte. Diese Fassung war wohl von dem sehr schönen Entwurf inspiriert, den Tessenow einmal für einen Bau auf der Insel Rügen gemacht hat.

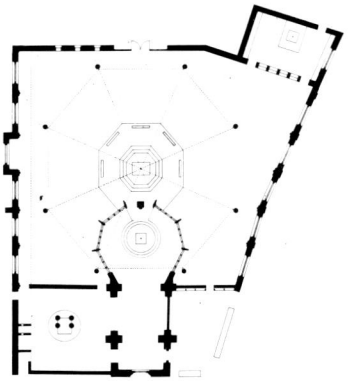

the church. According to the first of these schemes the chapel would have stood within a large regularly shaped hall that would also have had a suspended ceiling construction. These proposals were probably inspired by the lovely design Tes-

Ich wollte eigentlich bei Tessenow, der heute wenig bekannt ist, studieren. Ich habe ihn nie gesehen, aber ich kann sagen, er war einer meiner besten Lehrer.
Im zweiten Projekt war ein großes Oktogon geplant, das auch die Kapelle in ihrem Raum einschloß.

senow once made for a building on the Isle of Rügen. I had originally wanted to study under Tessenow, who is relatively unknown today. I never met him or even saw him, but I can truly say that he was one of my best teachers.
The second scheme proposed a large octagon, in which the chapel would also have been incorporated.

Den nächsten Kirchbau, St. Albert in Saarbrücken (1) kann ich nicht gut verheimlichen, da er doch ein recht typisches Beispiel der Einstellung der fünfziger Jahre darstellt. Es liegt dieser Zeit der Wunsch zu Grunde, mit dem Krieg alles, was nur traditionell überliefert war, abzulehnen und sich auf die unverfälschten Ursprünge und -zustände zu besinnen. Ich erinnere in dem Zusammenhang an das, was ich im Vortrag »Wohnungsbau« über Beton und das Bewahren der Echtheit des Materials gesagt habe wie auch über das Bedürfnis, das man damals hatte, alles scheinbar Morbide abzureißen.

In Saarbrücken war der Wunsch vorherrschend, im Bau nur das ausschließlich darzustellen, was in der Liturgie zeitgemäß

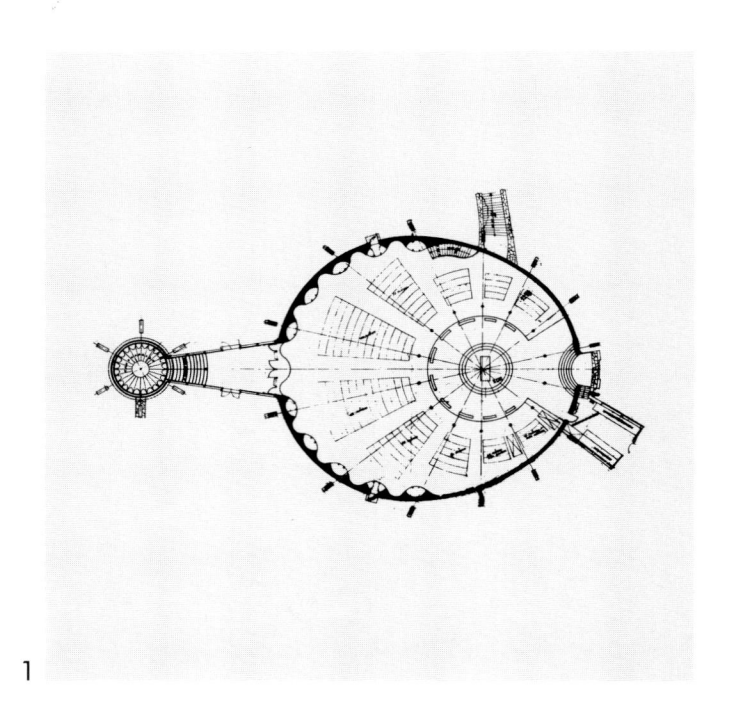

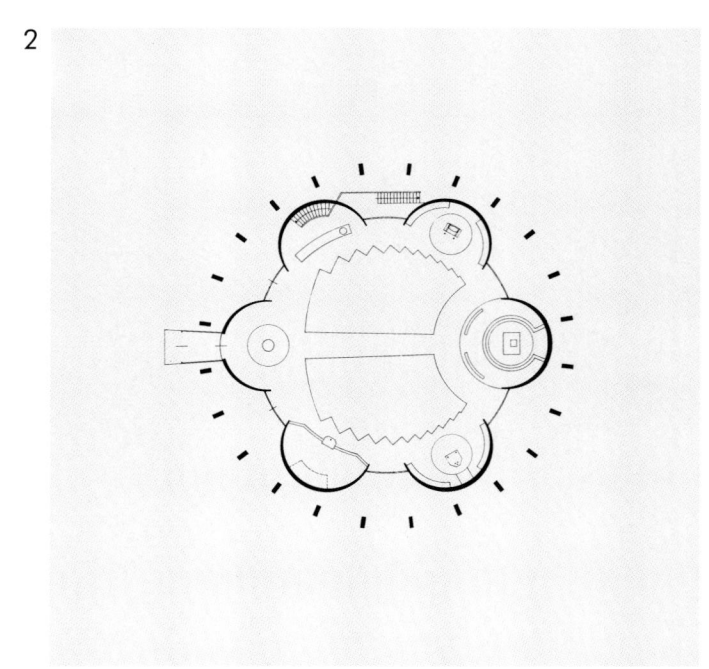

1

2

The next church project, St. Albert's in Saarbrücken (1), is one I cannot very well ignore, for it is a typical product of the attitudes prevailing in Germany in the 50s. Underlying this age was a desire to put behind us everything that had anything to do with the war, to reject all things handed down from tradition, and to return to our origins and to conditions that were pure and unadulterated. In this context I can remember what I said, in a lecture on housing, about concrete and the retention of the genuine quality of the material, and indeed about the need felt at that time to tear down all things seemingly tinged with a sense of morbidity.

In Saarbrücken there was an overriding desire to express in built form, exclusively those elements of the liturgy that ap-

wichtig erschien. So wurde der Raum allein auf das Abendmahl hin konzipiert. Er sollte die Gemeinde darstellen, wie sie sich auch ursprünglich um den Tisch des Herrn versammelt hat.

Die Kirchen von Blumenau (4) und Brusque in Brasilien (3) sind in der gleichen Konstruktionsart gebaut. Streben tragen gleichmäßig eine Segmenttonnenschale. Vom System her ähnlich ist auch die kleine Kirche in Kalscheuren (2). Dort haben wir über einem Stützenkranz eine große Betonsegmentkuppel gebaut, die sozusagen über dem Kirchen-»Platz« schwebt.

3

4

peared relevant to the times. As a result the space was focused solely about the sacrament of Holy Communion. It was meant to represent the community as it might originally have been gathered about the table of the Lord.

The churches in Blumenau (4) and Brusque in Brazil (3) use the same form of construction. Equally spaced struts support a segmental arched shell.

The small church in Kalscheuren (2) employs a similar system. There we constructed a large concrete segmental dome supported by a ring of columns. The dome floats in a sense over the central space of the church.

Im Süden Brasiliens habe ich die Kathedrale in Tubarao geplant. Vorhanden war eine kleine Kapelle. Wir hatten vorgesehen, sie als Taufkapelle zu nutzen, eingegliedert in ein großes offenes Atrium, in dem der Gottesdienst auch im Freien gehalten werden könnte. Der eigentliche Kirchenraum ist die Fortsetzung dieses Atriums. Er umschließt seinerseits wieder den Chorraum.

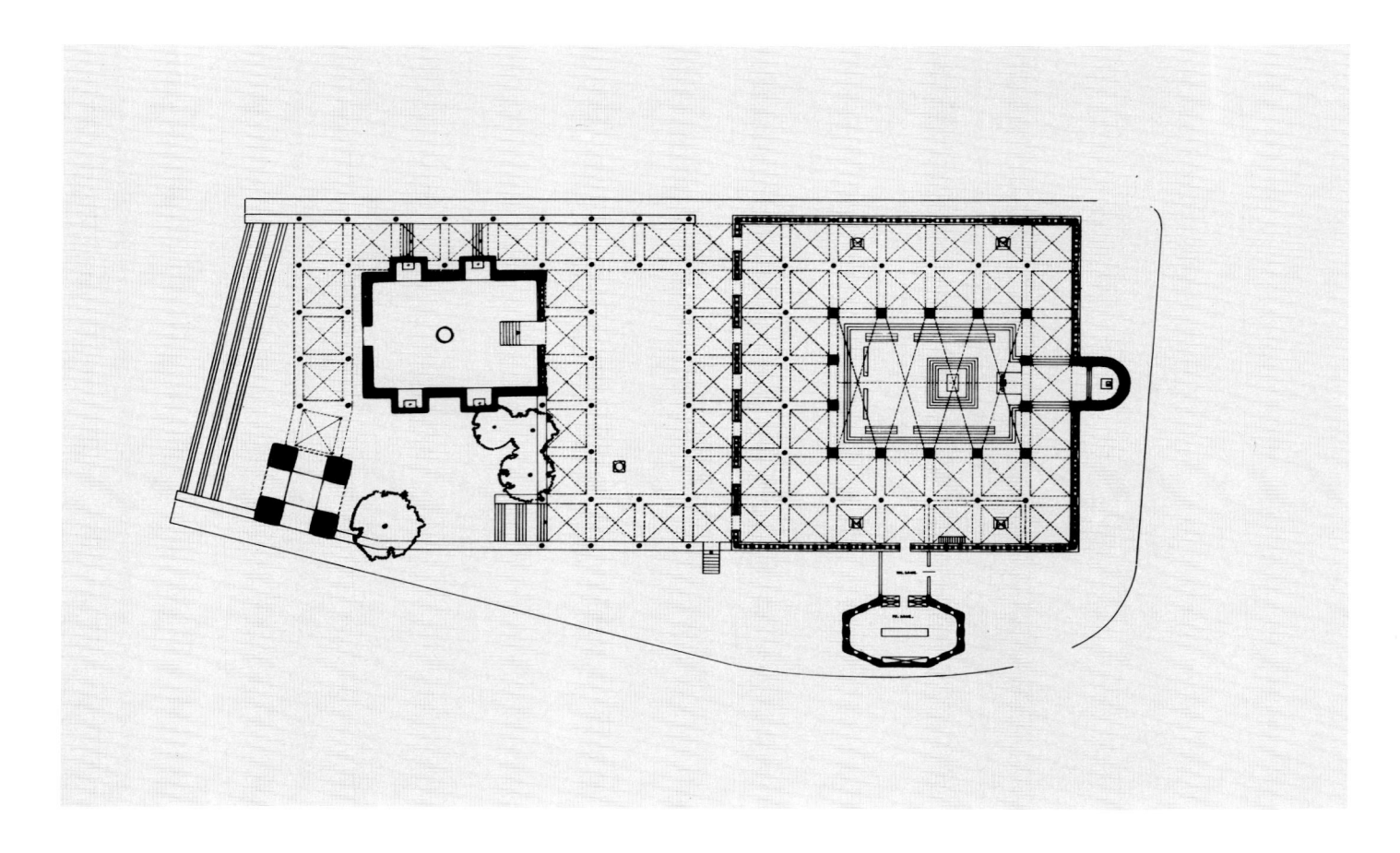

I also designed the Cathedral of Tubarao in the south of Brazil. There was a small existing chapel that we had intended to use as a baptistery, integrated into a large open atrium where services could also be held in the open-air. The actual church space is a continuation of this courtyard and encloses the chancel or choir at the centre.

Tubarão — Cathedral

Das Prinzip, den Ort bestimmter Funktionen mit markanten geometrischen Bauformen zu betonen, sie dann zu umschließen und zu verbinden, habe ich mehrfach ausgeführt, zum Beispiel in Schildgen. Eine große Mauer umgrenzt das ganze Areal einschließlich eines geräumigen Vorhofes, der von dem alten Saalbau, dem Pfarrhaus und den Neubauten gebildet wird. In diesem Hof steht der Glockenturm mit einer kleinen Kapelle. Ein Atrium mit Taufkapelle schließt sich an. Es ist Teil

I have often adopted the principle of stressing the location of particular functions with striking structural forms, enclosing them in space and creating links between them. It is something I did in Schildgen, for example. A high wall encloses the entire complex, including a spacious forecourt that is defined by the old hall structure, the presbytery and the new buildings. There is also a bell tower with a small chapel in this courtyard and an adjoining atrium and baptistery. It forms part of a

eines großen Umgangs, der in Gestalt einer Art Seitenschiff mit Beichtstühlen durch die Kirche fortgeführt wird und weiterhin auch den Chor umschließt. Alle besonderen Funktionen werden durch Türme betont und so auch von außen deutlich sichtbar markiert.

large ambulatory that continues through the church as a kind of aisle with confessionals and is drawn round the head of the chancel. The locations of all special functions are emphasized by towers, which provide a clear landmark on the outside as well.

Im System ähnlich ist ein Kirchenzentrum auf Formosa, das ich für eine katholische Missionsstation gebaut habe. Die Anlage besteht aus einer Kirche, Wohnungen, einer kleinen Schule und einem offenen Hofraum mit einem Glockenturm

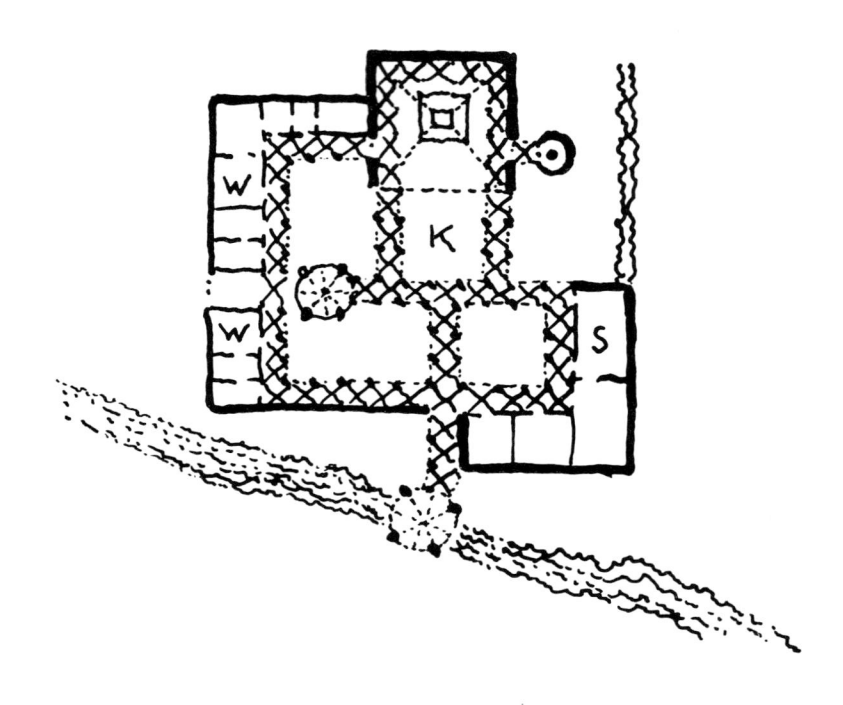

The church centre I built for a Roman Catholic mission on Formosa (Taiwan) is based on a similar system. The complex consists of a church, a number of dwellings, a small school and an open courtyard with a bell tower over the entrance. All

über dem Eingang. Alle diese Bereiche sind umschlossen von überdachten Gängen und durch diese Gänge miteinander verbunden. Eine kleine Brücke führt über den Bach und durch den Glockenturm auf den inneren Platz.

these realms are linked and enclosed by covered walkways. A small bridge leads across a stream and beneath the bell tower into the courtyard.

St. Christophorus in Oldenburg ist ein anderes Beispiel dieser Konzeption. Der streng umgrenzte Komplex umfaßt Kir-

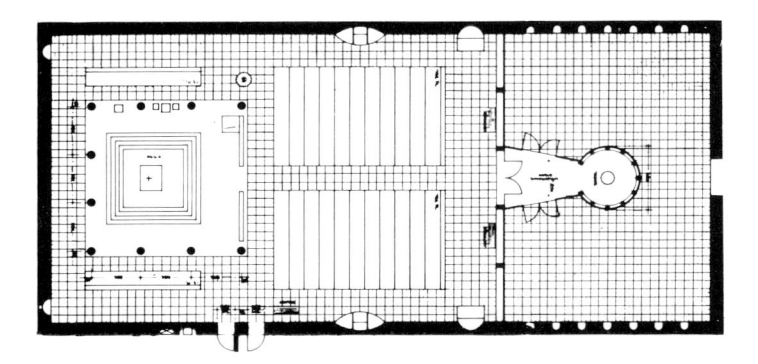

88 St. Christopher's in Oldenburg is another example of the same basic concept. The complex is bounded by a high wall

che und Vorhof. Türme markieren den Chorraum und die Taufkapelle im Vorhof.

and comprises a church with a forecourt. The chancel area and the baptistery in the forecourt are marked by towers.

Zu der Kirche in Kassel führt eine lange Straßenallee den Hang hinauf und geht in eine Treppenanlage über, die in den Kirchenraum hineinführt. Der Weg setzt sich im Inneren fort. Er wird betont durch die seitlichen Mauern sowie auch durch die Konstruktion mit dem gefalteten Träger, der vom Eingang bis zur Altarwand gespannt ist. Alles ordnet sich dem Gedanken des Weges unter.

Die verschiedenen Funktionen, die in den vorigen Beispielen betont als Einzelbaukörper in Erscheinung traten und durch ein neutrales Bauglied verbunden waren, sind in Kassel in einem Gehäuse zusammengefaßt.

Die Außenwände sind in rotgefärbtem Schüttbeton ausgeführt. Wir haben uns Mühe gegeben, die Arbeitsgänge im Schüttvorgang so durchzuführen, daß eine sehr lebendige und edle Oberflächenstruktur entsteht, die die Halle wie einen kostbaren großen Schrein wirken läßt.

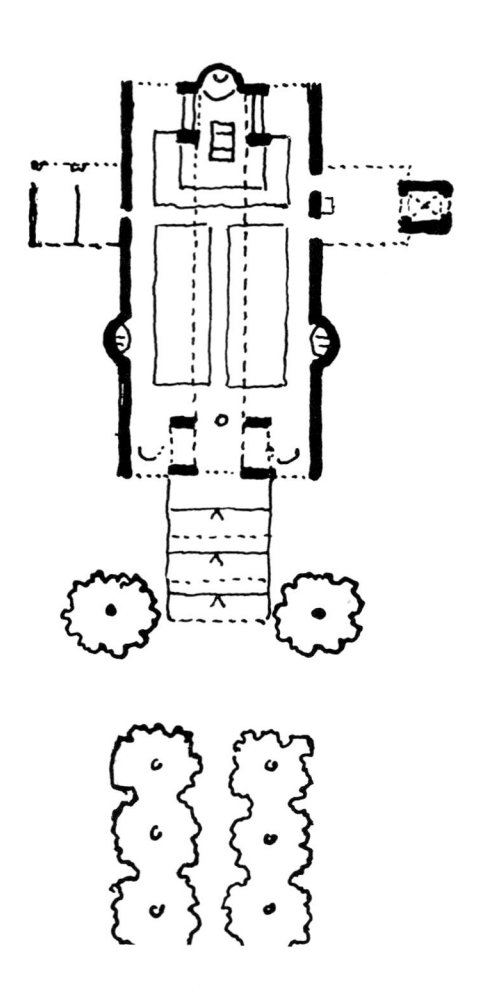

There is a long avenue of trees leading up the hill to the church in Kassel. This route is taken up by a broad flight of steps that leads one directly into the church. The path continues in a straight line inside and is reinforced by the side walls, and by the folded beam spanning from the entrance to the rear chancel wall. Everything is subordinated to the idea of this processional way.

The various functions in the examples above – stressed in the form of individual built volumes with neutral connecting links – are united in a single structure in Kassel. The external walls were built in red-coloured no-fines concrete. We took great pains to execute the various stages of the casting process so as to obtain a high quality, lively surface texture that would give the hall the appearance of a large and precious shrine.

Kassel — Marienkirche

Der gefaltete Träger, der in Kassel gleichsam als Unterkonstruktion die eigentliche Decke trägt, die sich wiederum mit den Wänden verbindet, war der Beginn für Überlegungen zu Faltwerkkonstruktionen an mehreren Kirchen. Die erste Realisierung erfolgte in Köln mit dem Bau von St. Gertrud. Diese Kirche liegt in einer geschlossen bebauten Straßenfront, die wir im Kirchenbereich so ausgeweitet haben, daß ein kleiner Vorplatz entstand mit dem Glockenturm, dem Jugendheim und

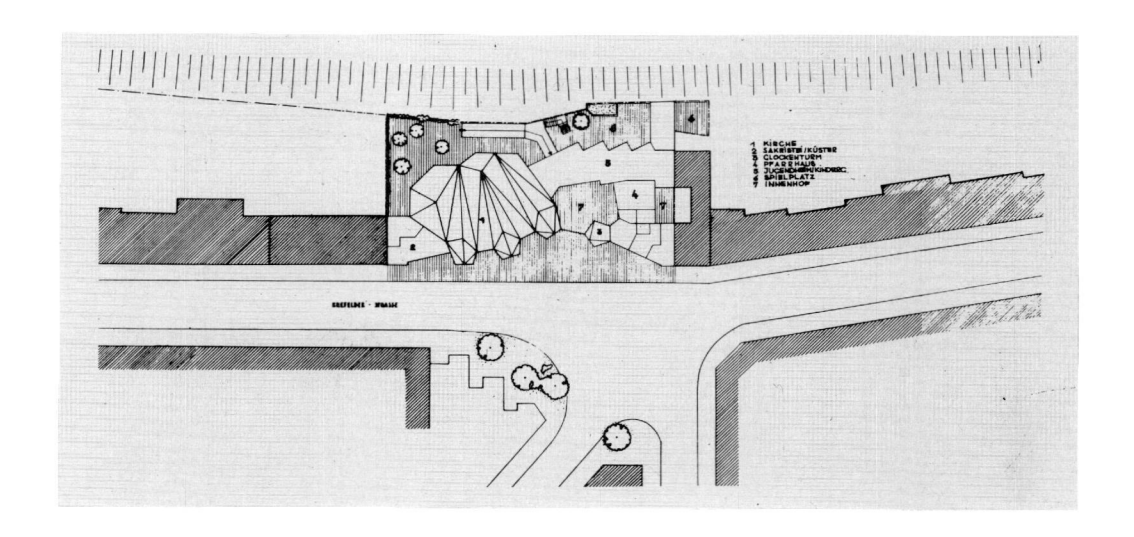

The folded beam in Kassel forms the load-bearing element supporting the actual roof, which in turn links up with the walls. This beam represented the beginning of a whole series of folded or prismatic structures used in churches. The first case in which we realized a design of this type was in St. Gertrude's in Cologne. This church is situated in a unbroken street front, which we pushed back along the length of the church to create a small forecourt with a bell tower, a youth centre and

dem Pfarrhaus.
Wir hatten Jahre zuvor schon einen Entwurf gemacht mit zusammengesetzten Einzelbaukörpern. Aufgrund der Faltwerküberlegungen kam mir aber der Gedanke, daß es konsequenter wäre, Decke und Wände mit der Faltwerkkonstruktion in eine räumliche Einheit zusammenzufassen. Dieses System wurde dann bei mehreren Kirchenprojekten weiterentwickelt,

a presbytery.
Some years previously we had already designed a scheme in which we had assembled a series of individual built volumes to form an ensemble. In view of our ideas of creating a folded structure, I felt it would be more consistent to unite the ceilings and walls in this structure to form a single spatial entity. This system subsequently underwent further development in a

Köln, St. Gertrud

1. und 2. Projekt

94 Cologne, St. Gertrude's

1st and 2nd Projects

Köln — St. Gertrud

Cologne — St. Gertrude's

so auch bei der Wallfahrtskirche in Neviges. Diese Kirche liegt an einem Hang, den wir zusammen mit einer Randbebauung als großen Wallfahrtsweg ausgebildet haben.
Der Weg führt zu einem offenen Kirchenvorplatz, der sich in den umschlossenen Kirchenraum fortsetzt. Der Altarraum ist dann das Ende des Weges.
Während in Kassel der »Weg« über den Altar hinweg einem fernen Ziel zustrebt, ist hier der Altar das Ziel, von dem aus

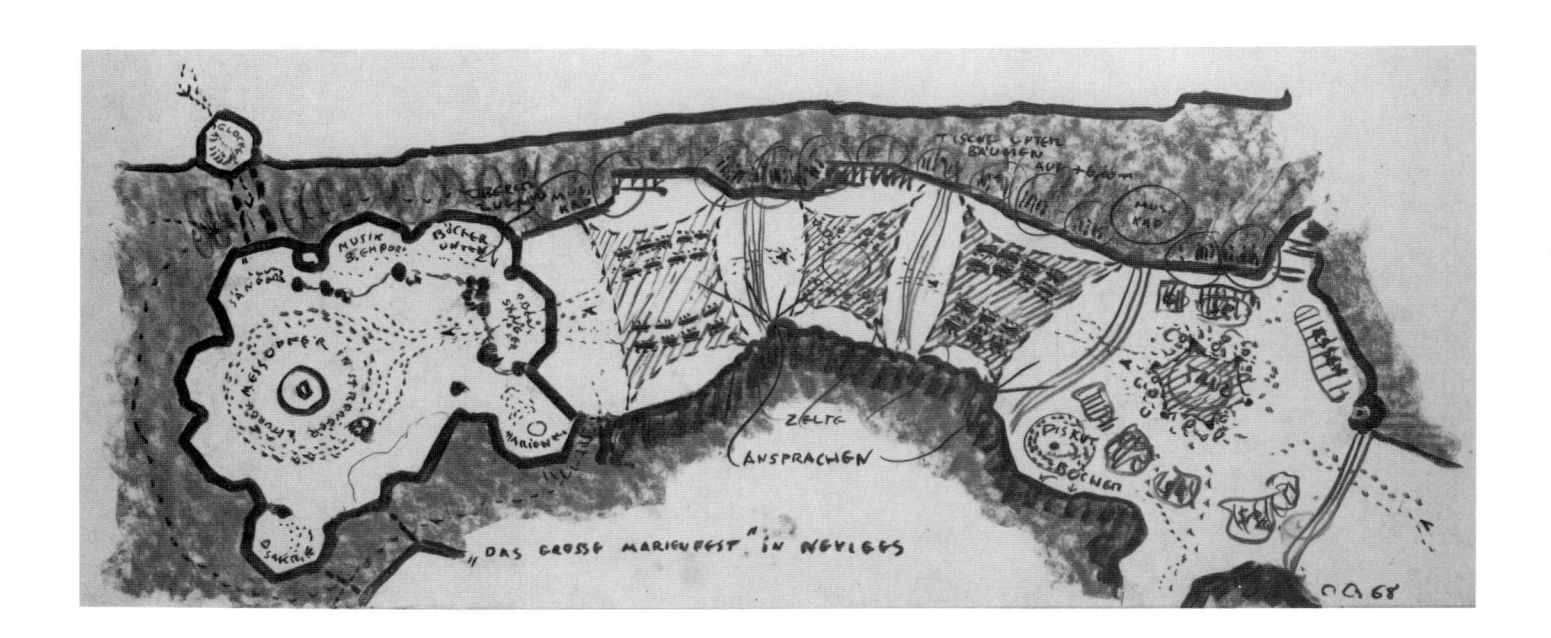

number of church designs, as for example in the Pilgrimage Church in Neviges. The church in Neviges is situated on a slope, which, in conjunction with a flanking development, we turned into a great processional way for pilgrims.
This route leads to an open forecourt in front of the church and continues into the space within, the altar area representing the culmination of this path.
Whereas in Kassel the »path« would seem to lead on beyond the altar to some distant goal, in Neviges it is the altar itself

sich der Blick nach oben wendet. In diesem Kircheninnenraum ist der Wille besonders sichtbar, aus Decken und Wänden eine konstruktive und räumliche Einheit zu bilden.
Seitlich des Wallfahrtsweges liegt vor der Kirche das Pilgerhaus mit Versorgungseinrichtungen für die Pilger und mit Schlafzellen im Obergeschoß. Der Vorplatz wird im Sommer bei großen Veranstaltungen mit genutzt und teilweise mit Zelten überspannt.

that is the goal, from where one's eyes are diverted upwards. In the interior of this church the desire to create a structural and spatial unity of walls and ceilings is particularly evident.
Situated in front of the church to one side of the path of pilgrimage is the pilgrims' house, containing welfare and service facilities and sleeping cells on the upper floor. In summer the forecourt approach is also used as an outdoor space for major events. Tent-like roofs can be spanned over part of its area.

Neviges — Wallfahrtskirche

Neviges — Pilgrimage Church

Neviges — Wallfahrtskirche

Neviges — Pilgrimage Church

Neviges — Wallfahrtskirche / Pilgrimage Church

Neviges — Wallfahrtskirche / Pilgrimage Church

Neviges, Wallfahrtskirche

Neviges, Pilgrimage Church

mit Elmar Hillebrand

with Elmar Hillebrand

Die Auferstehungskirche in Köln-Melaten bildet wohl den Abschluß meiner Bauten, die den Ausdruck der architektonischen Plastik sehr in den Vordergrund stellen. Eine lange Wasserstraße führt zum Kirchplatz hin: eine sehr schöne Situation mit dem Wasser und den hohen Bäumen auf beiden Seiten, die den Eingangsbereich der Kirche umrahmen.

Köln-Melaten, Kirche, Grundriß

rechts: 1. Skizze

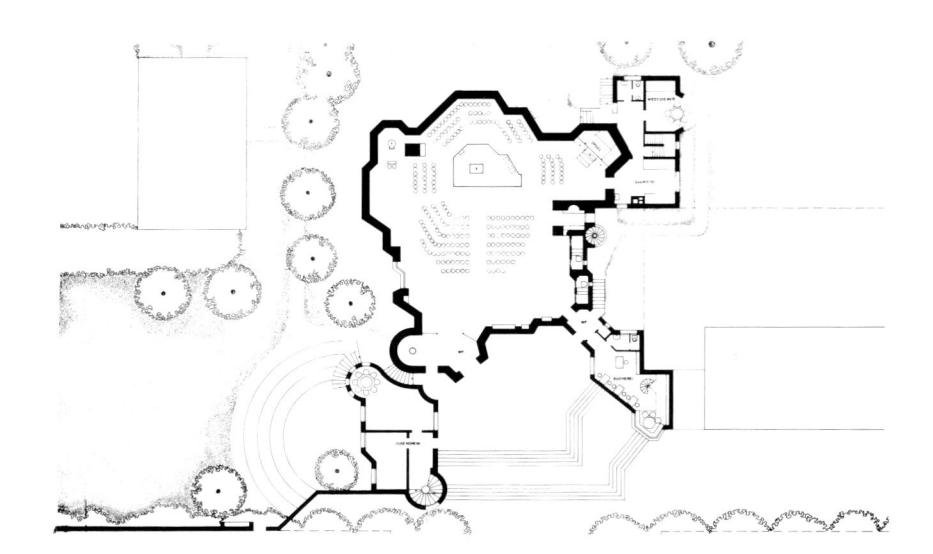

Melaten, Cologne, Church, ground plan

on the right: 1st sketch

The Church of the Resurrection in Melaten, Cologne, probably represents the culmination of that line of development in my buildings, where the expression of the sculptural element in architecture predominates. A long strip of water leads up to the open space in front of the church. It is a very beautiful situation, with the water and the tall trees to both sides framing the entrance to the church.

Im Innern sind es tragende Betonsäulen, die sich wie Bäume nach oben verzweigen und immer dichter schließlich zur Decke werden. Die Zwischenfelder sind ausgemauert. Für die Fenster haben wir Kunststoffplatten mit Nägeln musterartig belegt und mit verschiedenfarbigem Kunststoff eingegossen. So entstanden starke Kunststoffplatten, die ein ganz eigenartiges Licht geben.

Inside, load-bearing concrete columns branch out like trees at the top, growing denser and denser until they merge with the ceiling. The intermediate spaces are closed with masonry filling. For the windows we laid out nails in pattern form on plastic sheets and then poured plastic of various colours on to this. The resulting thick plastic slabs were used for fenestration, and the light admitted through them is of a quite remarkable quality.

Köln-Melaten

Melaten, Cologne

Auferstehungskirche

Church of the Resurrection

Köln-Melaten — Auferstehungskirche — Schnitt

Melaten, Cologne — Church of the Resurrection — Section

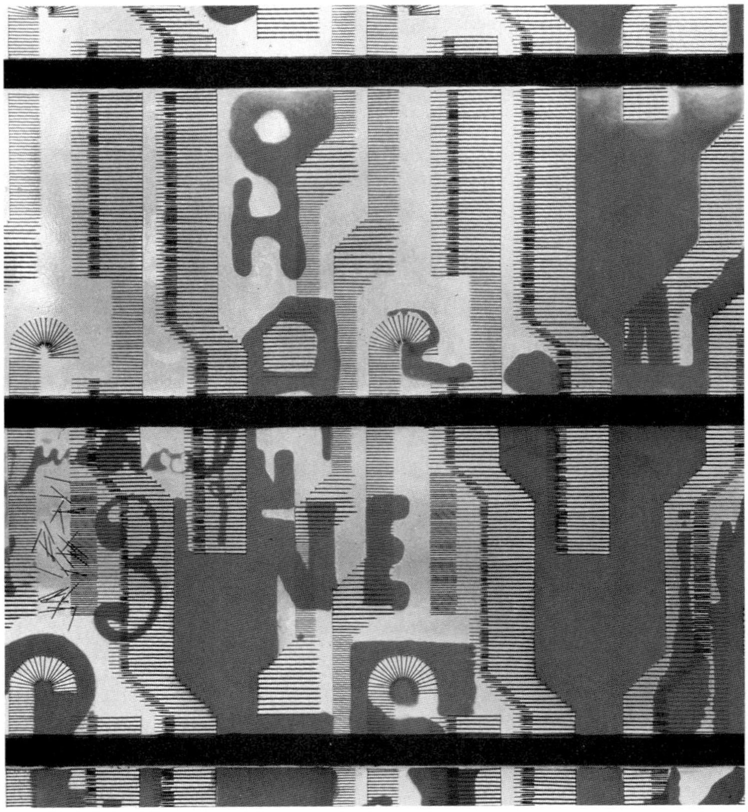

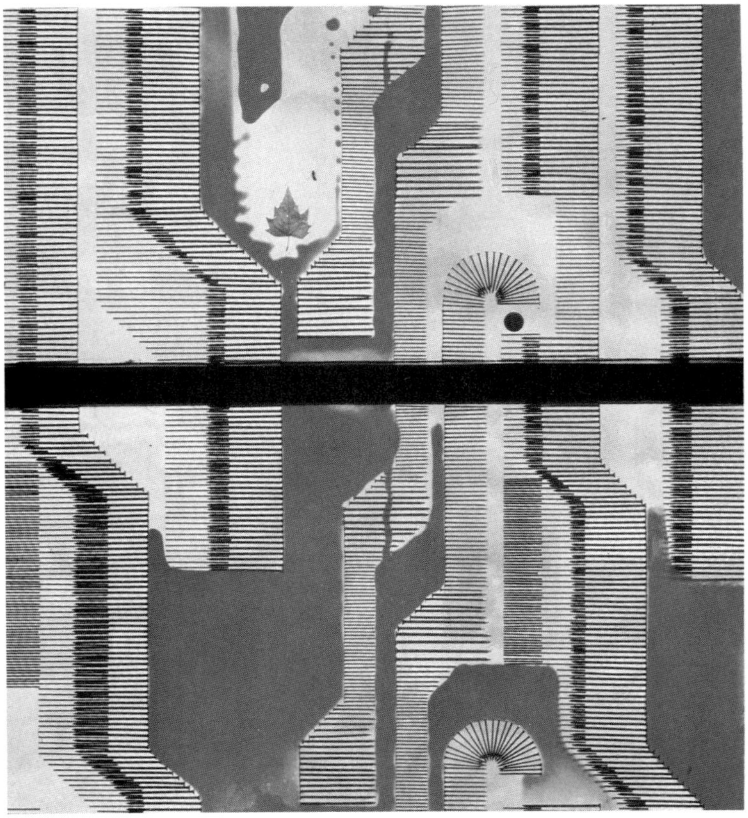

Es war eine interessante Aufgabe, viele Jahre später in Kettwig ein Kirchenzentrum zu schaffen, das zugleich der katholischen wie auch der evangelischen Kirche dient. Da ging es ganz besonders darum, das Gemeinsame, Verbindende sichtbar zu machen, ohne das Eigenständige zu verschleiern. Verbinden ohne zu vermischen, das ist doch immer wieder das Problem für uns als Städtebauer und als Architekten bis hinein in jedes Detail.
Der große Saal des katholischen Teils ist vor allem Kirchenraum; der große Saal des protestantischen Teils wird wohl auch

Kettwig   Gemeindezentrum

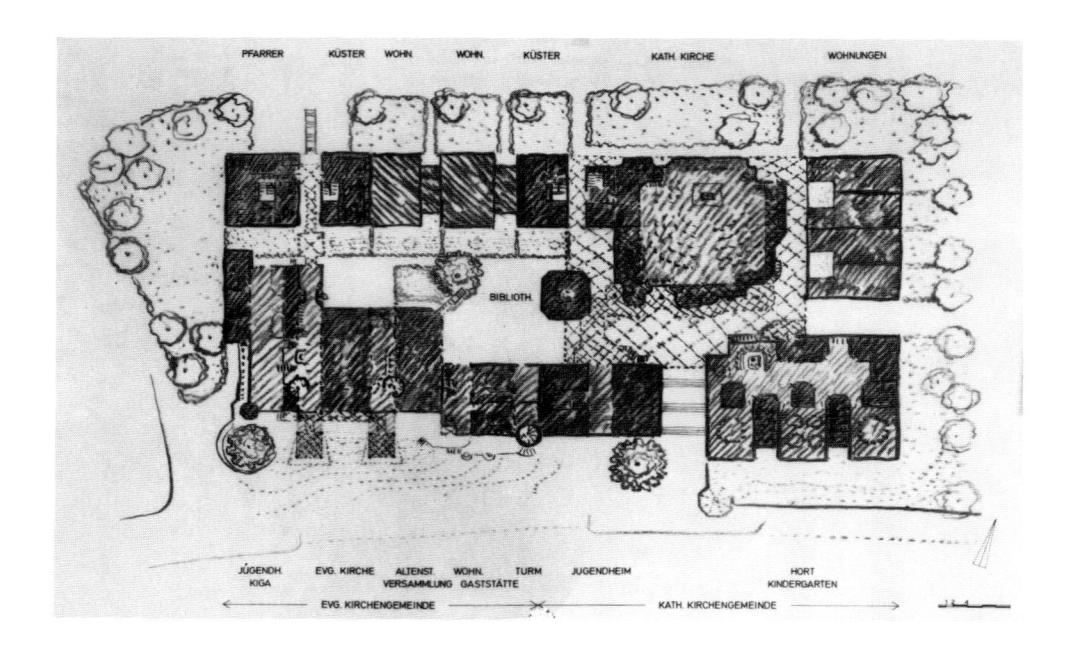

Kettwig   Community Centre

It was an interesting commission many years later to design a church centre in Kettwig for both the Catholic and Protestant Churches. Here we are particularly concerned with making visible the common, uniting elements of the two Churches without blurring the differences. How to connect things without mixing them up is the recurring problem with which we, as urban designers and architects, are faced; and it is a problem that continues through the design work down to the very last detail.

als Kirche genutzt, ist aber doch eher ein Mehrzweckraum für vielerlei Funktionen.
Unter einem Dach gruppieren sich mit diesen großen Haupträumen ein Jugendheim, Kindergärten, eine Bibliothek, eine Kneipe und Wohnungen, die zum Teil von kleinen Gassen erschlossen werden. Die ganze Anlage hat eine sehr deutliche Verbindung zur Straße, die ich mir zu einem Straßenplatz ausgeweitet wünschte, damit der Ortsteil dort eine Mitte erhält.

The large hall of the Roman Catholic section of this centre is first and foremost a church space. The large hall in the Protestant section is also used as a church, but it is essentially a multi-purpose space for a variety of functions.
Grouped about these two main spaces are a youth hostel, a kindergarten, a library, a bar, and a number of dwellings, access to which is in part via small lanes. The entire complex has a strong orientation to the road, which I wished to expand at this point to form an open space and thus create a centre for the district as a whole.

Kettwig

112 Kettwig

Gemeindezentrum

Community Centre

Die Wallfahrtskirche in Wigratzbad im Allgäu ist aus vielen zeltartigen Teilen zusammengesetzt. Es handelt sich hier um eine Wallfahrt, die sich nach dem Kriege entwickelt hat. Es ist zu erwarten, daß die Kirche nur für eine beschränkte Zeit in der jetzigen Größe benötigt wird. Wir hatten deshalb den Gedanken, so zu bauen, daß einzelne Zeltabschnitte wieder entfernt und anderswo errichtet werden können. Sozusagen eine verwandelbare Kirche oder eine auf dem Wege dorthin,

The Pilgrimage Church in Wigratzbad in the Allgäu consists of a large group of tent-like elements. The act of pilgrimage to this place was something that developed after the war. The church will probably be required in its present size only for a limited period. Our concept was therefore to build it in such a way that the individual »tent« segments could be removed again and erected elsewhere; it is a transmutable church, so to speak, or a church on its way to the place where it

wo sie gebraucht wird. Der Bau ist deshalb ganz in Stahlkonstruktion ausgeführt.
Im Innern gibt es eine kleine Empore, die sich durch den Kirchenraum zieht. So ist, wenn notwendig, für viele Leute Platz, ohne daß der Raum zu groß wird.

is needed. For that reason the construction was entirely of steel. Inside there is a small balcony that extends through the space of the church, thus helping to provide adequate room for a great number of people without the space seeming too large.

Bei dem Wettbewerb für den Dom zu Trier hat mich ganz besonders der Zwischenraum vom Dom und der anschließenden gotischen Marienkirche interessiert. Ich kannte die Situation von früher sehr gut und fand vor allem den Raum der Marienkirche, der in den fünfziger Jahren von Rudolf Schwarz restauriert wurde, sehr schön. Er ist inzwischen durch stark farbige Fenster ziemlich verdorben worden.

Der Dom selbst war von einer protzigen Kälte, so daß ich ihn eigentlich gar nicht mochte. Ich habe mich deshalb mit Vehemenz auf die Zwischenzone gestürzt. Das eigentlich Interessante war für mich, das Beieinander von Dom, Marienkirche und Kreuzgang zu betonen und so zu einer einheitlichen Anlage zu verbinden, daß die Einmaligkeit dieser Situation erlebbar wird.

Ich habe für den Zwischenbereich Entwürfe in zwei Varianten gemacht. Die eine sieht eine niedrige Verbindung mit einer Stahlkonstruktion vor. Inmitten der Halle, die sich so ergab, sollte eine kleine Sakramentskapelle für beide Kirchen stehen. Die zweite Variante zeigt eine hohe Halle, die nicht mehr als Zwischenbereich wirkt, sondern als wichtiger Teil der Gesamtanlage.

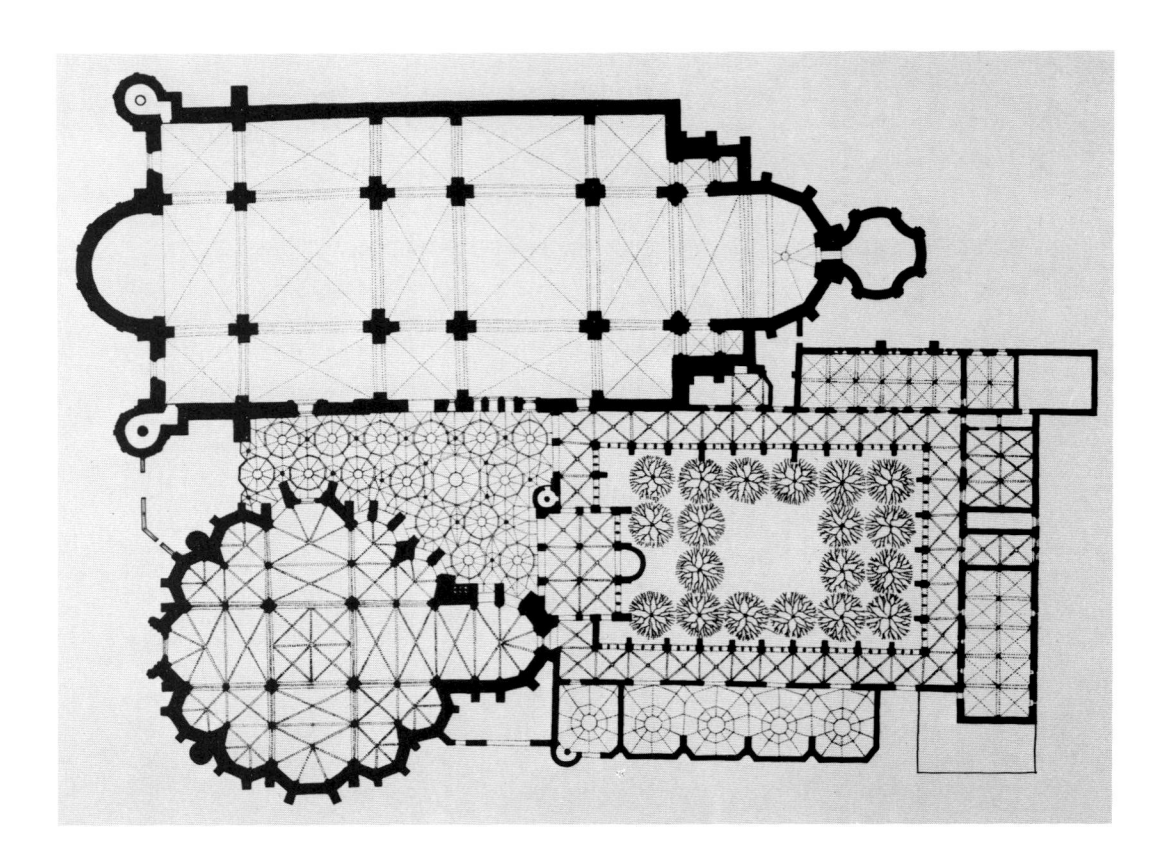

What particularly interested me about the competition for Trier Cathedral was the intermediate space between the cathedral itself and the adjoining Gothic church of St. Mary. I was well acquainted with the situation from a much earlier time, and I admired the fine interior space of St. Mary's, which Rudolf Schwarz had restored in the 1950s. (In the meantime it has been spoilt by the insertion of boldly coloured fenestration.)

The cathedral itself radiated an air of ostentatious coldness, and in all honesty I did not like it really. I therefore concentrated all my attention on the intermediate zone. What interested me was to stress the proximity of cathedral, St. Mary's Church and cloisters and to unite them all into a single entity, thus bringing out the uniqueness of this situation.

I made two alternative sets of proposals for the intermediate realm. The first was for a low steel linking structure. In the middle of the hall that was thus created would have stood a small sacramental chapel serving both churches. The alternative scheme proposed the building of a tall hall that no longer functioned as an intermediate zone, but would have represented an important new element of its own within the overall complex.

Nothing came of these ideas for an intermediate element. Instead, we were awarded the commission for the restoration

Aus dem Zwischenteil ist nichts geworden. Wir haben stattdessen den Auftrag für die Restaurationsarbeiten des Doms bekommen. Ich habe sie zusammen mit Nikolaus Rosiny durchgeführt und dabei den Dom während des Planens und Bauens immer mehr schätzen gelernt.

Der Grund für meine frühere Abneigung war der Umstand, daß alles ganz glatt verputzt und schmierig weißgrau gestrichen war. Die Sicherungsarbeiten ergaben, daß das ganze Mauerwerk überall verpreßt werden mußte. Der Putz kam dadurch natürlich herunter, es kam ein herrliches Mauerwerk zutage mit sehr interessanten Details aus allen Epochen. Vieles ist noch aus der römischen Zeit, und seither haben die Spuren der Geschichte sich in dem Mauerwerk vielfältig niedergeschlagen. Unsere Arbeit und unser einziges Verdienst war, dieses einmalig interessante und schöne Mauerwerk vor den Denkmalschützern geschützt zu haben, die unbedingt den vorherigen Zustand der Verputzung wieder herstellen wollten. Man kann heute kaum mehr nachvollziehen, wie sich der gesamte Raum durch die Freilegung des Mauerwerks verändert hat, wie alles viel größer und großartiger und reicher geworden ist, wie die früher protzig kalte Monumentalität sich in einen gewaltigen, aber ruhigen, beschaulichen, andächtigen Raum verwandelt hat.

work to the cathedral, which I carried out in collaboration with Nikolaus Rosiny. In the process of planning and construction I came to esteem the cathedral more and more.

The reason for my earlier aversion was the fact that everything had been plastered over smooth and smeared with a greyish coat of paint. Preliminary investigations revealed, however, that the entire brickwork had to be injection grouted. The whole of the plaster was of course removed in the process, revealing the most marvellous brickwork with interesting details from many different periods. Quite a lot of the structure still dates from Roman times. Since then, of course, history has left its marks in a variety of ways. Our work, and the only credit we can take, was to have saved this uniquely interesting and beautiful brickwork from the conservationists who were determined to restore the previous state with the plaster covering. One can scarcely imagine nowadays, how the interior space as a whole was changed by the exposure of the brickwork, how everything became much larger and grander and richer, and how the previous cold, ostentatious monumentality was transformed into a mighty, yet calm, tranquil, devotional space.

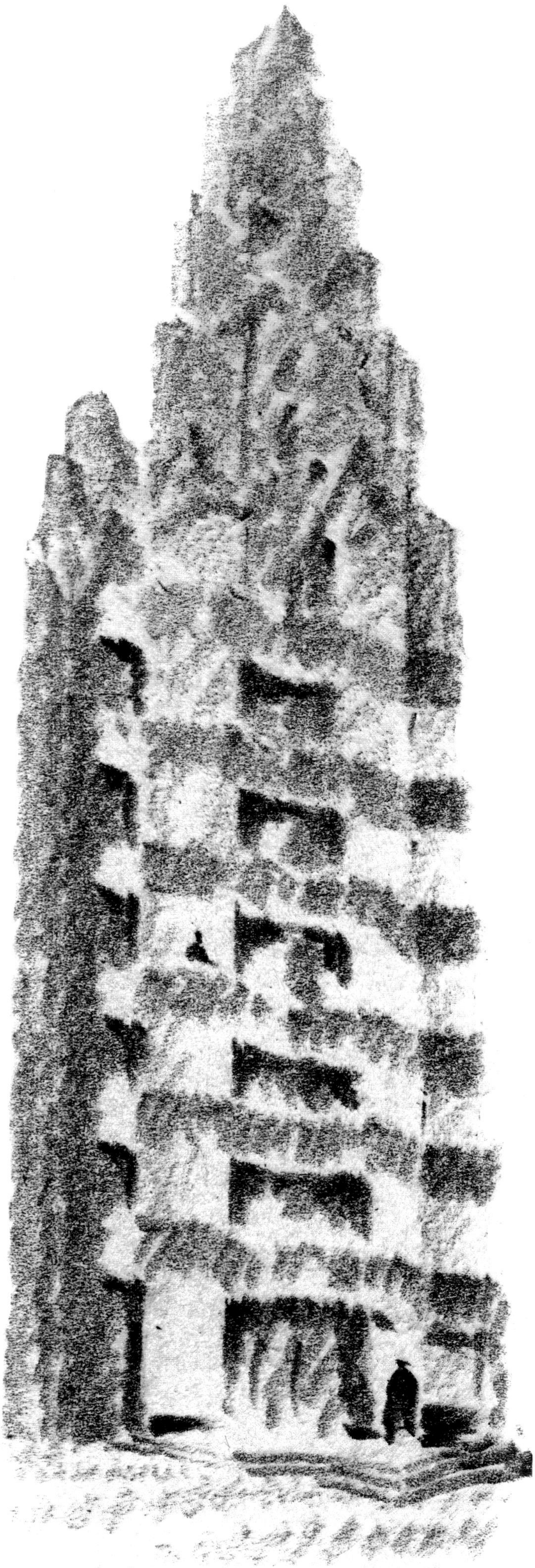

Rathäuser

Köln	Rathaus, Wettbewerb, 1960, mit Kurt Günßler, Peter Martini, Reinhard Stapper
Bensberg	Rathaus, 1964, mit Werner Finke, Hans Schmalscheidt, Günter Kaintoch
Amsterdam	Rathaus, Wettbewerb, 1973, mit Dieter Basilius, Manfred Jäger, Hans Schmalscheidt
Bocholt	Rathaus und Kulturzentrum, 1977, mit Gerhard Wagner, Günther Frings, Dieter Kokula, Arnold Kirchner, Federico Valda
Rheinberg	Rathaus und Bürgerhaus, 1980, mit Georg F. Adolphi, Katja Hrankovicova, Gerhard Wagner, Markku Kari, Ulrich Kuhn, Fritz Steinigeweg, Gudrun Wurlitzer
Köln	Technisches Rathaus, Wettbewerb, 1975, mit Gerhard Wagner, Katja Hrankovicova, Miroslav Volf
Köln-Kalk	Rathaus, in Planung 1986, mit Hans Linder, Franz Kilian, Hasso Breuer
Wesseling	Rathaus, Wettbewerb, 1969, mit Gerhard Wagner, Franz Kilian

City Halls

Vergleicht man einmal Kathedralen und Rathäuser früherer Zeiten, merkt man einen interessanten Gegensatz: Eine Kathedrale, wie zum Beispiel die in Reims, wirkt so, als sei der Himmel auf die Erde geholt und mit ihr fest verwurzelt. Rathäuser aus der selben Zeit, wie zum Beispiel die in Aachen und Bremen, sind in der Würde des Gehäuses den Kirchen sehr ähnlich und dennoch scheinen sie, in Umkehrung, dem Boden enthoben, als seien sie aus dem Getriebe der Stadt herausgestellt, gleichsam in einer Sphäre dem Himmel näher gerückt, wo es weniger Fehler und Schwächen gibt.
Welcher Rat oder Senat würde heute diesen Anspruch ertragen?

If one compares the cathedrals and city halls of earlier times, one becomes aware of an interesting contrast. A cathedral, such as that in Reims, creates the impression that heaven has been drawn down to earth and firmly implanted there. City halls dating from the same period, such as those in Aachen or Bremen, are very similar to churches, so far as the dignity of the outer shell is concerned, but they appear to be raised from the ground, as if removed from the bustle of the city to a sphere that is closer to heaven, where there are fewer errors and weaknesses. What council or senate would be able to live up to such a claim today?

Es bleibt aber für uns Architekten doch die Aufgabe, dem Bau der Volksvertretung oder doch wenigstens dem Ratssaal eine Würde zu geben, die mehr und anders ist als die einer Bank oder eines Versicherungsgebäudes.

Bei dem Wettbewerb für den Wiederaufbau des Kölner Rathauses schien mir diese Würde von selbst gegeben, wenn man den alten erhaltenen Ratssaal von Umbauung freihält, so daß er zusammen mit dem schönen Turm als deutliches Zeichen seiner Aufgabe inmitten der Stadt steht. Alle anderen Funktionen, wie Eingangshalle, Büroräume, zusätzliche Sitzungsräume und Ratskeller wurden ihm untergeordnet.

For us architects, however, the task remains to give buildings that house representatives of the people, or at least the council chamber itself, a certain dignity that exceeds and differs from that of a bank or an insurance building.

In the competition for the reconstruction of the City Hall of Cologne this dignity seemed to me to be assured, if one were to keep the old, surviving council chamber free from further developments, so that it would stand, together with the fine tower, as a symbol of the function it performs in the middle of the city. All other functions — entrance hall, offices, additional assembly rooms and the cellar inn — were subordinated to this.

In Bensberg stand das alte Burggelände für das Bauvorhaben zur Verfügung. Schon die Lage auf dem Berg und die mit der alten Burg verbundene Grundrißform mit dem Spiel der alten und neuen Türme heben das gesamte Gebäude hervor.

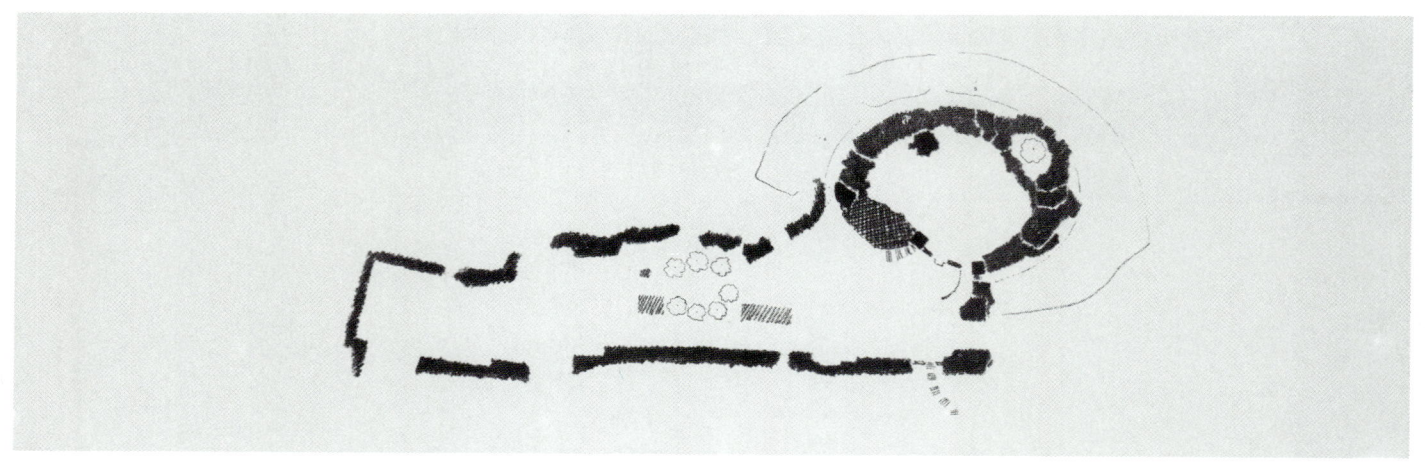

The area of the old castle in Bensberg was designated as the site for the town hall development. The entire complex stands out through its situation on the hill, the form of the ground plan, which links up with the old castle, and the interplay of old

Zudem nimmt auch hier der Ratssaal in dem alten Gemäuer eine Sonderstellung ein. Er öffnet sich zum inneren Platz hin, so daß auch eine größere Anzahl von Bürgern am Geschehen im Saal teilnehmen kann.

and new towers. In addition the council chamber occupies a special position within the old walls, opening out to the courtyard on the inside, so that an even larger public can participate in the proceedings within the chamber.

Eine besondere Aufgabe war der Wettbewerb für das Rathaus in Amsterdam, den wir im Lehrstuhl der Aachener Hochschule bearbeiteten. Neben dem Ratssaal waren mehrere andere Säle für die Repräsentation der Stadt gefordert.
Die Situation in Amsterdam ist ganz eigener Art. Anstelle von Straßen zieht sich das Wasser durch die städtische Struktur.

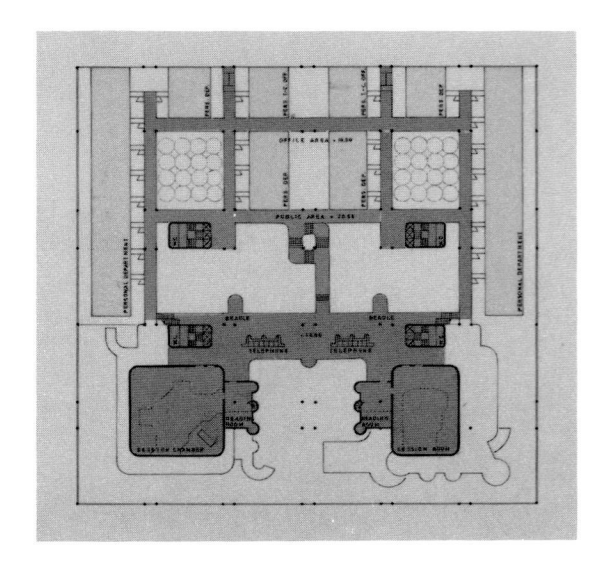

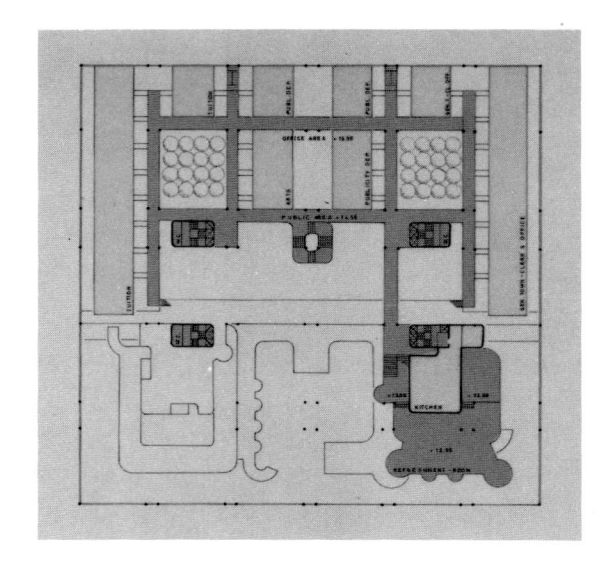

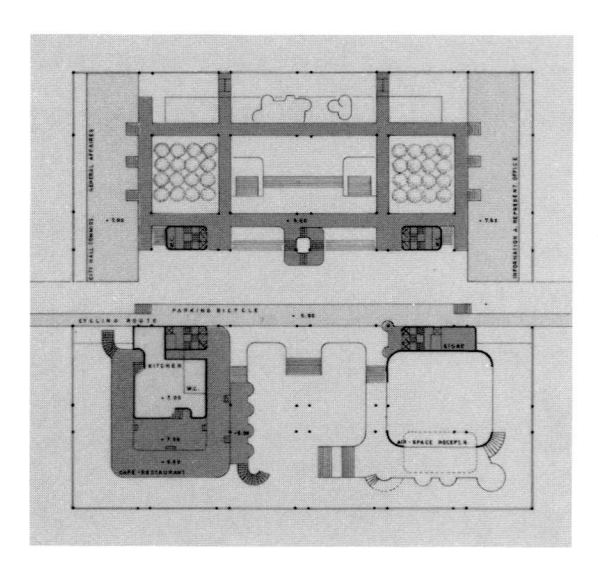

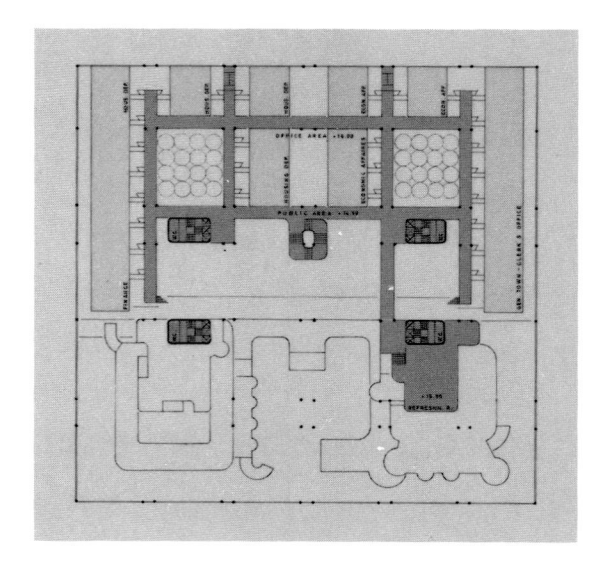

The competition scheme for the City Hall in Amsterdam was the subject of a special project we undertook at Aachen University. In addition to the council chamber, the brief required a number of other halls for various formal functions. The situation in Amsterdam is quite unique. The urban fabric is dissected not by roads but by waterways. We accentuated the

Wir haben nun das Rathaus aus dem Stadtgefüge hervorgehoben, indem wir das Wasser gleichsam als große Platzfläche zusammengeschlossen haben, in der das Rathaus wie eine Insel erscheint, die vom städtischen Getriebe abgerückt und so hervorgehoben wird.

position of the city hall within the urban structure by creating a larger area of water, in which the complex lies like an island, a precious object removed from the bustle of everyday urban life.

Auch das Rathaus Bocholt ist inselähnlich in einer Wasserfläche geplant worden, die leider zu klein ist, so daß die Insel eigentlich nur von einer Seite als solche richtig erkennbar ist. Der Grund für die Lage war vor allem die Tatsache, daß das

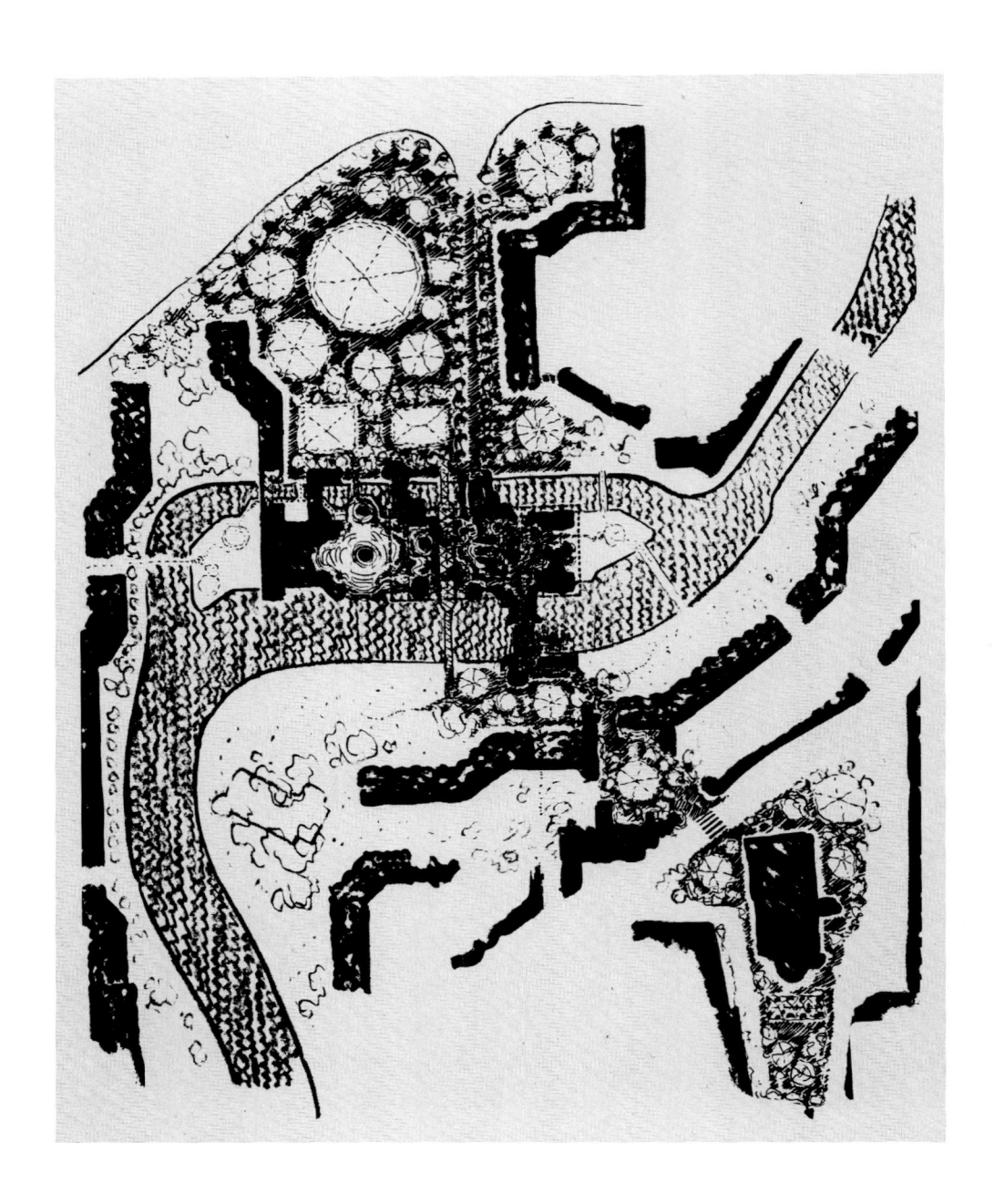

Bocholt Town Hall was also designed to have the features of an island surrounded by water. The area of water is unfortunately too small, however, and as a result the island character of the scheme only really manifests itself on one side. The

Rathaus gleichsam zwei Stadtteilen in gleicher Weise zugehört, und dann auch der Wunsch, beide auf eine neutrale Weise miteinander zu verbinden.

location of the site was dictated by the fact that the town hall was meant to serve two parts of the urban area to an equal degree and by the wish to link these two parts in a neutral manner.

Rathaus Rheinberg. Hier war unser Gedanke, den Marktplatz und Kirchplatz über einen Vorhof gleichsam in einen glasüberdachten inneren Platz – den Ratssaal – weiterzuführen. Dieser wird als Endpunkt der Platzfolge, aber auch durch seine

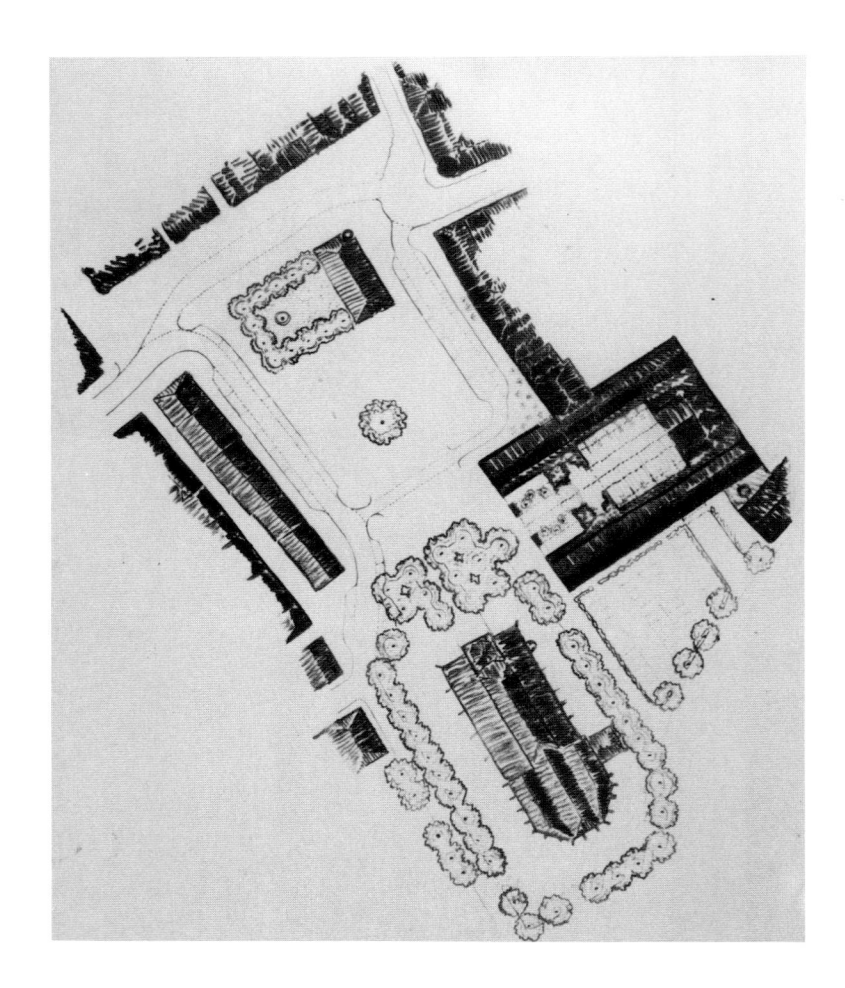

Rheinberg Town Hall. Our concept here was to extend the market place and the church square via an enclosed forecourt into a glass-covered internal space; i.e. the actual council chamber. As the culminating point of this sequence of open spaces, and by virtue of its central position, the chamber would be removed from the everyday events outside. The other

zentrale Lage aus dem täglichen Geschehen hervorgehoben. Die übrigen Räume für Verwaltung, Sitzungen und für ein Restaurant umschließen den Saal wie Straßenwände mit Fenstern und Balkonen.

spaces required for administration, committee meetings and a restaurant are laid out round the outside of the council chamber and provide the development with a street face, articulated with windows and balconies.

Rheinberg — Stadthaus / Town Hall

Rheinberg — Stadthaus

Rheinberg — Town Hall

Das Technische Rathaus in Köln. Ein Technisches Rathaus ist kein Rathaus im üblichen Sinn. Es beherbergt nur den Verwaltungsapparat einer Stadt und kann also nicht die Würde beanspruchen, die sonst dem Sitz des gewählten Rates der Stadt zusteht.

Als Standort war ein Gelände in Deutz neben dem Deutzer Bahnhof vorgesehen. Erschwerend für die Aufgabe waren bereits vorhandene Planungen der Stadt für eine Hochstraße, eine Schnellstraße und zusätzlich eine U-Bahnuntertunnelung an dieser Stelle. Wir haben deshalb den Bau ähnlich einer großen Brücke geplant, die sich zwischen dem Stadtrand Deutz und dem Bahndamm spannt.

Parallel zum Stadtrand läuft in einem Anschlußbau ein passagenartiger Weg mit Läden, Restaurants usw. Hier liegen auch die Zugänge zu den verschiedenen Erschließungskernen des Technischen Rathauses. Es gibt also keinen repräsentativen Eingang. Alle Zugänge sind dezentralisiert, man geht von der Ladenstraße aus über Treppen oder Aufzüge zum Tiefbauamt oder zu einem der anderen Ämter.

Im Rathaus selbst ordnen sich die Büros im Kammsystem jeweils um einen Hof. Da vom Bauherrn wegen der enormen

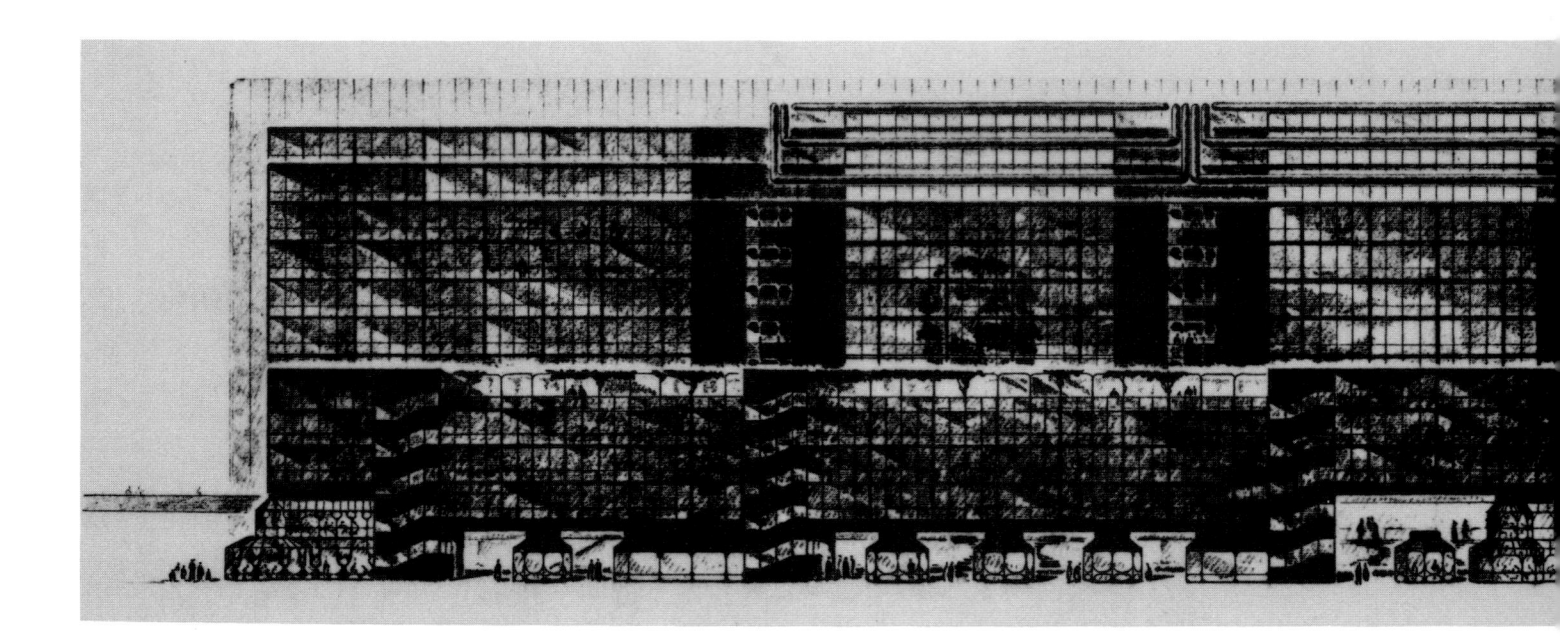

Technical City Hall, Cologne. A technical city hall is not a city hall in the usual sense of the term. It houses purely the administrative apparatus of a municipality and cannot therefore claim the dignity of the actual seat of the elected city council. The site for this complex was in Deutz, close to the local station. Further complications were created by existing plans on the part of the administration to build a raised highway, an expressway, and an underground railway tunnel at this point. We therefore designed the building rather like an enormous bridge spanning between the urban periphery of Deutz and the railway line.

Parallel to the edge of the town is a linking structure in the form of an arcaded strip with shops, restaurants, etc. Located along its length are also the entrances to the various access cores of the Technical City Hall. There is, therefore, no single formal entrance. All points of access are decentralized. From the main road one proceeds via stairs or lifts to the department for roads, or civil engineering, or one of the other sections.

The city hall itself is laid out in the form of a double comb along a central spine. The offices are grouped round individual courtyards between the »teeth« of the comb. Since the client required a fully climate-controlled system, on account of the

Lärmbelästigung durch Straßen und Bahn ein klimatisiertes System gewünscht worden war, war es das vernünftigste, die Glashaut nicht entlang dem Fassadenumriß zu führen, sondern Büros und Höfe mit einer Glashaut zu schließen. Ganz abgesehen von dem räumlichen Gewinn ist die dadurch entstehende Außenfläche viel geringer als bei einer Verglasung sämtlicher Räume an den Hofseiten. Es entsteht damit jeweils eine geschlossene Hofsituation wie in einem Theater mit mehreren Rängen. Die Klimatisierung erfolgt von den Mittelgängen her durch die Arbeitsräume hindurch in die Halle des Hofes und wird dann im oberen Teil wieder abgesaugt.

Natürlich ist es nicht nur das Technisch-Architektonische, was uns interessiert und zu diesem Vorschlag animiert hat. Die Raumwirkung der Höfe schafft eine ganz besondere Arbeitswelt, in der die Gemeinsamkeit der Arbeit stark betont ist, wobei die Einzelperson, gleichsam in einer Loge sitzend, ihren eigenen Bereich in der Gesamtheit hat. Bei einem Rathaus, egal ob es eine repräsentative Funktion hat oder nicht, ist es doch naheliegend, zum Ausdruck zu bringen, daß der dort Arbeitende als Einzelpersönlichkeit in der Gemeinschaft und für die Gemeinschaft tätig ist.

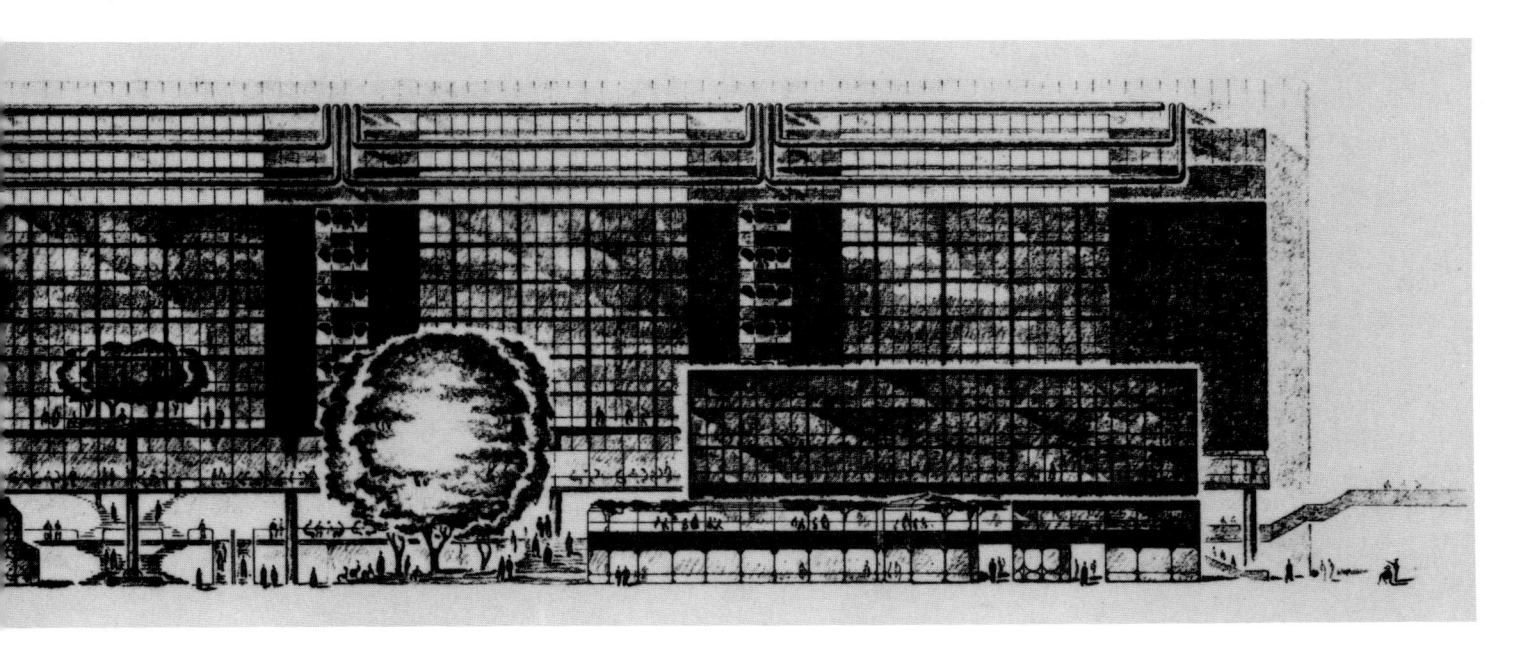

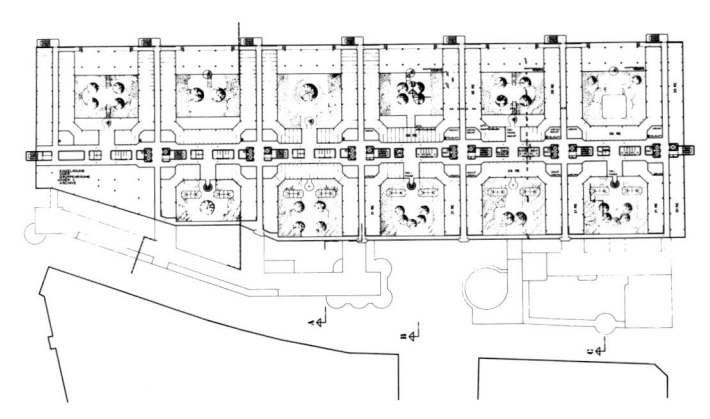

very high level of noise disturbance from the adjoining roads and railway line, the most sensible solution was not to draw a glass façade round the indented outline of the building, but to enclose both courtyards and offices with a skin of glazing. Apart from the spatial gain achieved by this, the actual skin of the building has a much smaller area than would have been the case, if all the rooms had been glazed along their courtyard faces. The present solution creates a series of closed courtyards that are not unlike a theatre auditorium with a number of tiers or balconies round the edges. Air-conditioning proceeds from the central corridors, via the working areas, out into the courtyard hall, the air being extracted again at the top. What interested us in this scheme and animated these proposals was not merely the technical element in the architecture. The spatial effect of the courtyards creates a unique working environment in which the sense of working together is strongly accentuated. At the same time, individuals sitting in one of the »boxes« or balconies have their own particular realm within the whole. Whether a town hall has a formal, representational function or not, it seems only appropriate to express the fact that the members of the staff, as individual persons, are working within a community for the community.

Köln-Kalk, Rathaus

Kalk, Cologne: Town hall

Projekt, 1986

Project, 1986

Wesseling, Rathaus für eine Industriestadt

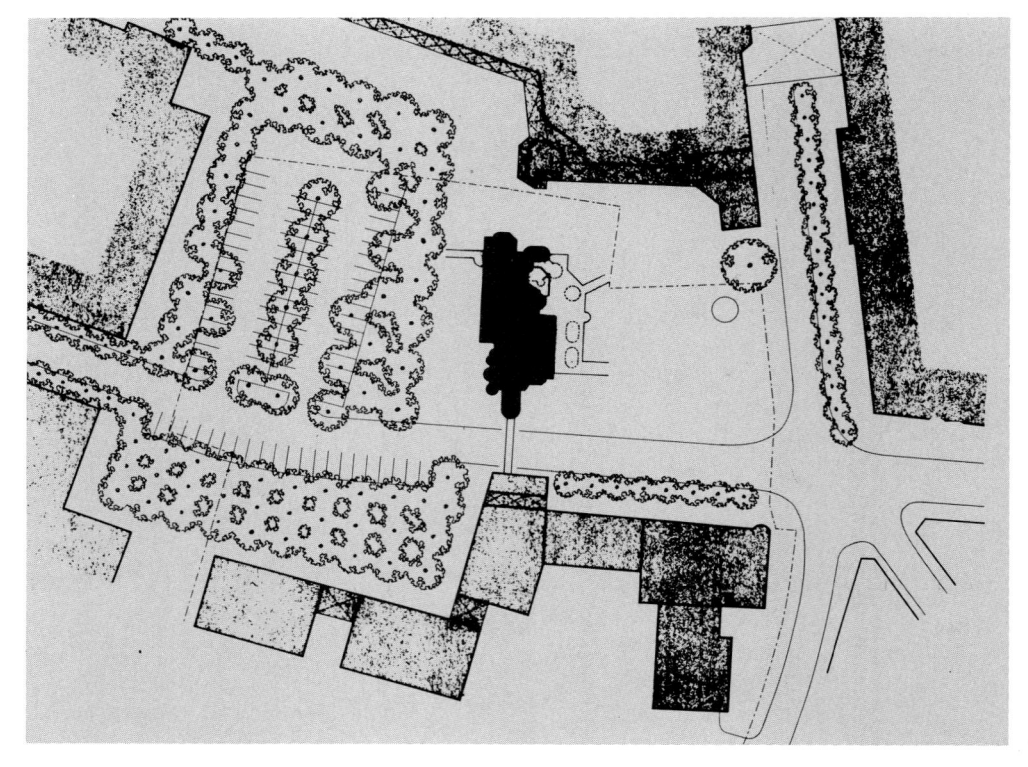

Wesseling, Town hall for an industrial town

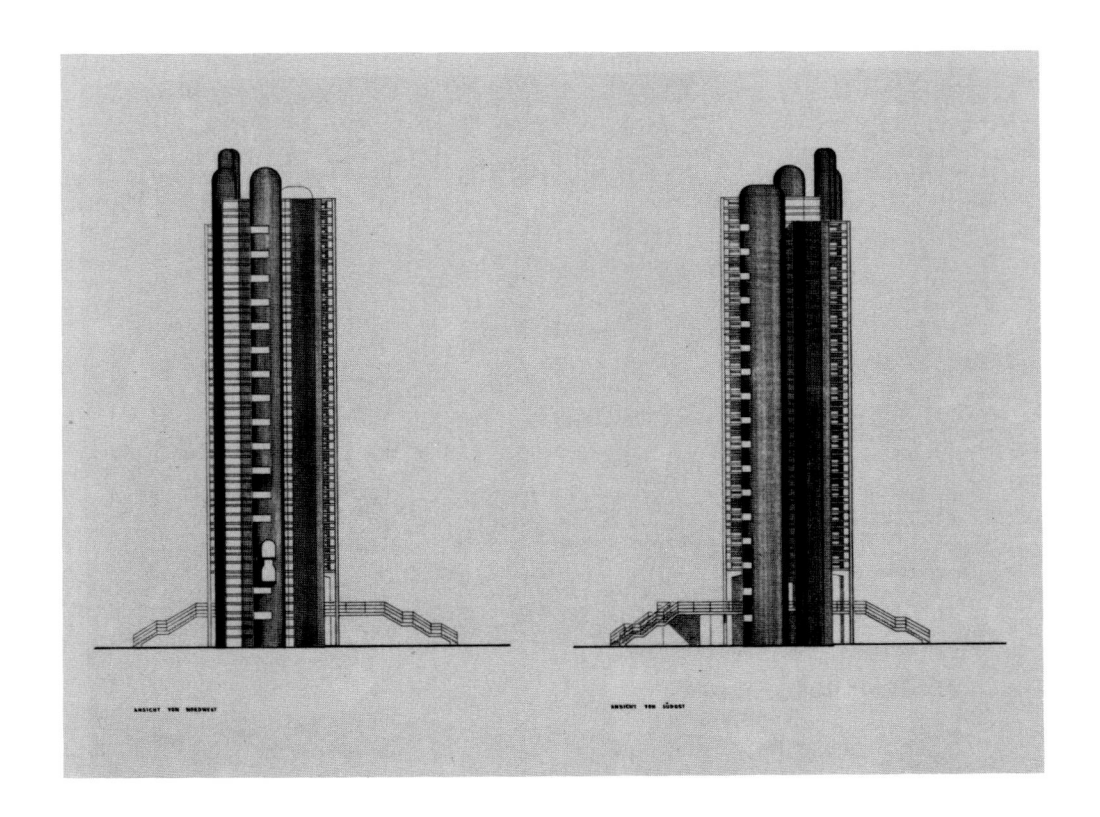

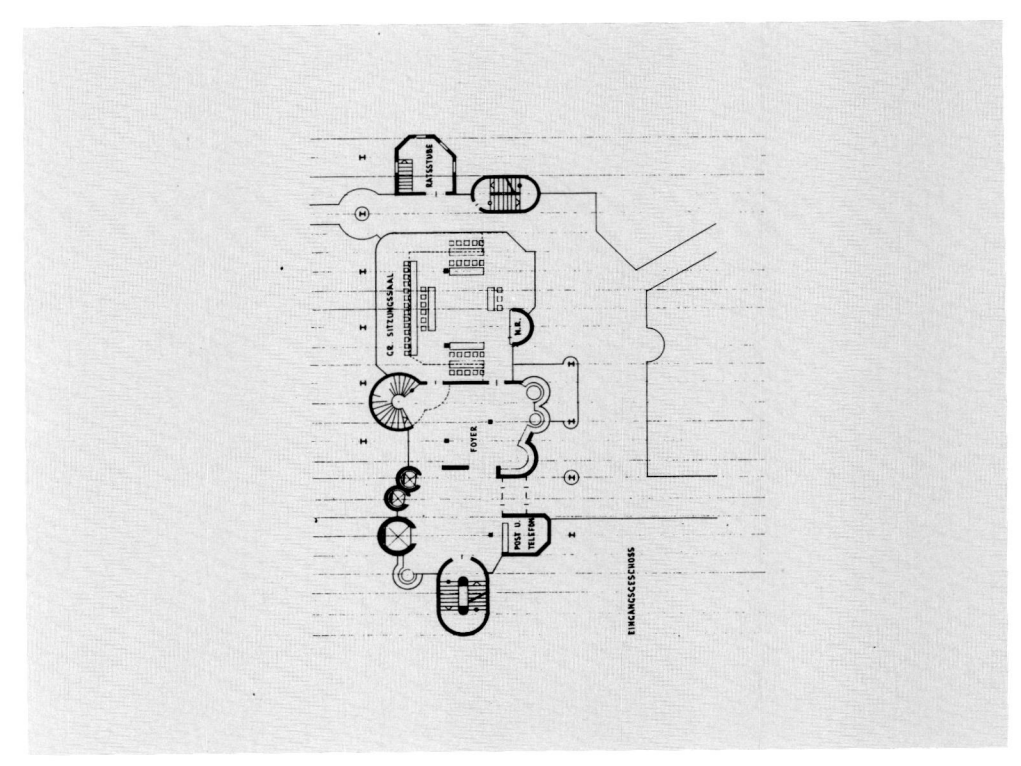

Wettbewerb, 1969

Competition, 1969

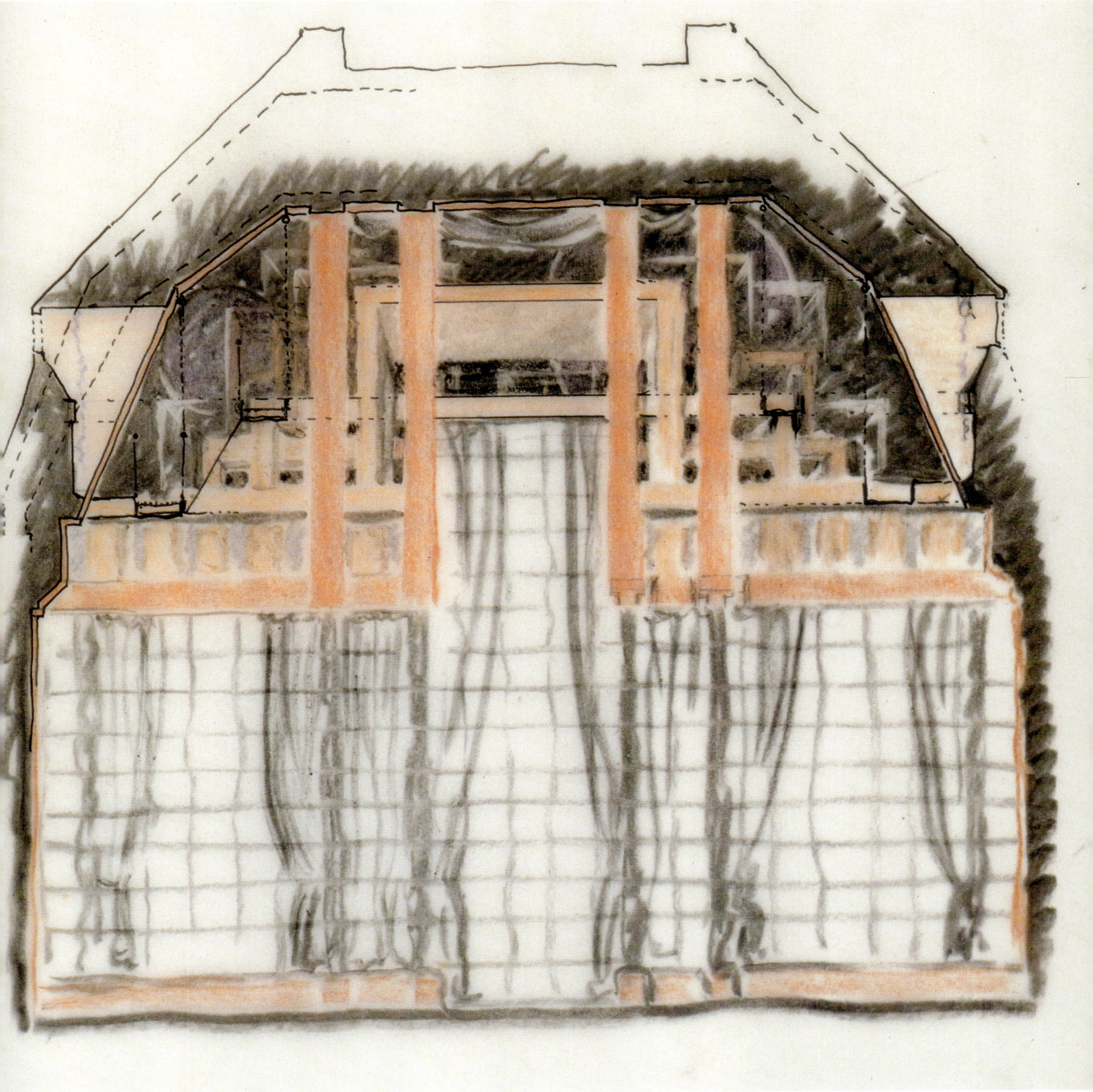

Theaterbau

Bonn	Theater am Rheinufer, Wettbewerb, 1959, mit Kurt Günßler, Hans Linder, Peter Martini, Franz Kilian
Trier	Theater am römischen Thermengelände, Wettbewerb, 1959, mit Kurt Günßler, Reinhard Stapper, Peter Martini, Franz Kilian
Bocholt	Theater im Rathaus, 1977, mit Gerhard Wagner, Günther Frings, Dieter Kokula, Arnold Kirchner, Federico Valda
Dudweiler	Theater im Bürgerhaus, 1979, mit Katja Hrankovicova, Miroslav Volf, Günther Kaesbach
Bergisch-Gladbach	Theater im Bürgerhaus, 1980, mit Hans Linder, Stefan Abelen, Stefan Conrad, Franz Kilian, Hans Klumpp
Itzehoe	Stadttheater, 1984, im Bau, mit Jürgen Minkus, Dörte Gatermann, Federico Valda, Wolfgang Jung
Stuttgart	Umgestaltung des Opernhauses, Wettbewerb, 1981; Pavillonanbau, 1984, mit Hermann Neuerburg, Elisabeth Böhm, Gudrun Wurlitzer, Bruno Kauhsen
München	Umgestaltung des Residenztheaters, Wettbewerb, 1983
Essen-Werden	Folkwangschule, Theater- und Konzertsaal, 1986–87, in Zusammenarbeit mit Stefan Böhm, mit Monika Adolphi, Stefan Abelen, Klaus Bölkow, Georg Rattay

Der Theaterbau der Griechen begeistert uns bis heute. Sie bauten ihre Theater in die Landschaft hinein und nutzten eine Geländemulde für den Zuschauerraum. Das Faszinierende daran ist, daß sie allein durch den Bau von Stufen das Gefühl eines architektonischen Raumes vermitteln konnten, dessen Form den Zuschauern in besonderem Maße das Gefühl des Zusammenseins gegeben hat. Das Außergewöhnliche an dieser Architektur ist, daß sie zugleich auch immer Landschaft beinhaltet. Das Bühnengeschehen, das Spiel, steht immer vor einem realen – teils gebauten, teils landschaftlichen – Hintergrund.

The theatre design of the ancient Greeks is something that still inspires us today. They built their theatres into the landscape und used a natural hollow in the ground to create an auditorium. One of the fascinating features of this is that, simply by the construction of steps, they were able to convey a sense of architectural space, the form of which communicated a pronounced feeling of community to the members of the audience. The extraordinary thing about this architecture was that it always contained the dimension of landscape at the same time. The events on the stage, the play, always took place in front of a real background, – partly built structure, partly natural panorama.

Die Römer haben das Prinzip des Amphitheaters übernommen, nur mit dem Unterschied, daß es sich meist nicht im Gelände mit der Landschaft verbindet, sondern zu einem in sich geschlossenen Gebäude wird und als ein gebauter Teil der Stadt erscheint. Palladio greift mit dem Teatro olympico in Vicenza das römische Muster wieder auf, einschließlich der Andeutung eines oberen Ranges. Das Gefühl der Gemeinsamkeit im Erleben des Spiels steht auch bei diesem Theatertyp sehr im Vordergrund.

The Romans adopted the principles of the amphitheatre, with the one difference that it did not usually accommodate itself to the topography and merge with the landscape, but was housed within a closed structure, forming part of the built urban fabric.
With his Teatro Olimpico in Vicenza Palladio takes up the Roman model again, including the suggestion of an upper balcony or gallery level. In this type of theatre too the experience of being part of a community whilst watching the play is dominant.

Der Gedanke des geselligen Zusammenseins im Theater unterlag Veränderungen und wurde in der Barockzeit dann auch baulich anders ausgedrückt. Als Beispiel möchte ich das herrliche alte Markgräfliche Opernhaus in Bayreuth anführen. Die orchestra des griechisch-römischen Amphitheaters ist nun dem meist ebenen, manchmal auch leicht ansteigenden Parterre gewichen, das als Zuschauerraum, aber auch als Aktionsfläche genutzt werden konnte. Die steile Stufung des Amphitheaters wurde durch die senkrecht übereinander stehenden Logen ersetzt. Die Theateraufführung wurde hier fast zur Nebensache. Sie war nur ein Teil des »Spiels« im ganzen Raum, in dem jeder Zuschauer ein Akteur des gesellschaftlichen Ereignisses war, das nun das eigentlich Primäre darstellte.

Giuseppe Galli-Bibiena   Opernhaus, Bayreuth

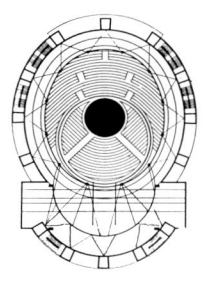

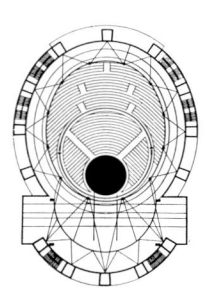

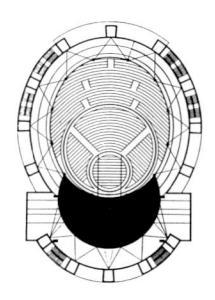

Walter Gropius   Totaltheater

This sense of social gathering in the theatre underwent certain changes and in the Baroque age found a different architectural expression. As an example, I should like to cite the splendid old margraval opera house in Bayreuth. In the Baroque theatre the orchestra of the Graeco-Roman amphitheatre gives way to a usually flat, or sometimes gently sloping »stalls« area which could be used as an auditorium or as a space for other activities. The steeply-rising steps of the ancient amphitheatre were superseded by tiers of boxes stacked vertically above each other. Here the theatrical presentation itself is reduced almost to a secondary event. It represented merely one part of the »performance« that took place in the space as a whole, in which every member of the audience had a role to play as part of a social occasion that was in itself the central event.

Für unsere Zeit möchte ich ein Beispiel nennen, das mir für eine heutige Auffassung sehr typisch erscheint und das in krassem Gegensatz zum barocken Theater steht. Das ist die Schaubühne von Sawade in Berlin. Hier steht nun das Theaterspiel vollkommen im Vordergrund, und alles ist diesem Spiel untergeordnet. Der Zuschauer befindet sich wie in einer Maschinerie, wo alles so optimal auf das Bühnenspiel hin ausgerichtet werden kann, daß ein totales Aufgehen in diese Spielsituation möglich gemacht wird. Das Spiel allein ist Sinn genug, und alles, was architektonischer Raum wäre, erschiene störend. Die Schaubühne zeigt eine sehr konsequente Darstellung dieses Prinzips.

Sawade   Theater-Umbau, Berlin

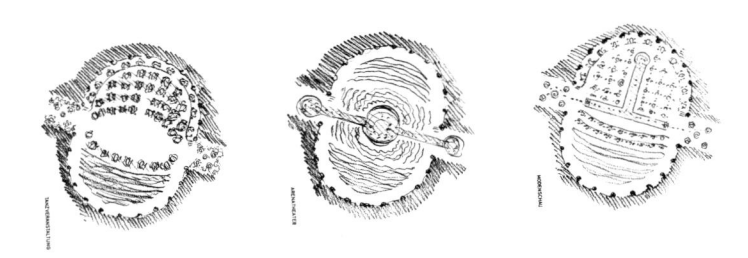

Gottfried Böhm, Projekt für das Stadttheater in Itzehoe, 1984

As an example of theatre design in our own age and of an attitude that seems to me to be quite typical today — and which stands in stark contrast to that underlying Baroque theatre — I should like to mention the Schaubühne by Sawade in Berlin (the former cinema complex built by Erich Mendelsohn). Here it is the theatrical performance that is placed in the foreground; everything else is subordinated to the drama. The audience finds itself as if within a machine, in which every part can be focused so optimally on the events on stage that total immersion in the performance is made possible. The play is sufficient in itself; anything that might be regarded as architectural space would seem distracting. The Schaubühne theatre is an uncompromising demonstration of this principle.

Unser erstes Projekt für ein Theater entstand für einen Wettbewerb in Bonn Ende der fünfziger Jahre. Wir haben das gemeinschaftbildende Prinzip des Amphitheaters der Griechen übernommen, jedoch so, daß man die volle Bühnentiefe sichtbar hat.
Wohl ist es wichtig, wie der Bühnenraum mit dem Zuschauerraum verbunden ist. Ebenso wichtig war für uns aber der Zusammenhang von Zuschauerraum und Bühne mit der Realität, der so eindrucksvoll hergestellt war beim griechischen Theater mit seiner gebauten, das heißt realen Bühnenarchitektur inmitten der realen landschaftlichen Situation. Wir hatten deshalb vorgeschlagen, die Rückwand hinter der Bühne zu verglasen, so daß der Raum sich nach außen öffnet und man

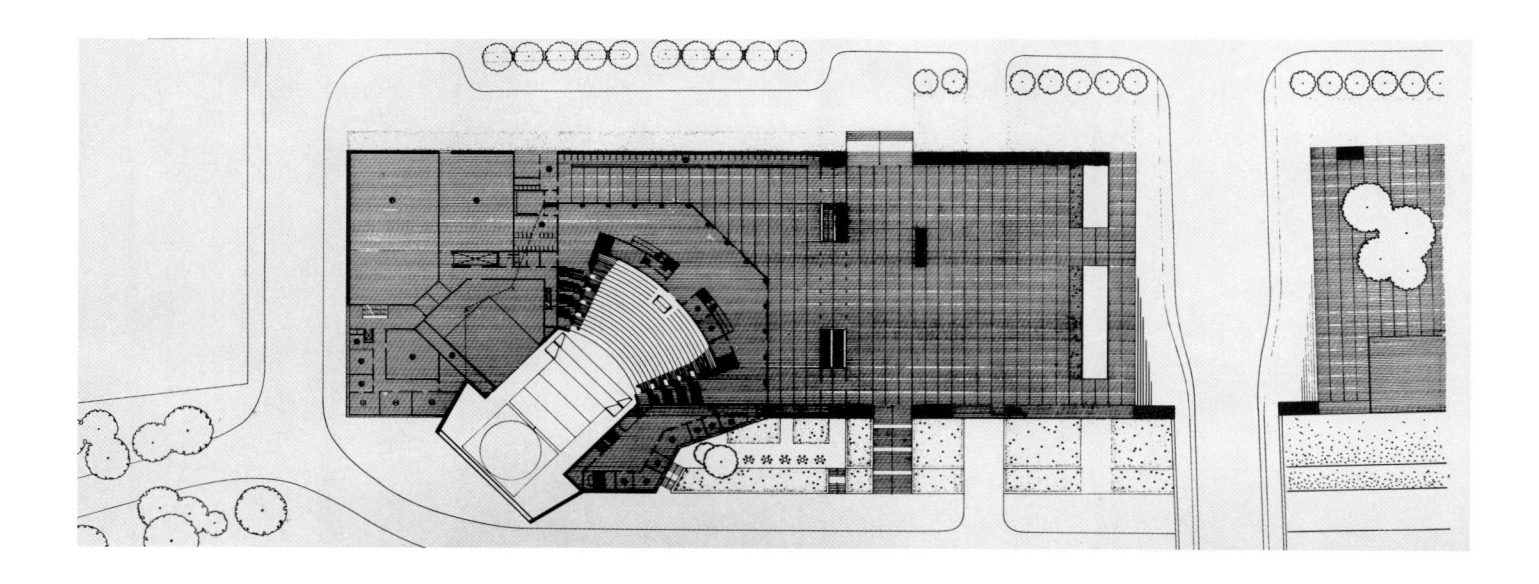

Our first project for a theatre was a competition entry for a building in Bonn towards the end of the 1950s. We adopted the socially unifying principle of the amphitheatre from the Greeks, but modified the form so that the full depth of the stage would be visible.
The way the stage area is linked with the auditorium is certainly an important factor; but just as important to us was the link between auditorium and stage, and reality, a link that was so impressively created in the Greek theatre with its built (i.e. real) stage architecture set in the midst of a real landscape. We therefore made proposals to glaze the rear wall behind the stage, so that this space could be opened up to the outside world; and beyond the stage one would see the city with the

hinter der Bühne die Stadt mit dem Rhein und die Landschaft sieht. Dadurch wird das Spiel und in ihm das Wort mit dem Alltäglichen in direkten Bezug gesetzt. Von außen her nimmt ihrerseits die Stadt, wenn auch nur ganz entfernt, am Geschehen im Theater teil. Jedermann in der Stadt kann ahnen, daß dort etwas Außergewöhnliches geschieht.

Wir haben die Zuschauerebene und die Foyerebene ineinander übergehen lassen. Das Foyer steigt etwas an und führt über den rückwärtigen Bühnenteil hinweg, so daß ein Umgehen des gesamten Theaters ermöglicht wird. Es ist auf diese Weise ein integrierter Teil des Theaterraumes entstanden, der zugleich zur Stadt hin geöffnet ist.

Rhine and the surrounding landscape. As a result of this the drama, and the words within the drama, are set in direct relationship to everyday life. On the outside the city also plays a role in the theatrical events, even if only at a considerable distance; and everyone in the city would have some idea that something unusual was taking place here.

We designed the auditorium and the foyer on a continuous level, so that the two spaces would flow into each other. The foyer rises somewhat and also leads round over the rear part of the stage. It is thus possible to walk round the entire theatre. In this way the foyer becomes an integral part of the theatre space and at the same time opens out to the city.

Den Gedanken einer Öffnung der Bühnenrückwand haben wir auch bei dem Wettbewerb für das Theater in Trier in das Projekt aufgenommen. Hier war die Situation besonders reizvoll, weil das Theater am Rande der römischen Thermen ge-

The idea of opening up the rear wall of the stage was something we also adopted in the competition project for the theatre in Trier. In this case the situation was particularly attractive, since the proposed site of the theatre adjoined a Roman baths.

plant war. Durch diese Bühnenöffnung hätte im Sommer das ganze Gelände mit dem Ruinenfeld genutzt werden können (z.B. Wallenstein kommt mit seinem ganzen Gefolge und Gefährt aus dem wirklichen Gelände mit der großartigen Architektur).

By opening the stage space in this way it would have been possible in summer to use the whole site including the ruins. (E.g. Wallenstein enters with his entourage and carriages from the authentic ancient site to the rear with its superb architecture.)

In Bocholt ist das Theater an die Bürgerhalle des Rathauses angeschlossen, die verschiedenen Nutzungen dient. Sie enthält Ausstellungsflächen, eine Bar, Läden, Zugänge zum Ratssaal, zur Verwaltung, zum Restaurant und eben zum Theater. Der Zuschauerraum des Theaters hat mehrere Ränge. Sie verbinden sich über das Bühnenportal hinweg und sind so angelegt, daß auch hier eine Theateraufführung als gesellschaftliches Ereignis erlebt werden kann.

In Bocholt the theatre forms part of the town hall complex. It adjoins the civic hall, which serves a number of different purposes. It contains exhibition space, a bar and shops. From this point one has access to the council chamber, to administrative offices, to a restaurant, and last but not least to the theatre itself. The theatre auditorium contains a number of balcony tiers, which are linked by stairs and a bridge across the proscenium arch, and which are laid out in such a manner that a

Eine Verbindung des Bühnengeschehens mit dem Zuschauerraum, das heißt mit dem Publikum wird durch übergreifende Ränge, Logen, Podeste, Treppen und seitliche Rampen ermöglicht. Auf diese Weise wird etwas vom Charakter der Bühne in den Zuschauerraum hineingetragen.

visit to the theatre here can also be experienced as a social occasion.
A link between the events on stage and the auditorium (i.e. the audience) is facilitated by the overlapping and interconnecting balconies, boxes, stairs, landing areas and side ramps. In this way something of the character of the stage spills over into the auditorium.

In Dudweiler handelt es sich weniger um ein Theater als um einen Mehrzweck- oder Gemeinschaftsraum. Meist wird er für gesellschaftliche Veranstaltungen verwendet, bei denen auch auf den Rängen Tische stehen. In der Mitte wird getanzt

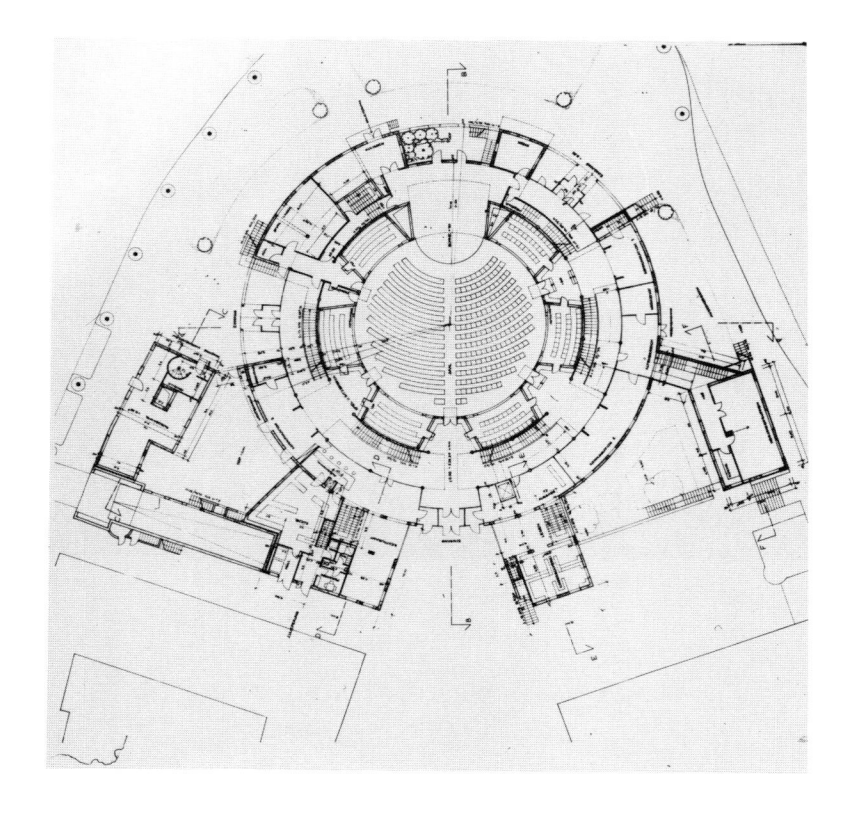

In Dudweiler the project was not so much for a theatre as for a multi-purpose or community space. In the majority of cases it is used for social functions at which the various balcony levels can be furnished with tables and chairs. In the middle is a

oder es findet in einem Teil des Saales eine bestimmte Aktion statt. Der Saal kann bewirtschaftet werden. So ist dies allenfalls ein Theaterraum für eine kleine Heimatbühne oder dergleichen.

dance floor. Alternatively, various events can be held in certain sections of the hall. Food and drinks can be served in the hall as well. It is at most a theatre space for small local stage groups and the like.

Dudweiler — Bürgerhaus — Flur

Dudweiler — Civic Hall — Vestibule

| Dudweiler | Bürgerhaus | Mehrzweckraum |
|---|---|---|･

| Dudweiler | Civic Hall | Multi-purpose space |

Städtebaulich schließt das Bürgerhaus in Bergisch-Gladbach den Marktplatz mit dem Rathaus, der Kirche und der alten Villa nach Osten hin ab. Wir haben das alte Gasthausgebäude »Bergischer Löwe« mit seinem Saalbau in den neuen Baukomplex einbezogen. Die Wohnbebauung in den oberen Geschossen, die im Wettbewerbsentwurf vorgesehen war, wurde nicht ausgeführt. Heute befinden sich im Dachbereich eine Diskothek, eine Hausmeisterwohnung und Jugendräume mit einer großen Terrasse. Sie sollte eigentlich mit einer Brücke Anschluß an den Stadtteil bekommen, der jenseits der Verkehrsstraße auf dem Berg liegt. Im Erdgeschoß befindet sich der Eingangsbereich mit der mehrgeschossigen Halle für Ausstellungen, Treffen und Feste. Auch die Märkte auf dem Marienplatz dehnen sich oftmals über die ganzen Treppengeschosse

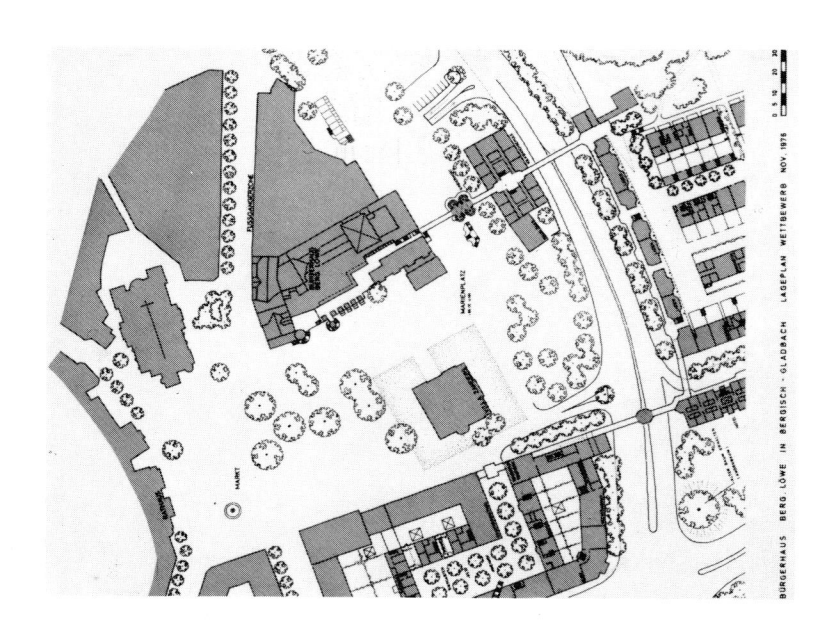

Within the urban planning context, the market place in Bergisch-Gladbach, with the town hall, church and old villa, was closed to the east by the new civic centre building. In our project we integrated the old hall structure of the »Bergischer Löwe« inn into the new building complex. The housing on the upper floors that was foreseen in the competition design was not executed. Today the attic storey accommodates a discotheque, a caretaker's flat and rooms for youth activities with a large terraced area. The development was to be linked by a bridge over the main road to the part of the town situated on the hill. On the ground floor is the entrance area with a hall extending over a number of floors and used for exhibitions, receptions, festivities, etc. On occasion the markets held in Marienplatz extend inside and spread out over the various staircase storeys into the heart of the building, to the theatre auditorium itself. Last but not least, this hall serves as a foyer to the

bis in den Kern des Gebäudes, den Theaterraum aus. Schließlich dient die Halle als Foyer für den kleinen und den großen Saal des Theaters.
In diesem Theater umgreift die Vorbühne den Zuschauerraum, so daß sich der Zuschauer gleichsam im Spielbereich befindet.
Wir wollten bei dem auf Seite 148 gezeigten Projekt für das Bonner Theater durch öffnen der Bühnenrückwand den Bezug zur wirklichen Welt der Stadt und Landschaft herstellen. In Bergisch-Gladbach dagegen ist die Vorbühne wie eine den Raum übergreifende städtische Architektur gebaut, in dem das Spiel stattfinden kann, in dem aber auch die Sitzreihen der Zuschauer eingreifen, so daß das Publikum sich teilweise schon in der Vorbühne und in dem Geschehen dort befindet.

larger and smaller auditoria of the theatre.
The apron stage of this theatre reaches out into the auditorium, so that the audience has the sensation of being drawn into the acting arena.
In the project illustrated on p. 148 for the theatre in Bonn, we wished to establish a relationship between the theatre and the real world of the city and the surrounding landscape by opening up the rear wall of the stage. In Bergisch-Gladbach, in contrast, the apron stage area is designed as a piece of urban architecture that interpenetrates with the auditorium, creating a space in which the play can be performed, and conversely into which the rows of seating for the audience extend, so that the audience has the sensation of being part of this space and of the action taking place within it.

Bergisch-Gladbach

Theatersaal

Theatre auditorium 161

Bergisch-Gladbach

Bürgerhaus

Civic Hall

Bei dem Projekt des Bonner Theaters sollte die Aktion, das Spiel zwischen dem Zuschauerbereich und der realen Welt, die sich hinter der Bühne mit dem Blick in die Stadt und Landschaft auftut, stattfinden. In Bergisch-Gladbach schiebt sich die Vorbühne mit ihrer Architektur weit in den Zuschauerbereich hinein und bildet mit ihm eine Art städtischen Platz. Akteure und Zuschauer befinden sich im gleichen Raum, in einer gebauten und beständigen Struktur. Die Hauptbühne selbst mit ihrer ganzen Scheinwelt ist als ein eigener imaginärer Bereich angeschlossen.

Für Itzehoe, eine Stadt nördlich von Hamburg, planten wir dagegen einen Raum, der zunächst für vielerlei Veranstaltungen geeignet ist. Die vorwiegende Funktion aber ist auch hier das Theaterspiel. Hierfür wird die Bühneneinrichtung eingeschoben. Das Bühnenportal mit Vorhang, Beleuchtung und allem was dazu gehört, wird in zwei Teilen je nach Wunsch und

As one has seen in the project for the theatre in Bonn, it was our intention to allow the action, the play, to take place between the auditorium and the real world beyond the stage that the view to the city and landscape revealed. In Bergisch-Gladbach the apron stage area and its architecture extend far into the auditorium; this process of interpenetration of space creates a kind of urban forum. Actors and audience alike occupy one and the same space, which is contained within a permanent built structure. The main stage area with its whole world of illusion represents the continuation of this space into an imaginary realm.

In contrast to this, in Itzehoe, a town to the north of Hamburg, we have designed a space that can accommodate a variety of events, but where the principal function will be theatre, for which purpose the stage equipment can be slid into position. The proscenium arch, together with curtains, lighting and all necessary appurtenances, is in two parts. These can be pushed

Größe von den Seiten in die Mitte des Raumes geschoben. Der Platzraum selbst bleibt um die Bühne herum als beständige reale Architektur bestehen. Das ist ähnlich der Situation, wenn Kinder im Wohnraum eine Kiste als Puppentheater aufstellen, den Vorhang aufziehen und ein Spiel aufführen. Oder man kennt es von den vielen Freilichtbühnen auf Stadtplätzen, wo die Wirklichkeit den festen Rahmen bildet, zu der der Zuschauer immer wieder in Bezug treten kann. Auch da ist man von gutem Spiel fasziniert, vielleicht sogar nachhaltiger, weil man ein natürliches Verhältnis zum Spiel hat, wenn man sich des Spiels bewußt ist. Es ist eigentlich das Gegenteil der eingangs erwähnten Berliner Schaubühne, wo der Zuschauer ganz in der Illusionswelt aufgehen soll.

Wegen der Mehrfachnutzung haben wir den Raum mit Tageslicht versehen, und zwar nicht nur von oben, sondern auch seit-

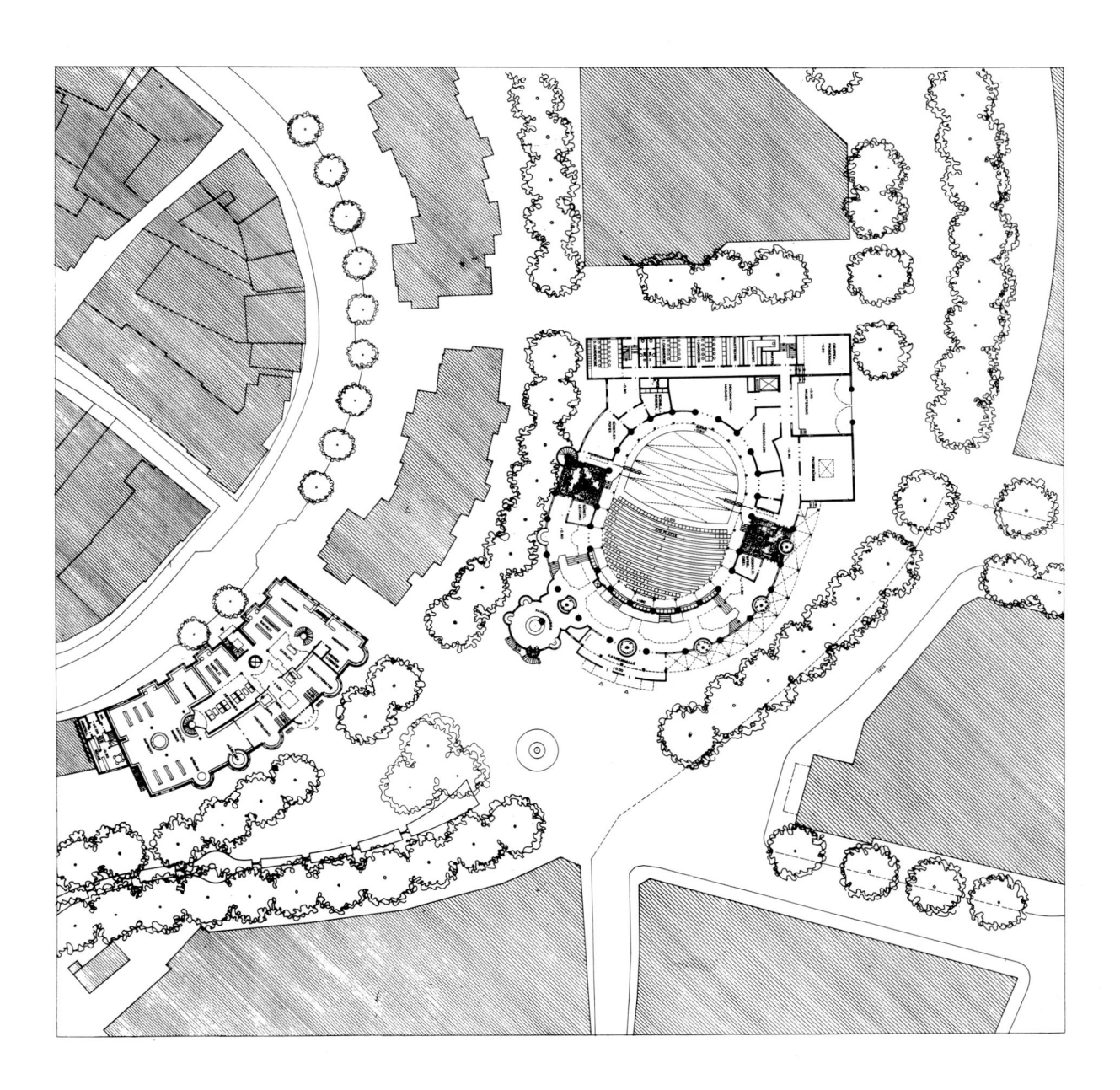

in from the sides to the centre of the space and assembled according to wishes and the size required. The main space is a permanent piece of real architecture, within which this stage is set.

The situation is not unlike that when children put up a box-like stage in the living room, raise the curtain and perform a piece of puppet theatre. Or one could find similar examples in the open-air stages that are erected in market places or other urban spaces, where the (built) reality provides a fixed background to which the members of the audience can refer at any time. Here too one is fascinated by a good performance, perhaps even more lastingly; because one has a natural relationship to the events on stage, if one is aware of the element of theatricality. This really represents the opposite case to that of the Schaubühne in Berlin, mentioned at the beginning, where the audience is meant to be absorbed completely into the world of illusion.

lich durch Höfe. Somit hat man auch direkten Kontakt nach draußen und fühlt sich bei Veranstaltungen am Tage nicht so eingeschlossen.
Das Foyer mit dem Eingangsbereich umschließt ringförmig den großen Saal und führt auf der einen Seite zu einem kleinen Saal, wo die Probebühne ist und wo auch kleine Veranstaltungen wie zum Beispiel Kammerkonzerte stattfinden können. Auf der anderen Seite führt es zum Künstlerfoyer, in dem sich in der Pause die Schauspieler mit den Zuschauern treffen können. Das Foyer bietet Zugang zu einem kleinen Restaurant.
Wichtig ist gerade für solche Theater, die viel mit Gastensembles arbeiten, die von außerhalb mit riesigen Lastwagen kommen, daß sie sehr gut anlieferbar sind. In diesem Fall kann nun direkt zur Bühne hin angeliefert werden oder die Wagen

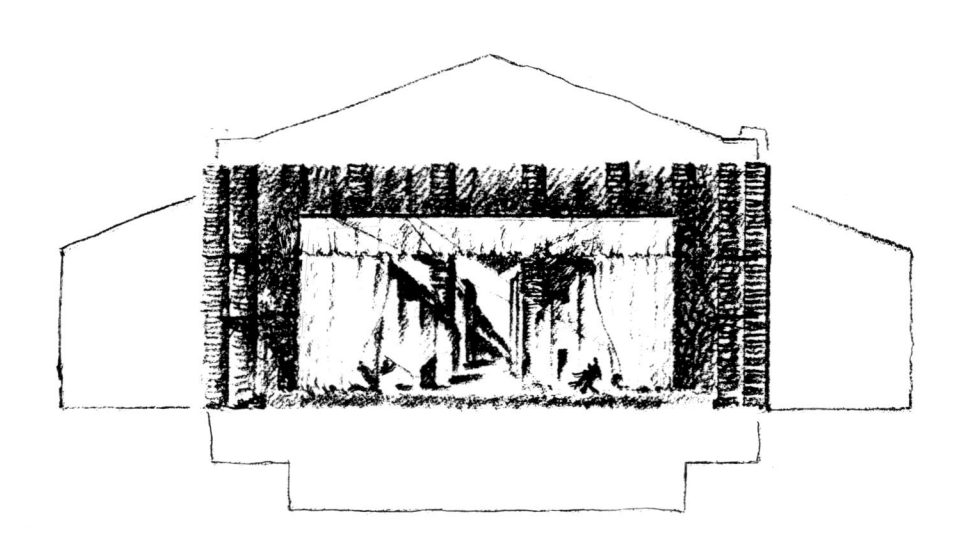

Because of the many different uses to which this space has to be put, we designed it to receive natural lighting, not merely from above, but from the sides, from courtyard areas. In this way one has immediate contact with the outside world and does not feel so confined during daytime events.
The foyer and entrance area are drawn round the large hall in a ring-like form. On one side this space leads to a smaller hall, where the rehearsal stage is situated and where smaller events such as recitals can take place; on the other side it leads to the artists' foyer, where actors can meet the public during intervals. From the foyer there is also access to a small restaurant.
What is important in the case of theatres of this kind, where many visiting ensembles from other towns arrive with enormous

fahren bis an den Dekorationsraum. Das läuft so ab, daß zum Teil schon während des Spielens wieder eingeladen wird, weil bereits am nächsten Tag an einem anderen Ort ein Auftritt stattfindet.
Die Art der Konstruktion des Theaters schafft eine sehr behäbige Ordnung, welche die besondere Bauweise der dortigen Gegend zum Ausdruck bringt. Die Säulen sollen in Ziegelmauerwerk ausgeführt werden. Runde Raumformen bringen akustische Probleme mit sich. Die dicken Säulen streuen aber den Schall. Es entstehen einzelne Raumteile, die den Schall unterschiedlich reflektieren. Im rückwärtigen Teil des Raumes werden die Flächen hinter den Säulen zum Teil schallschlukkend ausgeführt.

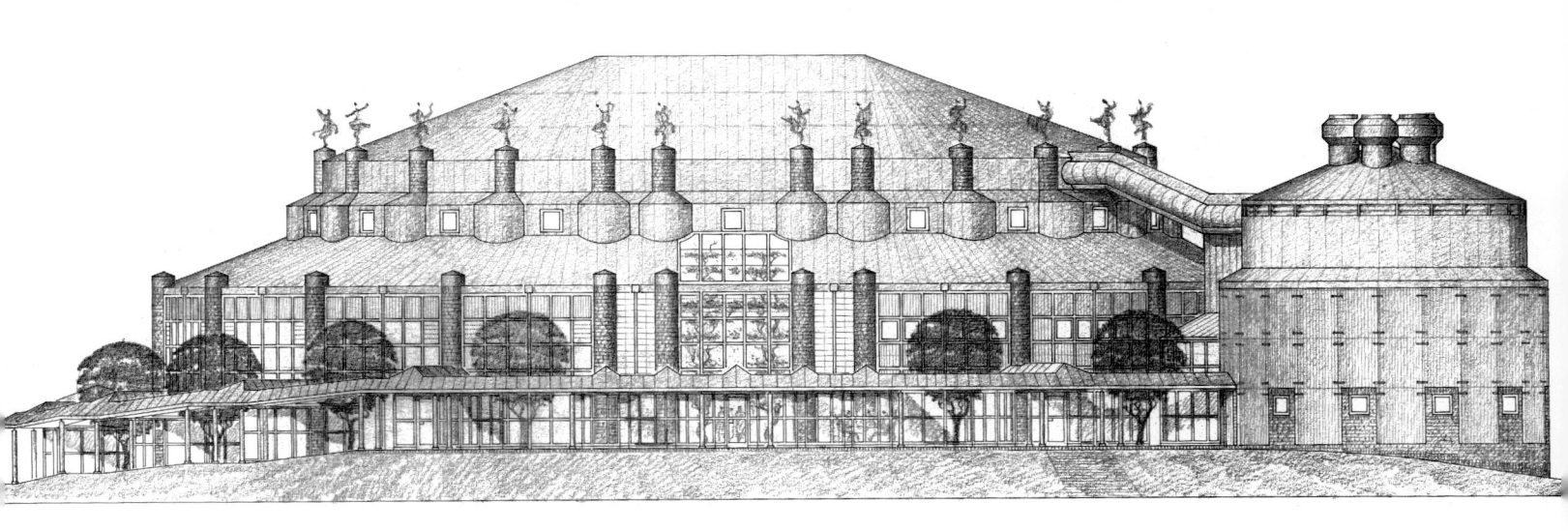

lorries, is that they are easily accessible for loading and unloading. In this case direct delivery to the stage is possible, or lorries can drive into the scenery store. The system functions in such a way that where necessary lorries can reload during an actual performance, when the ensemble has to perform again the following day in another town.
The structural form of this theatre helps create an extremely spacious and leisurely sense of order that is an expression of the particular type of construction in that region. The columns are to be executed in brickwork. Curved spatial forms give rise to acoustic problems. The thick columns help to disperse the sound, however. Furthermore, individual spatial realms are thus created that reflect the sound in different ways. At the rear of this hall the surfaces behind the columns are built in part in a sound absorbing form of construction.

Das Württembergische Staatstheater in Stuttgart ist ein altes, ziemlich großes Theater, das um die Jahrhundertwende von Max Littmann im barocken Stil gebaut worden ist. In den fünfziger Jahren wurde eine »Purifizierung« des Saales vorgenommen. Es sah dann dementsprechend aus.
Es handelt sich um einen fast runden Raum mit zwei Emporen, sehr auf die Bühne hin gerichtet. Wir haben vorgeschlagen, alles, was bei der »Purifizierung« nur verdeckt wurde, wieder freizulegen und für den Übergang des Zuschauerraumes zur erweiterten Bühnenöffnung eine neue Lösung zu suchen. Es ist der Versuch, den Charakter der Bühnenmaschinerie in

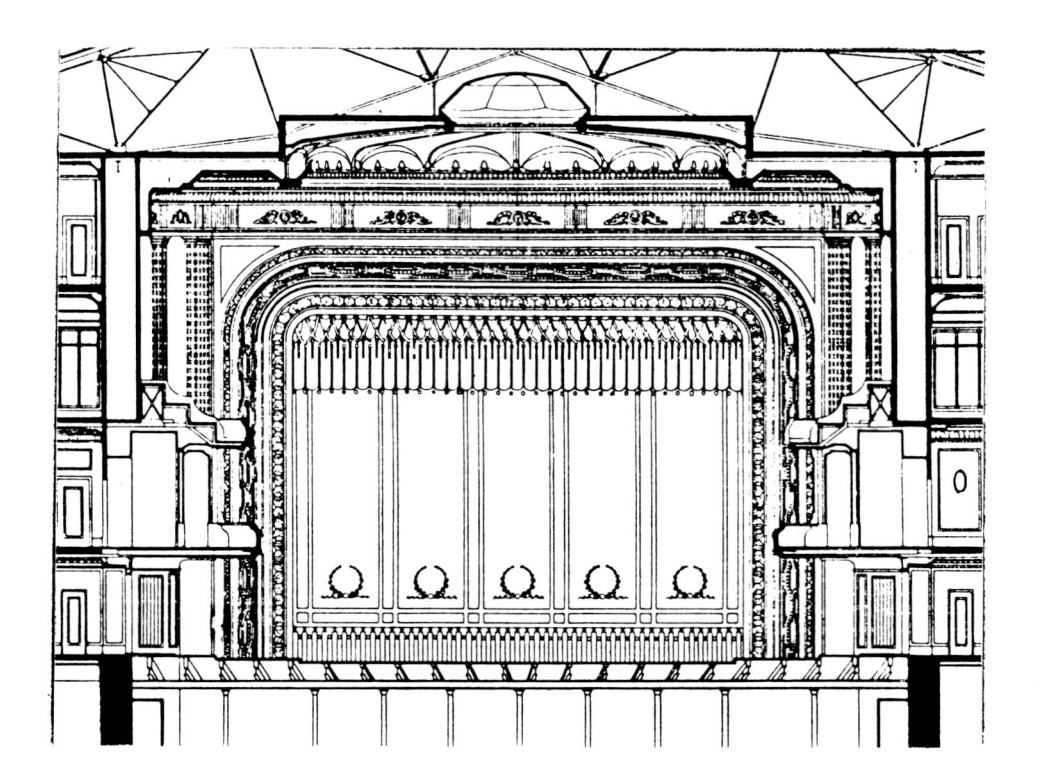

The Württemberg State Theatre in Stuttgart is an old and fairly large house, built at the turn of the century in Baroque style by Max Littmann. In the 1950s the auditorium underwent a »purification«, and the outcome was what one might expect. The auditorium is an almost circular space with two balcony levels, focused very much on the stage. We proposed the uncovering of all the things that had been concealed as part of the process of »purification«, plus a new solution for the transition between auditorium and the extended proscenium arch. It was an attempt to allow the character of the stage machinery to spill over into the auditorium. Small balconies and staircases were to be attached to the scaffold-like inserted struc-

den Zuschauerraum hinüberspielen zu lassen. Die gerüstartigen Einbauten sollten mit kleinen Emporen und Treppen versehen werden, so daß man sie auch zum Spielen vor der Bühne hätte nutzen können.

Wir haben zwar den ersten Preis erhalten, aber zum Bau ist es nicht gekommen. Eigentlich kann man das auch verstehen. Es wurde gesagt, unser Vorschlag sei wieder ein neuer Versuch, und man sei schon einmal mit dem »Verbessern« hereingefallen; wenn jedoch der Littmannbau getreulich restauriert werde, wisse man, was man bekomme.

tures, so that it would be possible to use them as an extension of the stage area.

Although we were awarded first prize for our scheme, it was never actually built, and one can perhaps understand why. It was said that our proposals represented yet another experiment, and that one had made a mistake with »improvements« once already. If, on the other hand, the Littmann building were faithfully restored, the client would at least know what he was getting.

Stuttgart, Staatstheater

Stuttgart, State Theatre

Umgestaltung, Wettbewerb, 1981

Alterations, competition, 1981

Für den Wettbewerb war auch noch eine Erweiterung des Foyers zu planen. Wir haben diesen Foyerteil als eigenen Baukörper in der Art eines Pavillons frei in den Hofraum gestellt. Er steht auf Stützen, damit die Feuerwehr weiterhin in den Hof hineinfahren kann. Zugänge führen von den beiden Rängen zu diesem Pausenpavillon. Sie sind durch eine Wendeltreppe mit dem Hof verbunden.
Über dem Pausenraum wölbt sich eine Glaskuppel, die von gekrümmten Eisenbahnschienen getragen wird. Zwischen und über den Schienen hängt eine Bleiverglasung, die teils aus verspiegelten, teils aus opalisierenden Gläsern hergestellt ist.

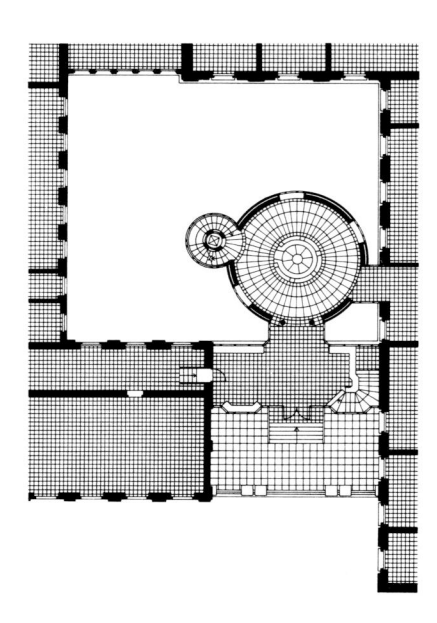

The competition brief also required an extension of the foyer. We designed this section of the foyer as an independent volume in the form of a pavilion, separate from the existing building and set in the courtyard. It is raised on columns, so that the fire brigade can still drive into the courtyard. There is access to this pavilion during the intervals from the two balconies, which are also linked to the courtyard below by a spiral staircase.
Over the foyer is a glass dome supported by a structure of curved railway rails. Laid over and between these rails are leaded lights, consisting partly of mirrored and partly of opalescent glass. During the day sunlight enters the space from above via the glass dome. At night the lights and the coloured dresses of the audience moving about in the foyer are re-

Bei Tage kommt von oben aus der Kuppel Sonnenlicht in den Raum. Abends spiegeln sich die Lichter und die sich bewegenden Menschen mit ihren farbigen Kleidern im Glasgewölbe kaleidoskopartig wider.
Der »Trinkbrunnen« steht unten in der Mitte des Raumes. Der oben umlaufende Balkon ist nur bei den Fenstern durch Brücken gehalten. Dazwischen führen Öffnungen das Licht an der Wandfläche nach unten.
Nun hat so ein runder hoher Raum oft etwas übertrieben Feierliches. Deswegen haben wir in leichten Grautönen Architekturen gemalt mit schattenhaften, tanzenden Figuren. So kommt eine gewisse Bewegung und Leichtigkeit in den Raum.

flected in the glass vaulting as in a kaleidoscope.
In the middle of this space is a »drinking fountain« for refreshments. The peripheral gallery is supported by spur projections only at the points where it passes window openings. Between these points there is a curved slit along the outer edge allowing light to descend down the face of the wall.
A tall, circular space of this kind often has an exaggeratedly formal quality about it. For that reason we had simulated architecture painted on the walls in pale grey tones with shadowy, dancing figures, thus lending the space a certain element of movement and lightness.

Stuttgart — Staatstheater

174 Stuttgart — State Theater

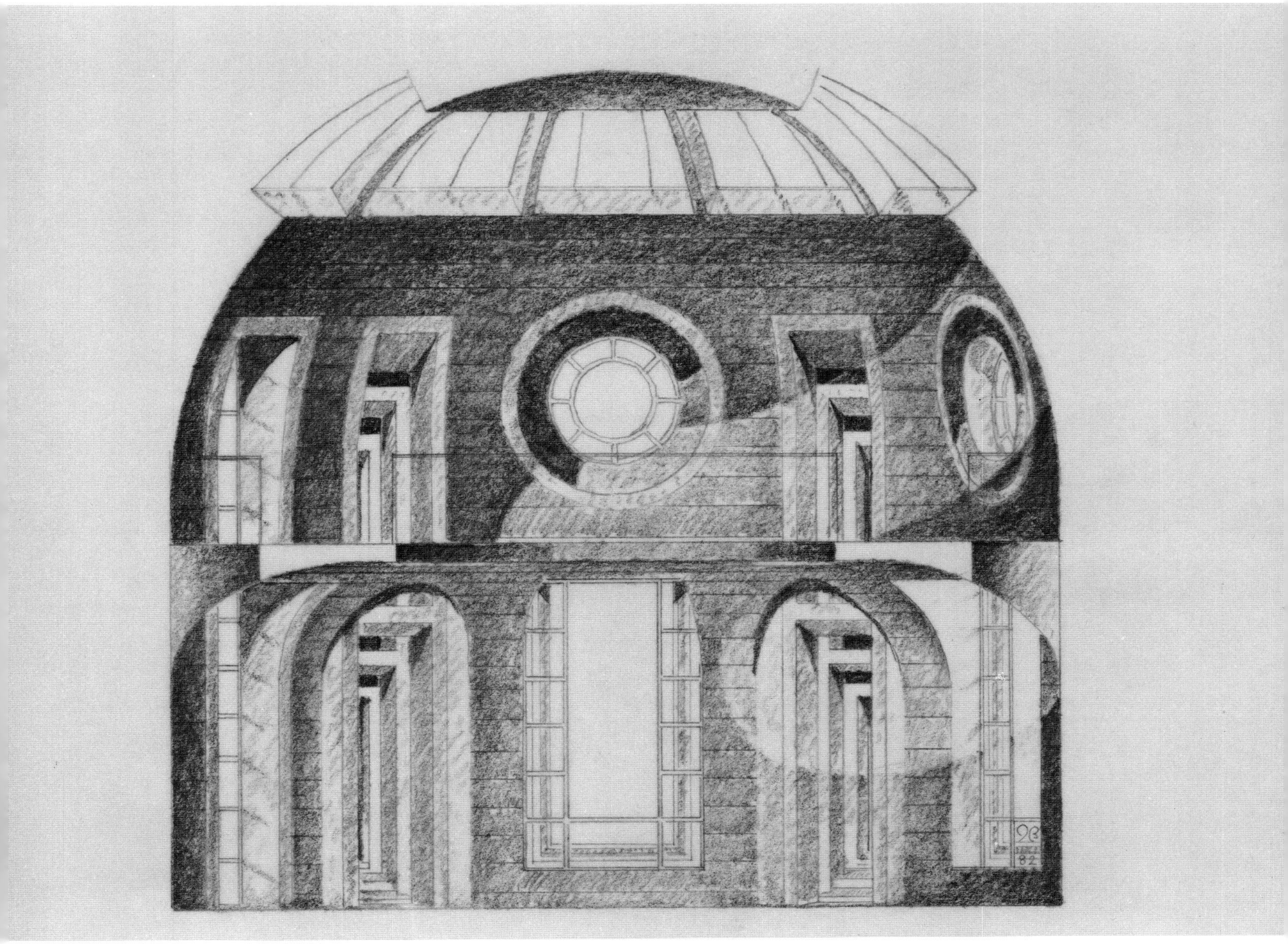

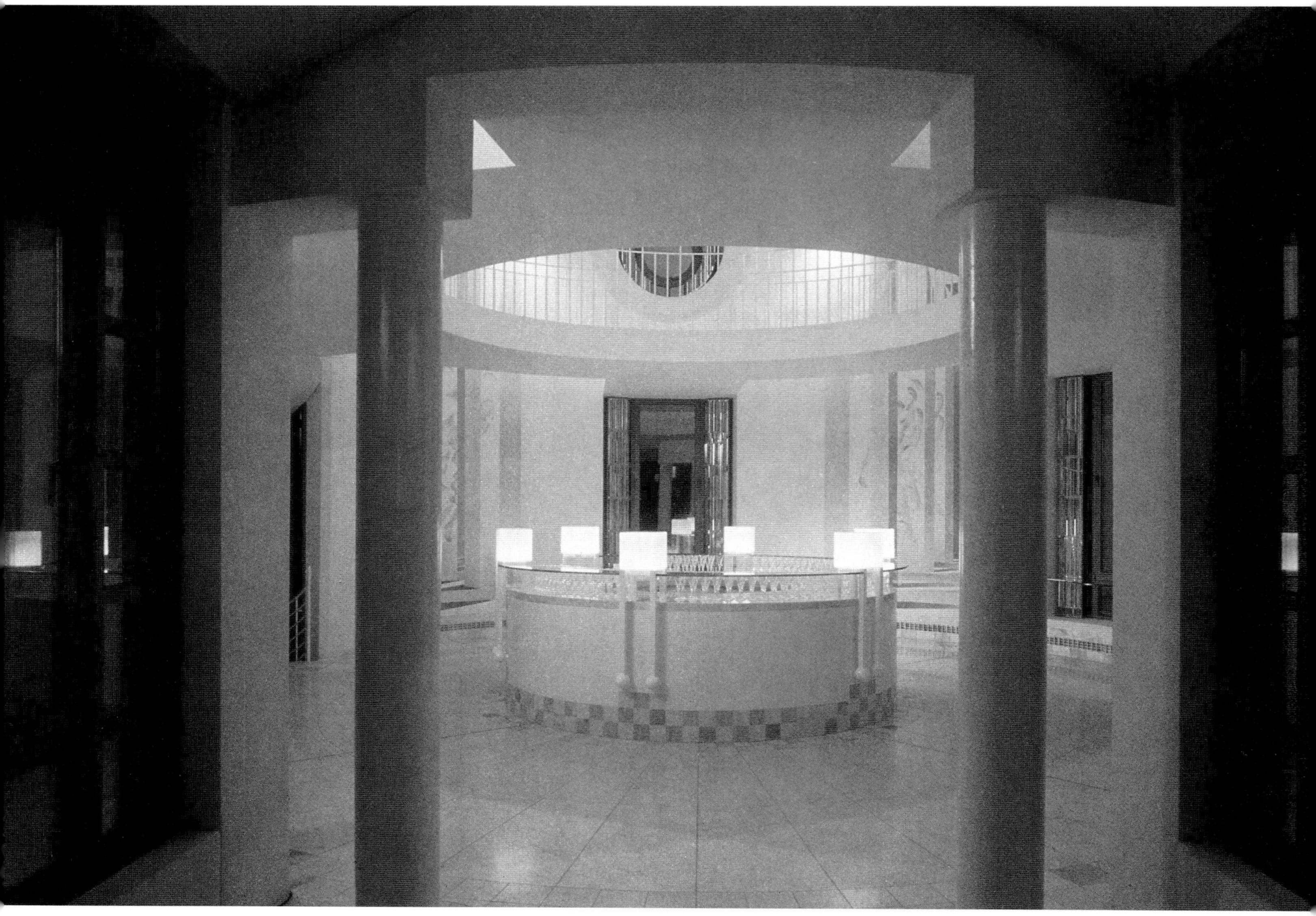

Stuttgart — Staatstheater – Opernhaus — Pavillon-Anbau

Stuttgart — Staatstheater – Opernhaus — Pavillon-Anbau

Stuttgart Staatstheater – Opernhaus Pavillon-Anbau

Stuttgart State Theatre – Opera House Pavilion extension

München, Umgestaltung des Residenztheaters

Munich, Alterations to Residenztheater

Wettbewerb 1984

Competition, 1984

Essen Theater- und Konzertsaal für Musikhochschule, 1985–1987

Essen Theatre and concert hall for college of music, 1985–1987

in Zusammenarbeit mit Stefan Böhm

in collaboration with Stefan Böhm

185

Öffentliche und öffentlich-private Einrichtungen

Bonn	Bundesbauten und B9, 1977, mit Lehrstuhl für Stadtbereichsplanung der RWTH Aachen
Bonn	Bundestag/Bundesrat, Wettbewerb, 1974, mit Gerhard Wagner, Günther Frings, Katja Hrankovicova, Dieter Kokula, Arnold Kirchner, Ulrich Kuhn, Klaus Burk
Saarbrücken	Schloß-Restaurierung, 1979, in Zusammenarbeit mit Nikolaus Rosiny, Krüger-Riegel
Saarbrücken	Schloß-Mittelrisalit-Neubau, 1987, in Arbeitsgemeinschaft mit Nikolaus Rosiny, mit Hans Linder, Hasso Breuer, Franz Kilian, Bernd Hellriegel, Günter Kaintoch
Paderborn	Diözesanmuseum, 1975, mit Hans Linder, Franz Kilian
Hamburg	Museumserweiterung, Wettbewerb, 1986, mit Jürgen Minkus
Köln	Schwimmbad Feuerwache, Wettbewerb, 1980, mit Hans Linder, Franz Kilian, Bruno Kauhsen
Berlin	Prager Platz, Schwimmbad, Projekt, 1977, mit Harald Thomä, Georg F. Adolphi, Fritz Steinigeweg, Hermann Neuerburg
Bad Kreuznach	Restaurant, 1976, mit Wilhelm Jungherz, Stefan Abelen, Elisabeth Böhm
Mannheim	Universitätsbibliothek, im Bau 1987, mit Jürgen Minkus, Corinna Schaade
Neulussheim	Brücke, 1986, mit Georg F. Adolphi, Günther Kaesbach

Public and Semi-Public Institutions

Bonn, Bundesbauten und B 9. Die Regierungsbauten, allen voran Bundestag und Bundesrat, bilden einen sehr bedeutenden Bereich innerhalb des Bonner Stadtgefüges. Deshalb haben wir an der Technischen Hochschule Aachen als Seminararbeit den gesamten Südteil der Stadt an der Achse nach Süden städtebaulich untersucht und planerisch bearbeitet.
Die alte Bundesstraße B 9 ist dort von einer Häßlichkeit, wie sie für Ausfallstraßen typisch ist. Dabei könnte diese wichtige Verkehrsader durch die Vielfalt bedeutender Nutzungen, die hier angesiedelt sind, besonders interessant sein.
Von der Universität ausgehend beginnt es noch vielversprechend mit dem herrlichen grünen Platz und weiter südlich mit

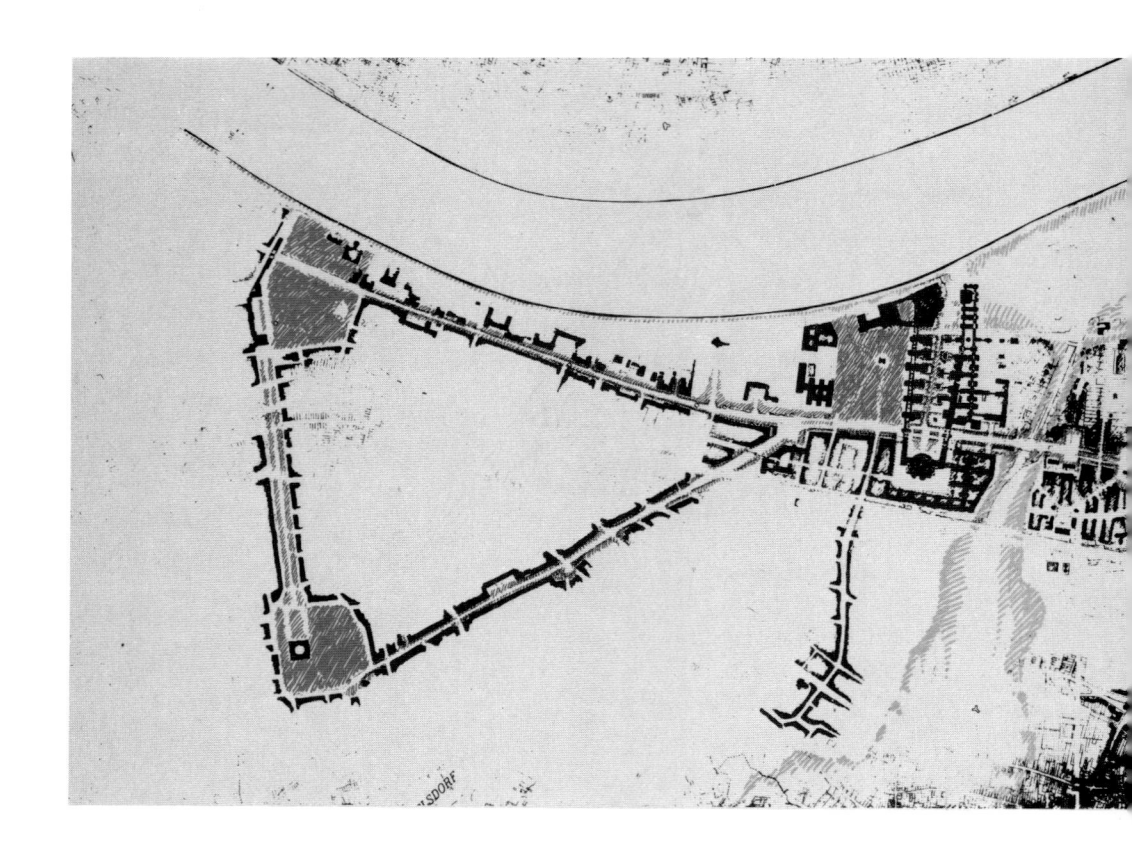

Government Buildings and B 9 Road, Bonn. The federal government buildings and in particular the Bundesrat and the Bundestag (the upper and lower chambers of parliament) form a major realm of their own within the urban fabric of Bonn. In the context of a project at the Technical University of Aachen we investigated the urban structure and drew up plans for the entire southern area of the city along the axis to the south.
The old B 9 Federal Highway in this area has the typically ugly appearance of most arterial roads; whereby this important traffic artery could be a most interesting route, in view of the variety of major functions situated along it here.
It begins at the university in a most promising manner with a wonderful green open space, and continues south past a series

einer Reihe schöner alter Bauten, die den Charakter der Straße prägen. Im neueren Stadtteil schon mit dem Kanzleramtsgebäude verliert sich die Beziehung zur Straße. Es ist mit seiner Zufahrt so angelegt, daß man nur »hinten herum« zum Bundeskanzler kommt. Auch die anderen Bundesbauten liegen hinten drin. Ebenso bedeutungs- und beziehungslos ist die Gesamtbebauung bis Bad Godesberg. Alles ist irgendwo irgendwie hingestellt.
Die Studenten haben für die einzelnen Bereiche detaillierte Vorschläge gemacht. Wir glauben, daß man dort auf längere Sicht eine ganz herrliche städtische Allee mit angrenzenden Gebieten unterschiedlichen Charakters bilden könnte.

of fine old buildings that lend a distinct character to the road. In the newer districts of the city, however, beginning at the Chancellery, the relationship between buildings and street is lost. The Chancellor's Office and its access drive are laid out in such a manner that entry is only possible from the rear. The other federal government buildings are also set back from the road. The entire development along this strip as far as Bad Godesberg is equally insignificant and devoid of any meaningful relationships. Everything has been set out haphazardly in the middle of nowhere.
The students made detailed proposals for individual parts of this area. We believe that it would be possible in the long-term to create a magnificent urban avenue there with adjoining districts of different character.

Für das Gebiet der Bundesbauten schlagen wir als Ausweitung dieser Allee einen großen grünen Platz vor, der in Größe und Gestalt in Analogie zu den Plätzen am Poppelsdorfer Schloß und an der Universität steht. Er ist gedacht als Kern des Regierungsviertels, dem das Bundespräsidialamt, das Bundeskanzleramt und nach Süden hin die Parlamentsbauten mit

Bonn, Fraktionsbereich am »Grünenplatz«   Vorschlag 1977

Bonn, Parliamentary party realm on »Grünenplatz«   Proposals, 1977

For the area in which the federal government buildings are situated, we proposed widening this avenue to form a large, green open space that would be comparable in size and form to the squares or open spaces at Poppelsdorf Palace and the university. It was seen as marking the heart of the governmental district, flanked by the official buildings of the West German president and the Chancellor and, to the south, by the parliament building with its yard. The regular, closed, elongated

dem Parlamentshof angeschlossen sind. Die strenge, geschlossene, langgestreckte Form des Hofes markiert den internen parlamentarischen Bereich mit den Polen Bundestag und Bundesrat. An der Längsseite zum grünen Platz hin denken wir uns im Anschluß an die Fraktionsgebäude Informationspavillons. Hier sollen die Bürger durch Ausstellungen und durch

Bonn, Bundestag, Plenarsaal   Wettbewerb, 1974

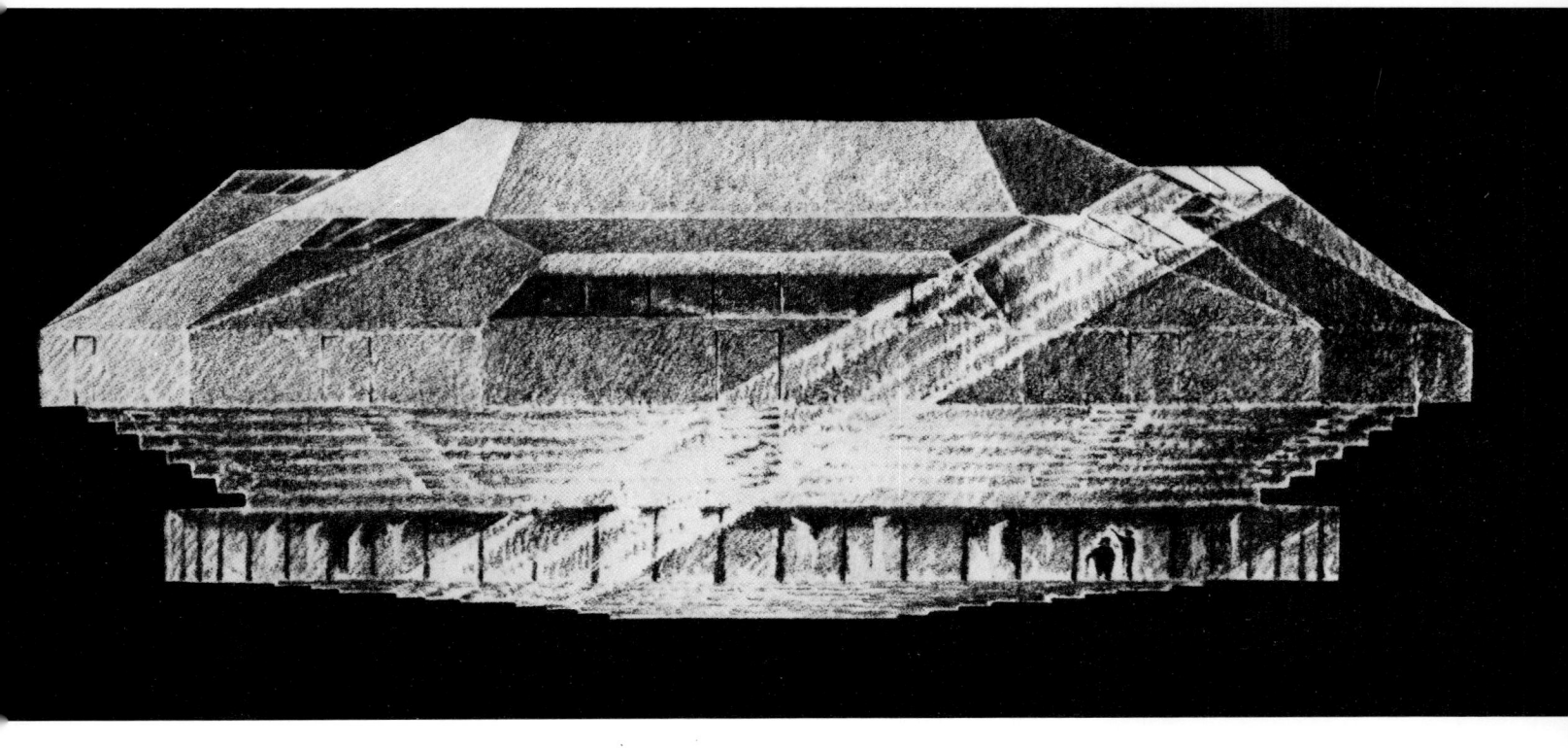

Bonn, Bundestag, parliamentary chamber of assembly   Competition, 1974

form of this yard defines the internal parliamentary realm with its two poles, the Bundestag and the Bundesrat. On the longer side, facing the green square and adjoining the party office buildings, we envisaged a number of information pavilions. Here citizens would be given the opportunity of informing themselves about current problems by means of exhibitions

Diskussionen die Möglichkeit haben, sich über anstehende Probleme zu informieren. Der Parlamentshof deutet durch seine Lage den Bezug zum Rhein an, der immerhin eine wesentliche Lebensader der Bundesrepublik ist.
An seiner Westseite wird der Hof von der B 9 durchquert. So ist der Ort der Gesetzgebung der Öffentlichkeit ständig präsent.

Bonn, Bundestag-Bundesrat — Wettbewerb, 1974

Bonn, Bundestag–Bundesrat — Competition, 1974

and discussions. The position of the parliamentary yard enables one to see the link with the Rhine, which is after all one of the vital arteries of the Federal Republic of Germany. At its western end the yard is cut off by the B 9 road. The legislature is thus located in close proximity to the public realm and to public awareness.

Zu einem kleinen Teil sind unsere Vorstellungen von dem großen grünen Platz in die neue Stadtplanung übernommen worden, aber das ist nur eine halbe Sache. Das Wesentliche ist nicht verstanden worden, denn die Hauptinstitutionen, Bundestag und Bundesrat, sind nach wie vor ohne richtigen Bezug zur Stadt.

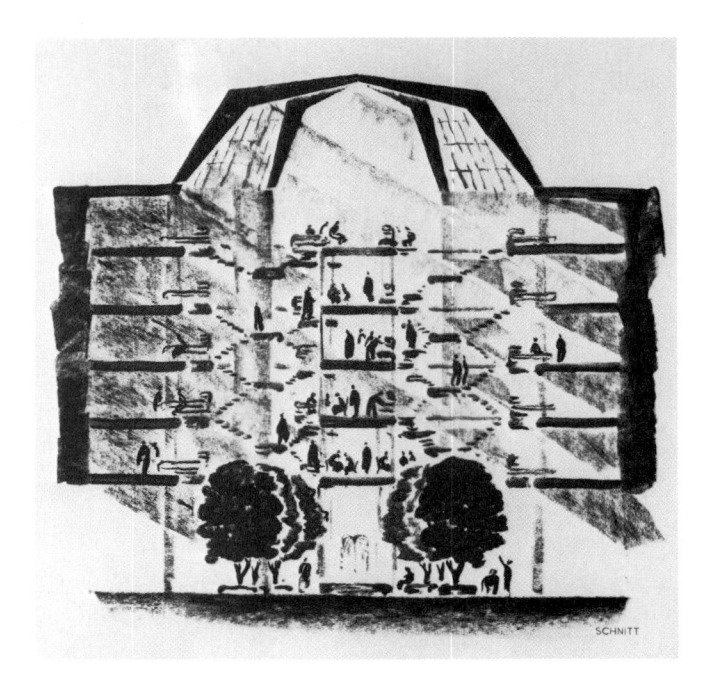

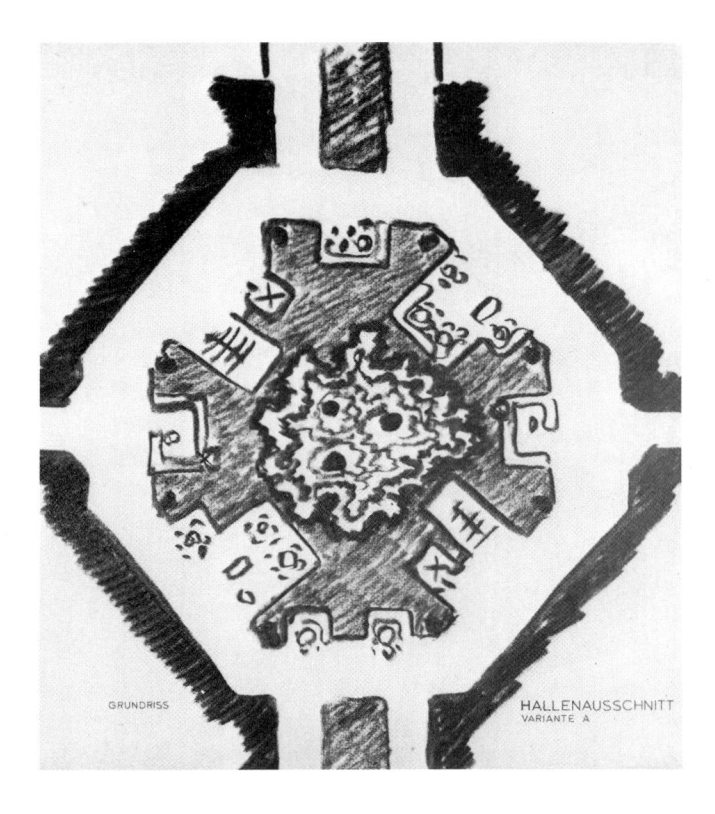

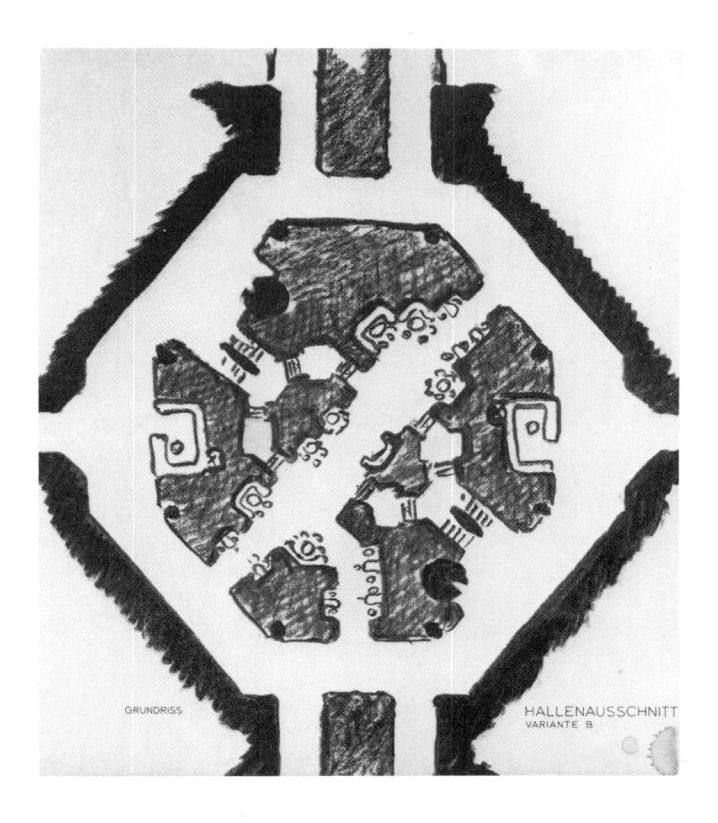

To a modest extent our idea of a large green open space has been adopted into the new planning proposals for the city, but unfortunately only in a half-hearted manner. The essence of our proposals was not understood, for the major institutions, the Bundestag and Bundesrat, have been left without any proper relationship to the city.

Vorschlag 1977: Bundespräsident (1), Präsidialamt (2), Museum für Deutsche Geschichte (3), Bundestag (4), Ausschüsse (5), Kanzleramt (6), Grünplatz (7),

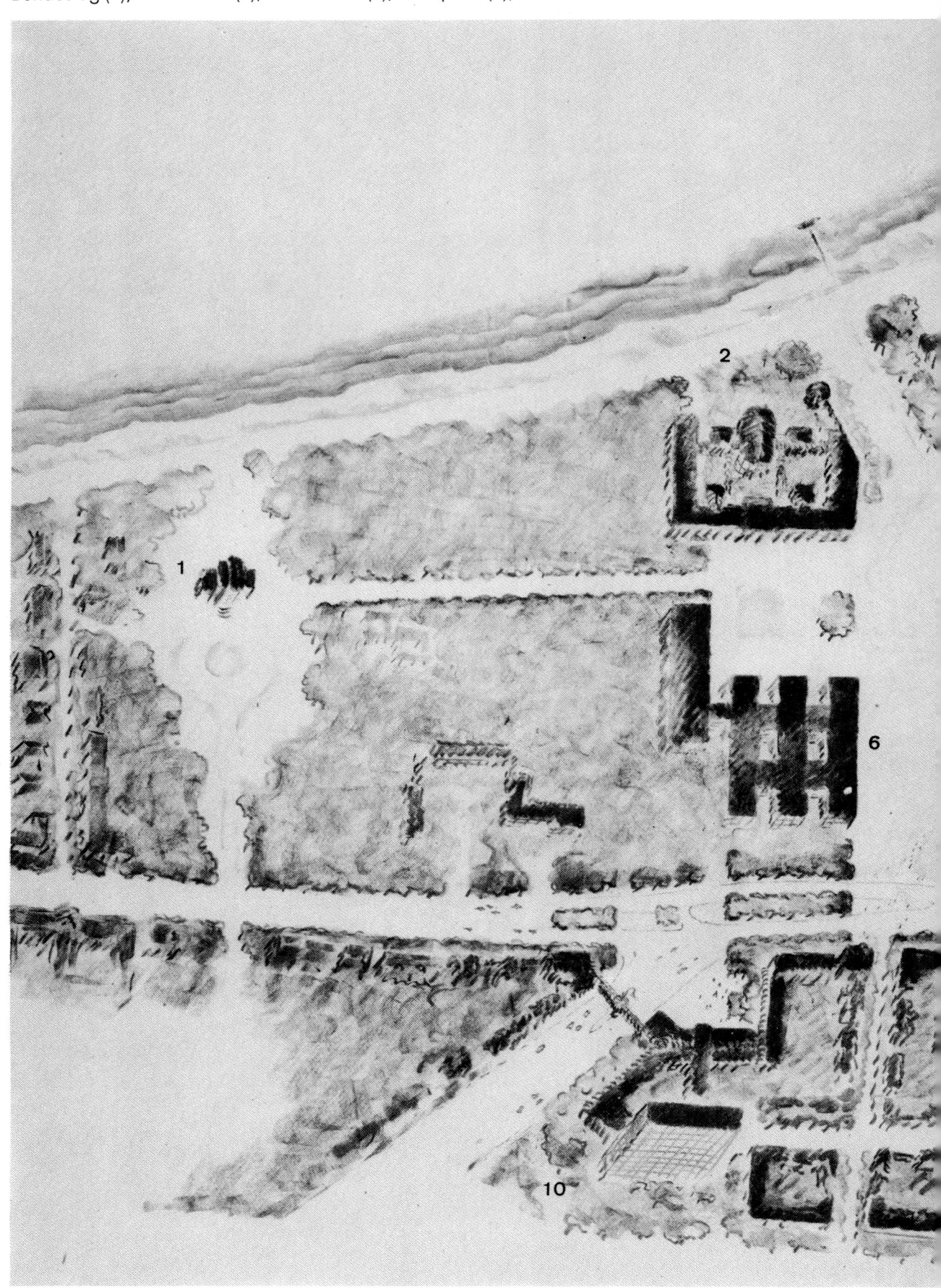

Proposals 1977: President of state (1), President's office (2), Museum for German History (3), Bundestag (4), Committees (5), Chancellor's office (6), Planted open space (7),

Abgeordnete, Fraktionen mit Informationspavillons (8), Dienste (9), Europahaus (10), Jugend-Gästehaus (11), Länder (11, 14), Bundesrat (13)

Members of parliament and parties, with info. pavilions (8), Services (9), Europa building (10), Guest house for young people (11), Regional state buildings (11, 14), Bundesrat (13)

Eine in gewisser Hinsicht ähnliche Aufgabe wie die Bundesbauten in Bonn, diesmal auf Landesebene, ist die Restauration und der Umbau des Schlosses in Saarbrücken. Auch hier möchte ich zunächst den größeren städtebaulichen Zusammenhang erläutern. Es handelt sich um ein ehemals zusammenhängendes Stadtgebiet, das durch den Fluß gegliedert war. Zwei Stadtseiten am Saarufer waren mit einer schönen Brücke verbunden, worauf sich der Name der Stadt bezieht. Durch Verkehrsbauten nach dem Krieg sind die beiden Stadtteile völlig voneinander getrennt worden. Am Ufer entlang läuft eine Autobahn, dann kommt noch eine Straße und wieder eine Straße, und erst dahinter fängt endlich die Stadt an, und irgendwo dort kommt auch noch das Schloß. Wir haben in einem Wettbewerb eine Überbauung der Autobahn vorgeschlagen mit einer marktähnlichen Verkaufszone, überdachten Höfen, einer Volkshochschule in Verbindung mit der alten Brücke sowie einem kleinen Bootshafen und anderen dazugehörigen Einrichtungen. Zur Saar hin wird dieser Komplex durch eine lange Reihe von Wohnhäusern mit Gartenhöfen abgegrenzt, die eine ideale Wohnlage und zugleich eine belebte Uferzone herstellen. Alle Bauten überbrücken die riesige Straßenfläche und lassen dabei die Zufahrten offen. Das ist eine Zukunftsvorstellung, die mit steigendem Grundstückswert immer leichter finanzierbar wird. Durch diese Planung würde der Stadtteil wieder in seiner zentralen Lage ans Ufer herangeführt und damit würde auch das Schloß deutlich zum Zentrum der Stadt gehören.
Aus diesem städtebaulichen Wettbewerb ergab sich schließlich der Auftrag für die Erneuerung des Schlosses. Das Parlament hatte beschlossen, das Schloß so wieder errichten zu lassen, wie es der Barockbaumeister Stengel gebaut hatte.

In Saarbrücken we were confronted with what is, in some respects, a similar task to that faced in the project for the federal government buildings in Bonn; – only in this case it was on a regional state level. It involved the restoration and conversion of the palace in Saarbrücken. Here too I should like to preface my description with an outline of the overall urban context. The palace is situated in what was once a cohesive urban area, articulated by the river flowing through its middle. The two parts of the city along the banks of the River Saar were linked by a beautiful bridge, from which the city derives its name. As a result of post-war road-building schemes the two halves of the city are now completely separated from each other. Along the bank of the Saar runs an autobahn and two further roads. The city itself begins only behind these traffic routes; and it is somewhere in this area that the palace lies. In a competition entry we proposed the construction of a market-like shopping zone, covered courtyards and an adult education institute, all built over the motorway and linking up with the old bridge, plus a small harbour for boats and other ancillary facilities. The edge of this development facing on to the River Saar would be defined by a long row of dwellings with garden courtyards, creating an ideal housing environment and at the same time a lively riverside zone. The buildings would be placed over the enormous area taken up by the roads, but leaving the access points open. That is, of course, a vision of the future. But with rising land prices it is one that will become increasingly feasible financially. These planning proposals would restore this area of the city to its old central position on the bank of the river, and the palace would be seen to belong to the heart of the city again.
The outcome of this urban planning competition was a commission for the rehabilitation of the palace. The regional parl-

Ursprünglich hatte das Gebäude einen betonten Mittelbau und hufeisenförmig angeschlossene Seitenflügel mit drei hohen Geschossen. Dieser Barockbau stand leider nicht sehr lange. Er brannte im 19. Jahrhundert völlig aus, und die zwei unteren Geschosse der Ruine wurden so ausgebaut, daß sich drei Geschosse daraus ergaben. Sie waren zeitweise bewohnt und dienten in letzter Zeit Büronutzungen. Ein neuer Mittelbau ist später hinzugebaut und in den dreißiger Jahren noch auf »altdeutsch« hergerichtet worden. Er wirkt sehr kleinlich in dieser großen Anlage.

Wir bekamen zunächst den Auftrag, das Schloß in der alten Art, also wie das Stengelsche Barockschloß, wieder zu errichten. Ein Schloß sollte es aber gar nicht mehr werden. Als Haus besonderer Art soll es den Landtag oder den Stadtverband aufnehmen mit dem dazu notwendigen großen und kleinen Plenarsaal. Diese Umfunktionierung bringt zunächst natürlich technische Schwierigkeiten mit sich. Das sind zum Beispiel die enormen Raumhöhen und Raumgrößen, die nicht für Büros geeignet sind. Das schwerwiegende Problem bei der Aufgabe war jedoch die Tatsache, daß schließlich eine zweihundertjährige Geschichte den heutigen Bau geprägt hat, wobei die architektonische Kraft durch Umbauten teilweise verloren gegangen ist.

Diese lange Geschichte aber durch Rekonstruktion gleichsam ungeschehen zu machen, schien uns nicht richtig, zumal für die Wiederherstellung des barocken Originalbaus außer der ursprünglichen Nutzung die entsprechende geistige Einstellung fehlte. Es ist ja ein Wiederaufbau nach einer Katastrophe wie Brand oder Kriegseinwirkung etwas ganz anderes, da die Verbundenheit mit dem Gebäude, dessen Zerstörung man selbst erlebt hat, noch lebendig ist.

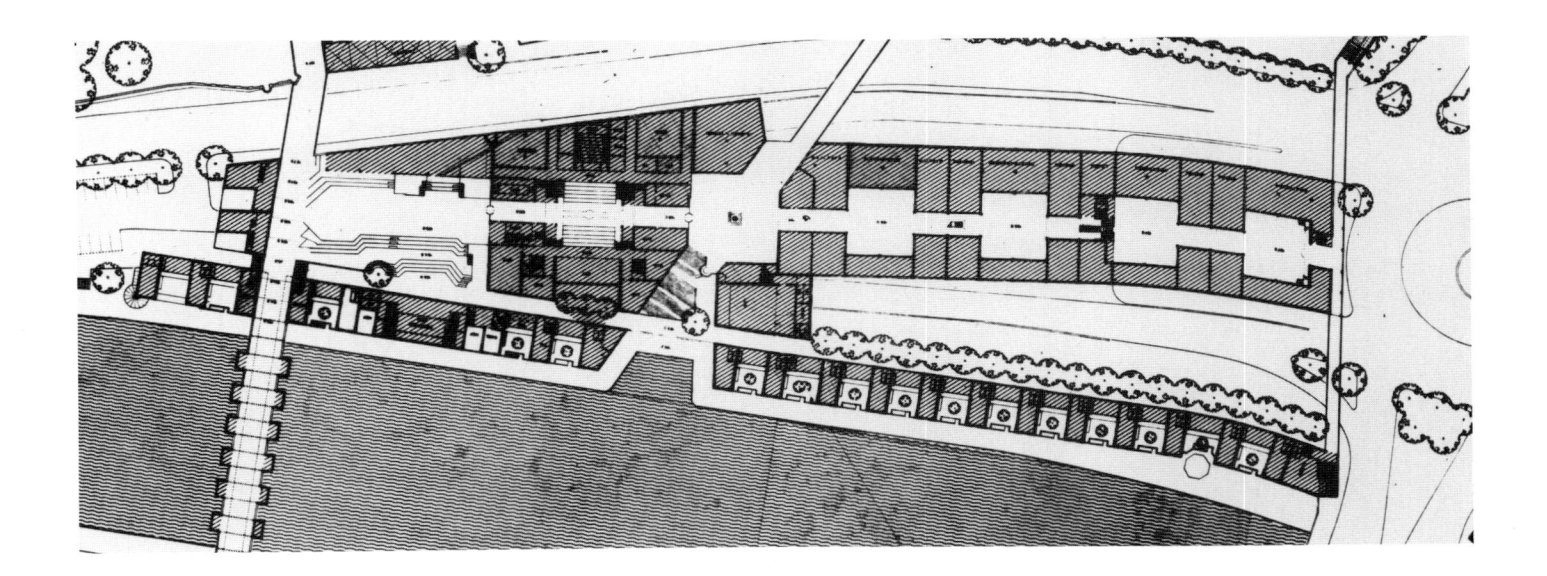

iament had decided to have the palace restored to its original form, as it was built by the Baroque master-builder Friedrich Stengel.

Originally there had been a salient structure in the middle of the palace with wings to both sides laid out in horseshoe form and containing three high storeys. This Baroque building did not stand for very long, unfortunately. In the 19th century it was almost completely destroyed by fire. The two lower floors of the ruins were rebuilt to accommodate three new storeys. These were inhabited for a time; but of late they served as offices. A new middle tract was added later and refurbished in »Old German« style in the 1930s. In the context of this large complex it has a somewhat dwarfed appearance.

Our initial commission was to rebuild the structure in its original form; i.e. the restoration of Stengel's Baroque palace, although it was no longer to be used as a palace. As a building of distinctive character, it was to house the state government of the Saarland or the organization of municipal authorities (Stadtverband), with the requisite larger and smaller chambers of assembly. This change of use inevitably gives rise to certain technical difficulties. For example, the great height and sizes of the rooms were not suitable for offices. But the major problem was the fact that the present building had been moulded by 200 years of history and that the architectural expression had been robbed of much of its force by the various alterations.

Simply to eradicate this long history by an act of reconstruction did not seem right to us. Furthermore, even though one might restore the original Baroque building, not merely was it impossible to put it to its original use, but the relevant mental attitude was lacking. A reconstruction after a catastrophe like a fire or war is something completely different; for the per-

Saarbrücken

198 Saarbrücken

Uferbebauung

Riverside development 199

Alle diese Überlegungen neben dem enormen finanziellen Aufwand für die Wiederherstellung des ursprünglichen Zustandes haben uns dazu bewogen, außer den Plänen für die Rekonstruktion (ich arbeitete da zusammen mit Nikolaus Rosiny) auch einen Vorschlag für die Erhaltung des jetzigen Bestandes der Seitenflügel mit Neugestaltung des Mittelteils zu erarbeiten. Dabei konnte der große Plenarsaal, der für die Nutzung die wichtigste Funktion einnimmt und auch für besondere Veranstaltungen von Stadt und Land außerordentliche Bedeutung hat, an der richtigen zentralen Stelle eingeplant werden. Ein wenig kann ich die Entrüstung verstehen, die dieser Vorschlag ausgelöst hat. War man doch sicher, daß man bei auch nur annähernder Rekonstruktion des Barockschlosses einen schönen und bedeutenden Bau erhalten würde.

Bei welchem Neubau hat man heute schon diese Gewißheit! Der an dem barocken Vorbild gemessene Anspruch für den Neubau ist ja so groß, daß uns selbst oft angst und bang wird, ob er bei aller Anstrengung zu erfüllen ist. Das Problem be-

sonal links one has with a building, the destruction of which one has experienced oneself, are still alive.
All these considerations, plus the enormous costs involved in a restoration of the building to its original condition, moved us to propose an alternative scheme to that of the reconstruction project (on which I collaborated with Nikolaus Rosiny). In this alternative, the present wing structures were retained and the middle section was redesigned. It was thus possible to give the large assembly chamber, which was to accommodate the most important function in the brief, and which was also of exceptional importance for special occasions held by the city and the state, the central position it deserved. To some extent I can understand the indignation to which these proposals gave rise. One was quite certain that, even with an approximate reconstruction of the Baroque palace, one would gain a building of beauty and significance.

With what new building does one have that certainty today? The criteria for any new building wishing to measure itself against the Baroque model were so high that we ourselves were often frightened whether they could be met, despite every

steht weniger in der Restaurierung der Seitenflügel und deren Nutzbarmachung für die Verwaltung als vielmehr in der Neugestaltung des so sehr verkümmerten Mittelbaus, ohne die auch hier schon geschichtliche Situation zu zerstören. Man wünscht sich einen Mittelbau mit mehr Kraft, damit der ganze Komplex wieder Zusammenhalt und Bedeutung bekommt. Obschon der Bau nicht mehr Schloßfunktion hat, dient er doch nicht einfach irgendeiner Verwaltung, sondern der demokratischen Regierung, die ihre eigene Bedeutung und Würde hat. Damit wird zum Beispiel auch die höfische Trennung hinfällig zwischen der »cour d'honneur« vor und dem abgeschlossenen Park hinter dem Schloß. Der heutigen Nutzung entspricht vielmehr ein offener städtischer Platz vor dem Schloß und ein Gebäude mit Durchlässigkeit zum Park, der nun ebenfalls der Öffentlichkeit zugänglich ist. Daher wollen wir den Mittelbau möglichst transparent gestalten. Die stark gegliederte Glaswand gewährleistet, daß immer Teile der Wand im Schatten liegen und die Durchsichtigkeit dort weitmöglichst

exertion on our part. The problem was not so much the restoration of the wing structures and their adaptation to the needs of the administration. The real difficulty lay in redesigning the truncated central section, without destroying the historic situation. A middle section with more power was called for, so that the complex in its entirety would acquire cohesion and meaning again. Although the building no longer has the function of a palace, it does not serve any ordinary administrative body. It is the home of a democratic regional state government that has an importance and dignity of its own. For these reasons the courtly division between the cour d'honneur at the front and the closed park at the back is no longer valid. The modern use to which the palace is to be put would find more appropriate expression in an open urban space in front of the palace and a building of some transparency that would allow a view of the park to the rear, which should also be accessible to the public now. That is why we wished to make the middle tract as transparent as possible. The bold articulation of the glass façade ensures that there are always certain areas of this elevation in shadow; but it also retains a maximum of

gesichert ist.
Ein Einblick in das Modell zeigt den Plenarsaal, der auch für Feste und Konzerte nutzbar sein soll. Er hat also unterschiedliche akustische Bedingungen zu erfüllen. Wir haben deshalb eine sehr stark gegliederte Decke vorgesehen, deren Tiefe durch eine Bemalung optisch verstärkt werden soll. Für die seitlichen Nischen sind Vorhänge vorgesehen, mit denen man durch verschieden abstufbares Öffnen und Schließen die Akustik beeinflussen kann. Die Dachfenster bringen den ganzen Tag über unterschiedliches Licht in den Raum.

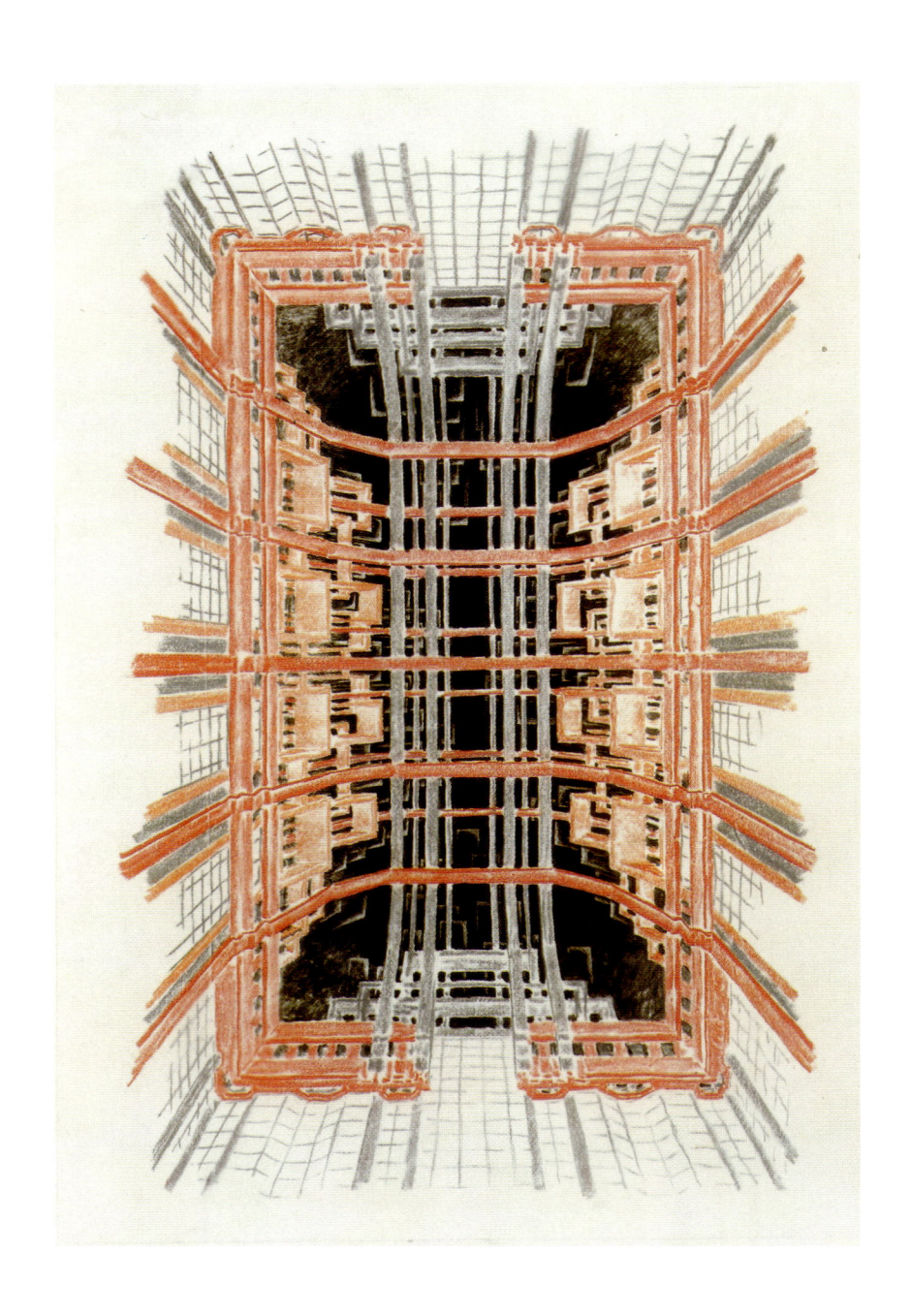

transparency.
A glimpse inside the model shows the debating chamber, which is designed to accommodate festive occasions and concerts as well. It thus has to meet quite different acoustic requirements. We therefore proposed a boldly structured soffit, the three-dimensionality of which would be visually accentuated by painting. Side niches are foreseen with curtains that can be opened to various degrees to help control the acoustics of this space. The roof lights allow changing light to enter the hall throughout the day.

Saarbrücken — Schloß — Mittelbau

Diözesanmuseum in Paderborn. In Paderborn greifen große Grünbereiche bis in den Kern der Stadt ein. Sie sind dadurch entstanden, daß in der Umgebung des Domes die Pader aus vielen Quellen entspringt und schon bald als kleiner Fluß die Stadt durchzieht. So bestehen noch im Herzen der Stadt ideale Wohnsituationen mit direktem Bezug zum Grünen im innerstädtischen Raum und weiter zur offenen Landschaft.

Im Krieg wurde um den Dom herum fast alles zerstört. Der Dom lag nunmehr frei auf einer riesigen Fläche, die sich zu ihm hin absenkt. Wir haben mit unserer Bebauung das Gelände wieder, wie vor der Zerstörung, in zwei Plätze gegliedert: in einen quadratischen Marktplatz und einen Längsplatz, der sich wiederum in zwei Platzniveaus aufteilt. Dadurch steht der Dom jetzt erneut auf einem eigenen Platzbereich.

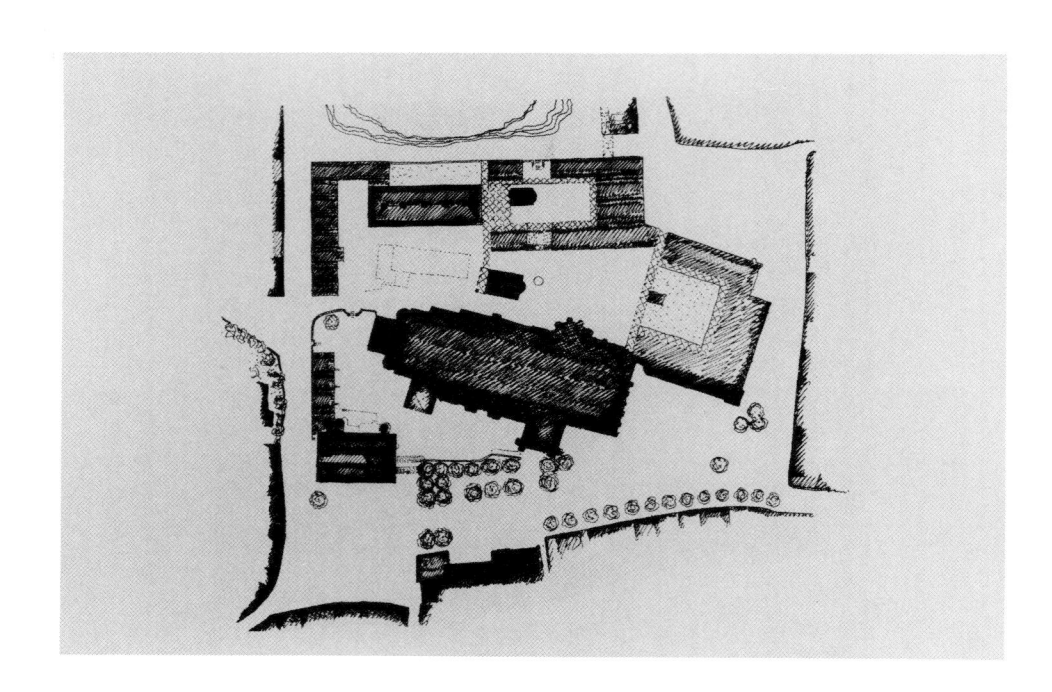

Diocesan Museum, Paderborn. In Paderborn there are large areas of natural landscape reaching right into the heart of the town. Their existence can be explained by the fact that the River Pader springs from a number of sources not far from the cathedral and these flow together to form a small river that winds its way through the town. As a result of this one finds ideal residential conditions at the very heart of the urban area in close proximity to green natural surroundings that in turn extend out to the open landscape.

During the war almost everything round the cathedral was destroyed, leaving it standing alone in the midst of an enormous open space that falls gently towards this building. Our development restructures this area, restoring to it the form it had before the destruction, dividing it into two open spaces: a square-shaped market place and an elongated open space that is subdivided into two different levels. As a result of this planning, the church now stands in its own cathedral square again.

Der neue Komplex mit Diözesanmuseum, Wohnhäusern, Büros und einem Café steht teilweise auf Stützen, so daß sich der Marktplatz unter dem Gebäude fortsetzt. Damit ergibt sich eine Blickbeziehung vom Platz in das Museum und durch das Museum hindurch zum Turm des Domes. Von den Caféräumen aus überblickt man den Marktplatz und hat zusätzlich einen Blick in das Museum.
Die Konstruktion des Gebäudes war besonders schwierig, weil auf dem Gelände sehr schöne alte Gewölbe existieren, die man nicht antasten wollte. Wir haben deshalb eine Konstruktion gewählt, die sich über das ganze Gewölbe stülpt. Vier Stützen sind in einem Trägerrost verbunden, von dem alle Decken und Wände abgehängt sind. Damit ist auch die Schale der Außenhaut von oben herunter gehängt. Sie ist deshalb relativ leicht konstruiert. So eine dünne Haut hat allerdings nur ge-

The new complex, comprising a diocesan museum, housing, offices and a café, is in part raised above the ground on columns, so that the market place continues under the building. A visual link is also established in this way from the square into the museum, and through it to the tower of the cathedral beyond. From the coffee house there are views over the market place and into the museum.
The construction of the building was extremely problematic, because there is some very fine old vaulting on this site that one did not wish to touch. We therefore chose a form of construction that straddles the entire area of the vaulting. Four columns are tied together in a load-bearing girder grid on which all floors and walls are supported. The outer wall membrane is also suspended from the top. For that reason it was given a relatively lightweight construction. A thin skin of this kind has

ringe Speicherfähigkeit, und es ist nicht leicht, das Raumklima künstlich konstant zu halten.
Dieses Museum ist kein Gebäude mit einer Folge von Räumen, die jeweils in ihrem Charakter den Besucher auf die Ausstellungsstücke einstimmen sollen. Der Bau ist eher wie ein großer Behälter, der wohl selber auch schön sein will, der aber zunächst dem Aufbewahren dient und der dabei in seiner Gesamtheit, durch seine Raumform, seine Maße, durch die aufsteigenden Ebenen und Durchblicke immer wieder zusammen mit kostbaren Exponaten einen gemeinsamen, zusammenhängenden Eindruck vermitteln will. Das ist eine Auffassung von Museum, wie sie wahrscheinlich nicht von allen Museumsleuten gerne gesehen wird.

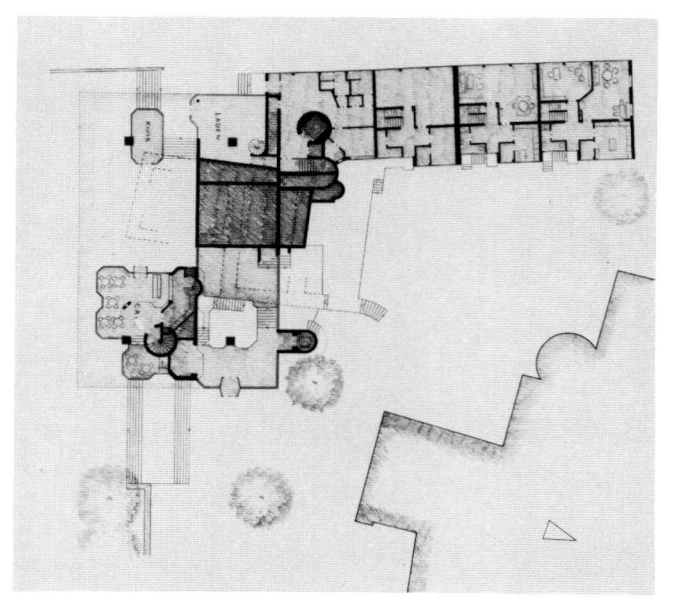

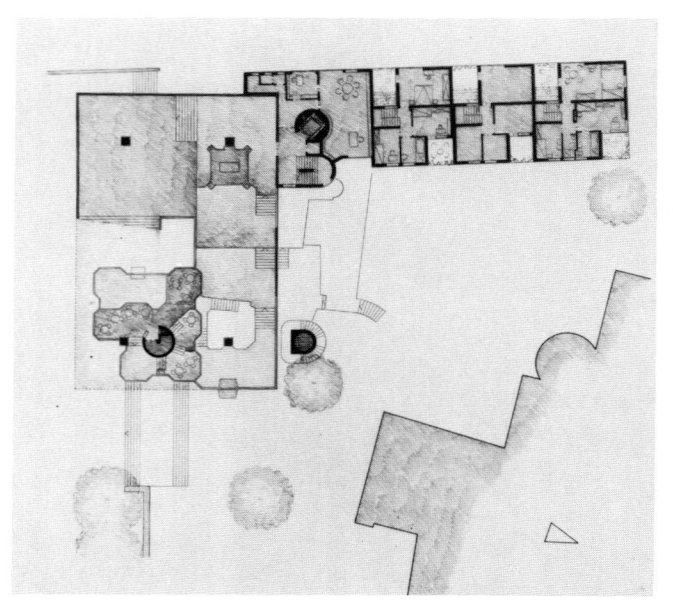

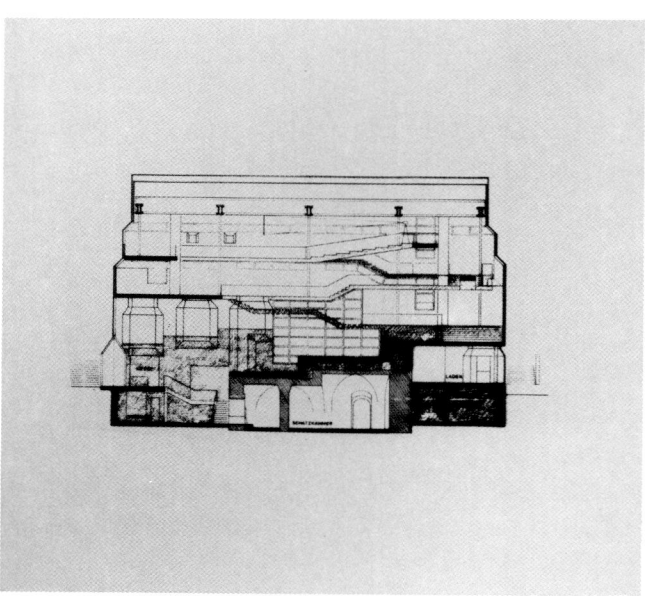

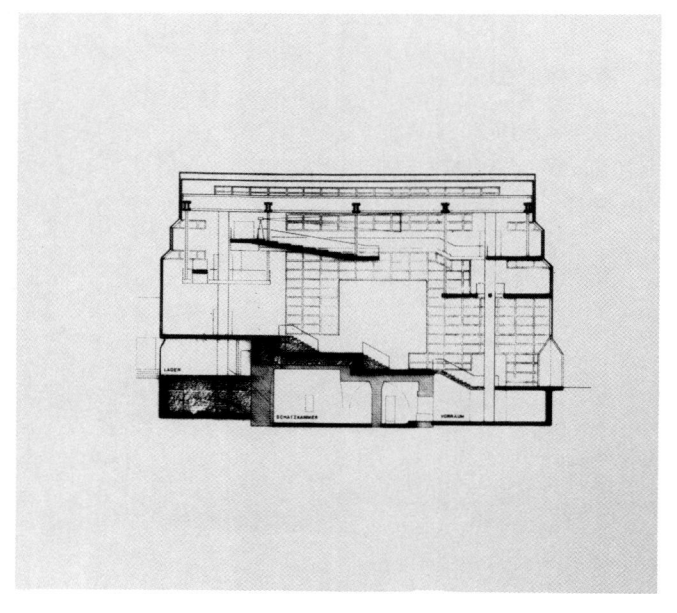

low heat retention properties, however, and it is not easy to maintain constant climatic conditions on the inside by artificial means.
The museum is not conceived as a sequence of spaces, the individual character of which is meant to put the visitor in the right frame of mind for the objects displayed. The building is more in the nature of a single large container, a structure that wishes to be beautiful in itself, but whose immediate purpose is that of conservation; that nevertheless, in its totality, through its spatial form, its proportions, its rising levels and the views it affords, tries to communicate, in conjunction with the precious objects on display, a coherent overall impression. This is a concept that probably not all museum people will accept.

Paderborn — Diözesanmuseum — Teilansicht

Paderborn — Diocesan Museum — Partial view

In dem Wettbewerbsprojekt für die Erweiterung des Museums in Hamburg haben, von der Auffassung des Museums her, ähnliche Gesichtspunkte wie beim Paderborner Museum eine Rolle gespielt. Wir haben den neuen Museumsteil, ohne den Altbau aus der Jahrhundertwende anzutasten, über den kubischen Neubau für moderne Kunst auf einer Stützenkonstruktion turmartig geplant. Unserer Ansicht nach sollte man vermeiden, den Grünbereich, der sich entlang der früheren Befestigung um die Stadt legt, mit einem breitgelagerten Bauvolumen abzuschließen, sondern eher durch einen vertikalen Baukörper den dortigen Knotenpunkt betonen.

Ähnlich dem Paderborner Museum entwickelten sich auch hier die Ausstellungsebenen in einem großen Gesamtraum mit

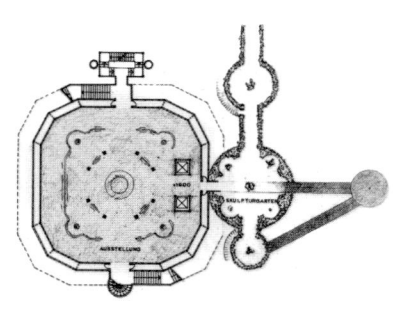

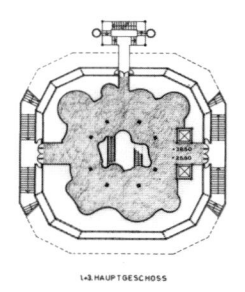

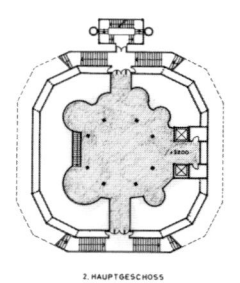

In the competition project for the extension of the Museum for Modern Art in Hamburg similar conceptual ideas were involved to those underlying the Paderborn Museum. Without touching the old building dating from the turn of the century, we designed the new section of the museum as a tower structure set on a column base over the cube of the new building for modern art. We felt it would be wrong to close off the green belt along the former city walls with a massive built volume. Instead, we decided to emphasize the centre of focus at this point with a vertical structure. In a similar form to that of the Paderborn Museum, various exhibition levels here unfold within a large overall space. A principal level and a number of

Hauptebene und eingehängten Galerieebenen, die unterschiedliche Geschoßhöhen ermöglichen. Sie sind untereinander mit Zwischentreppen verbunden.
Hier in Hamburg bildet eine großzügige spiralförmige Treppe innerhalb der doppelschaligen verglasten Fassade nochmals im Verein mit den Aufzügen den vertikalen Zusammenhang. Somit entsteht in etwa der Eindruck einer begehbaren Plastik. Ich muß noch dazu sagen, daß dieser Museumsneubau ausschließlich der modernen Kunst gewidmet ist, die ja die herkömmliche Museumsfeierlichkeit nicht wünscht. Wir haben mit unserem Entwurf versucht, Exponate und ihr Gehäuse als Einheit erleben zu lassen.

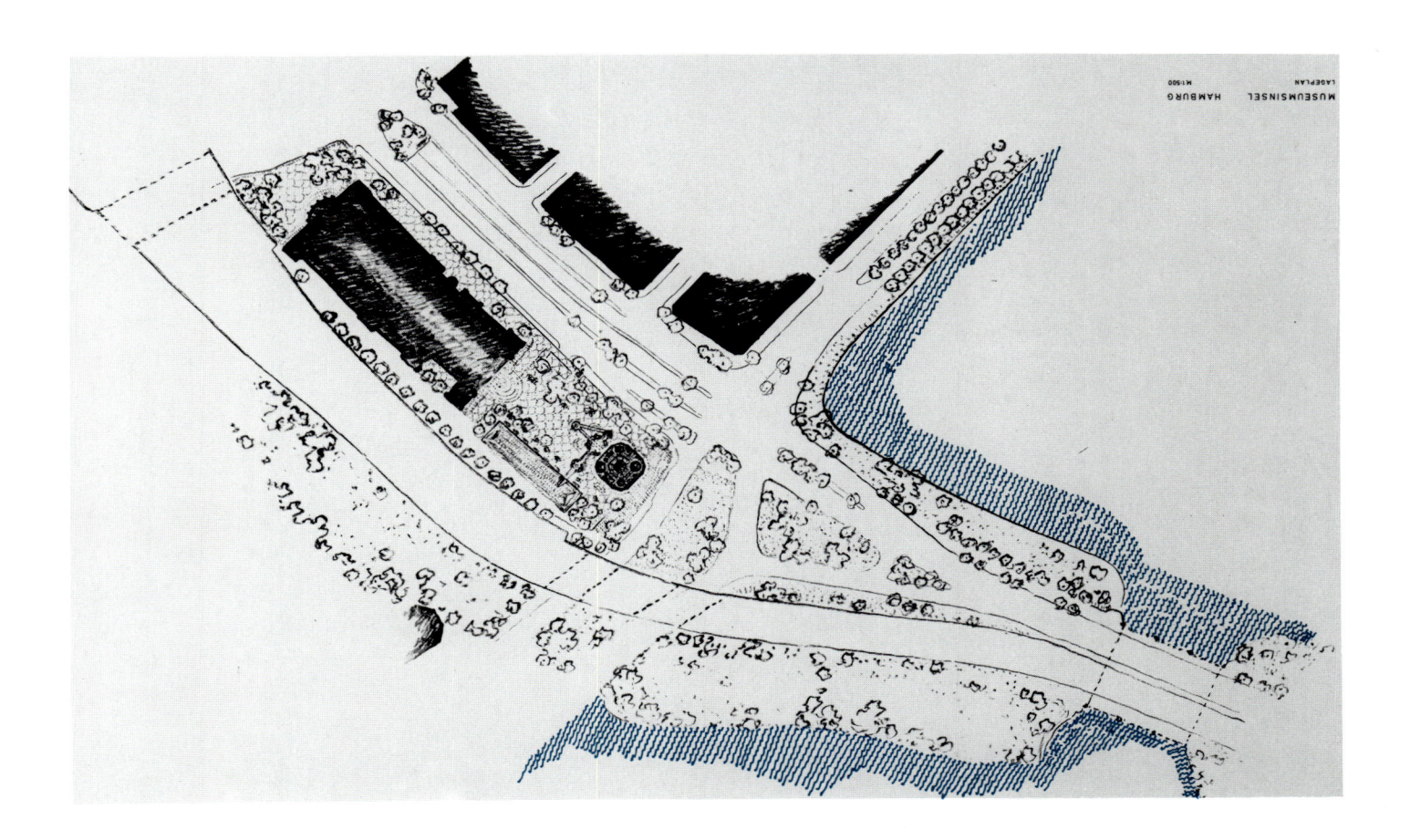

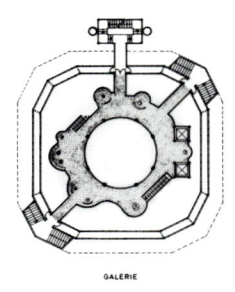

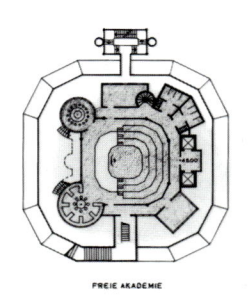

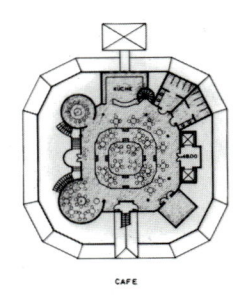

inserted gallery levels, linked by flights of stairs, create a variety of storey heights. Here in Hamburg the vertical line of access is formed, in conjunction with the lifts, by a broad spiralling staircase within the double skin of the glazed façade. One has the impression of a climbable sculpture. I should add that this museum is devoted exclusively to modern art, which is a realm where the pomp and circumstance of traditional galleries would be out of place. With our design we attempted to create a situation where the objects exhibited and the containing structure would be experienced as a unity.

Hamburg

Museum

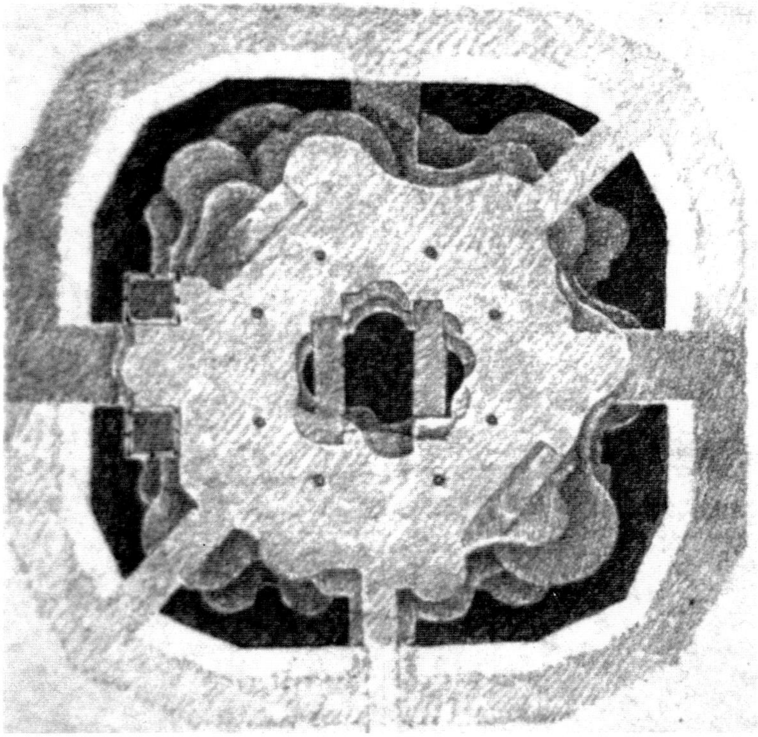

Hamburg Museum

Hamburg Museum

Schwimmbad – Feuerwache in Köln. Von der alten Feuerwache in Köln stehen noch einige Bauten mit unterschiedlicher Höhe, baukastenartig mit gelben und roten Ziegeln errichtet. Früher standen an der Platzseite hohe Häuser mit Geschäften und anderen Einrichtungen im Erdgeschoß. Dieser Teil ist im Krieg zerstört worden und sollte jetzt durch ein Schwimmbad ersetzt werden. Damit diese Platzseite nicht nur von einer einzelnen Funktion begrenzt wird, haben wir zusätzlich an den Ecken Flügelbauten mit Wohnungen, Läden und einer Kneipe vorgeschlagen. Das Schwimmbad wurde so geplant, daß es mit seinem Leben und Treiben auch von außen wahrnehmbar wäre. Außerdem soll auch eine Gasse vom Platz aus in das Innere der Gesamtanlage führen.

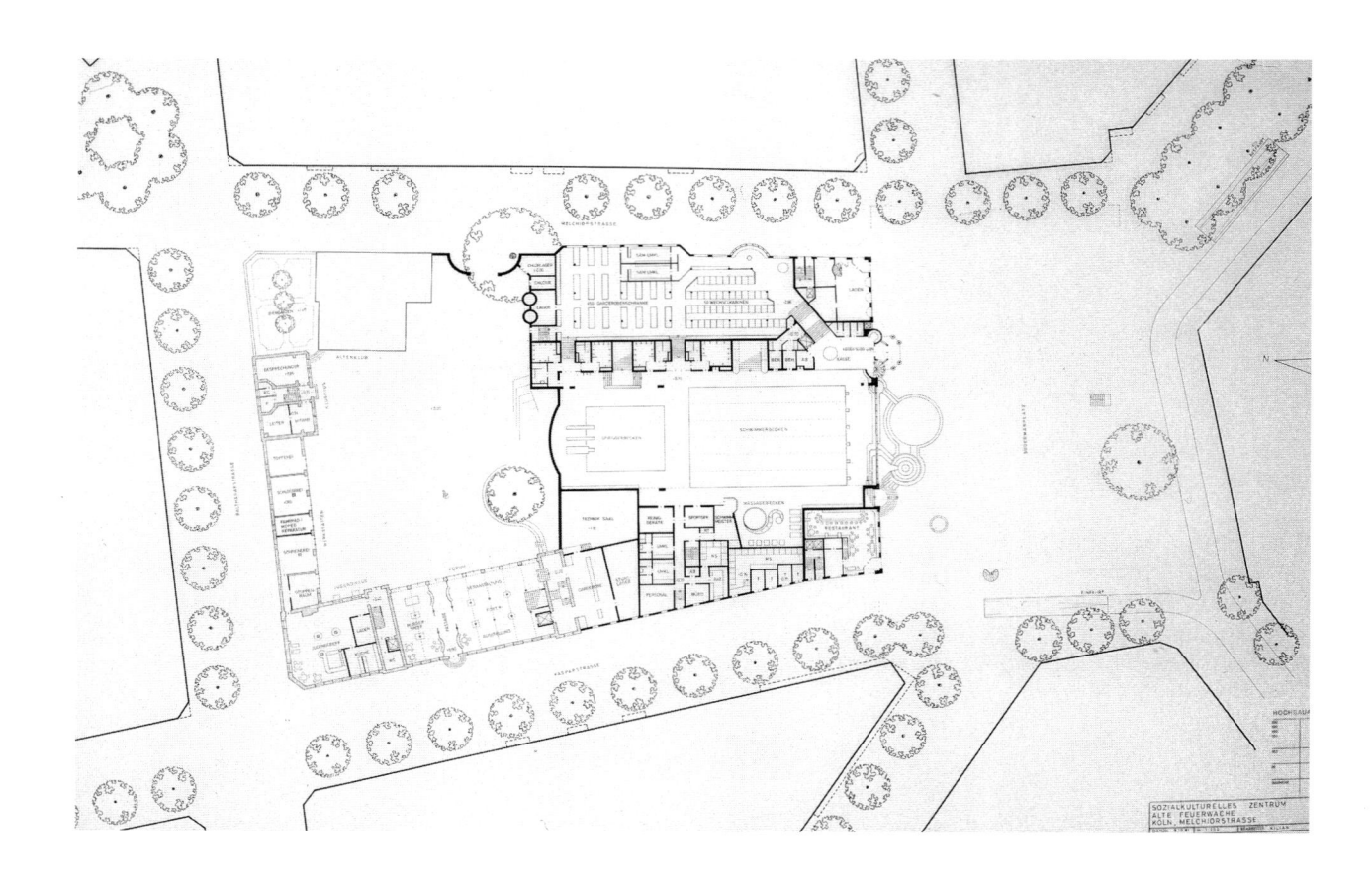

Swimming Baths, Fire Brigade Headquarters, Cologne. All that is left of the old fire brigade headquarters in Cologne are a number of buildings of different heights, erected in a kind of toy building block style with yellow and red bricks. Facing on to the square in former times were tall blocks with shops and other facilities on the ground floor. This part of the development was destroyed in the war and is now to be replaced by a swimming pool. In order that this side of the public open space should not be occupied by one function alone, we suggested inserting additional wing structures at the corners, accommodating housing, shops, and a bar. The swimming pool, was designed in such a way that its internal life and activities can also be seen from outside. In addition, a narrow lane was planned, leading from the square into the interior of the complex.

Köln · Schwimmbad – Feuerwache

Cologne · Public baths – Fire brigade headquarters

Schwimmbad – Prager Platz, Berlin. Zu dem Projekt am Prager Platz in Berlin gehört ebenfalls ein Schwimmbad. Dort ist die Aufgabe schon von den verschiedenen Badefunktionen her viel interessanter. Geplant ist ein großes Freizeitbad, dessen Vielfalt von Wasserbecken, Fontänen, Rutschbahnen usw. eine lustige Situation schafft, die sich in der geplanten Dachlandschaft auch nach außen hin ausdrückt. Die große Tonne des Bades stößt bis zur Platzwand vor. Ein kleiner Bach

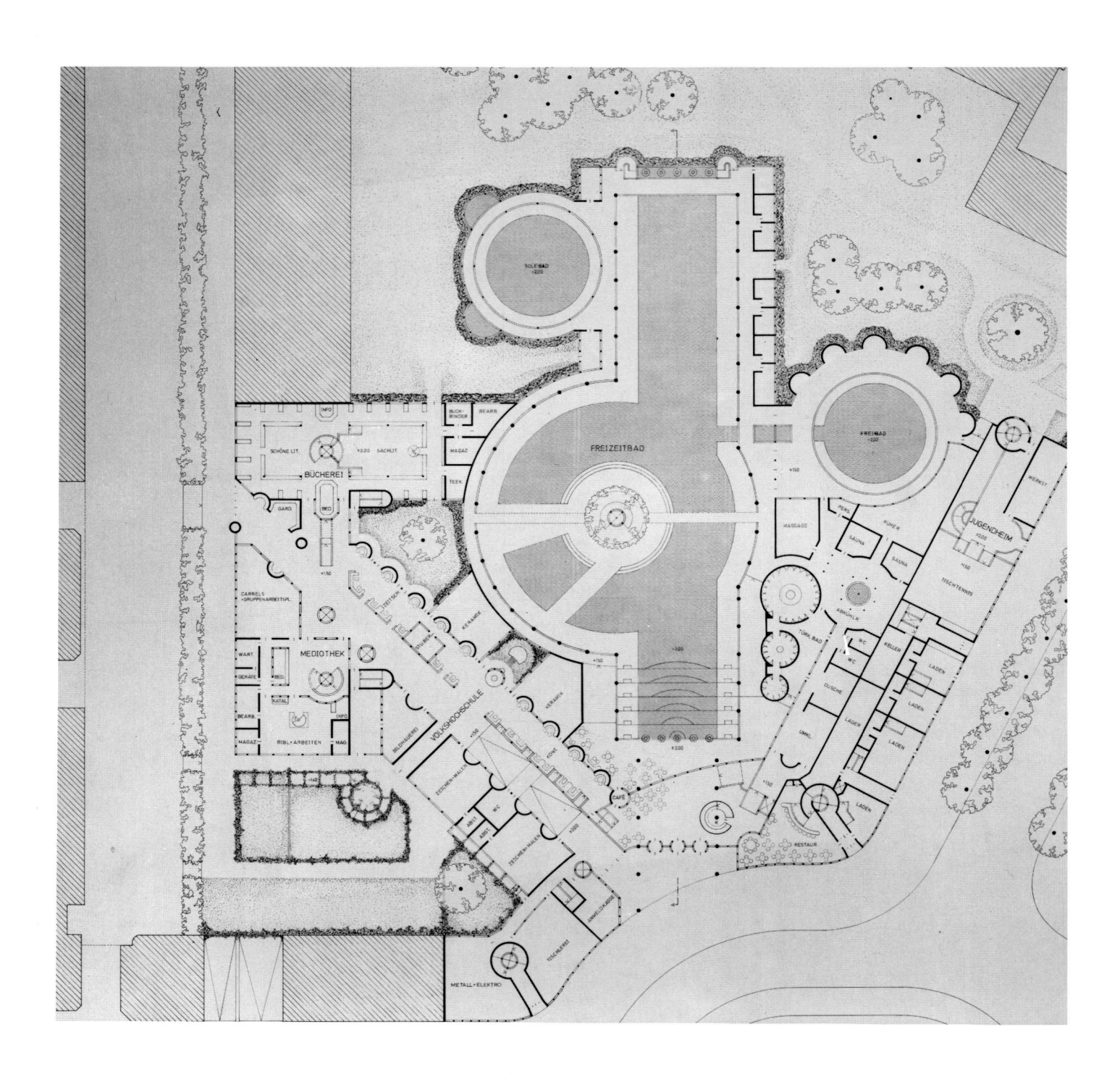

Swimming Baths, Prager Platz, Berlin. Amongst the amenities to be provided in the Prager Platz scheme are the swimming baths. The project is of greater interest here due to the range of bathing facilities foreseen. A large recreational baths complex is planned with a variety of pools, fountains, chutes, etc., the light-hearted atmosphere of which will also be expressed on the outside in the proposed rooftop landscape. The large barrel-vault roof of the baths is continued out to the

führt bis zur Mitte des Platzes, so daß im Sommer in einer großen flachen »Pfütze« mitten auf dem Platz Kinder planschen können. Der Durchblick vom Platz in die große Tonne der Badeanlage stellt eine enge Beziehung zwischen Platz und Freizeitbereich her.

edge of Prager Platz itself. A small stream flows to the centre of this public open space, and in summer children will be able to paddle and play in a large shallow pool in the middle of the square. The view from Prager Platz into the spacious barrel vault of the swimming baths establishes a close relationship between the public open space and the leisure realm.

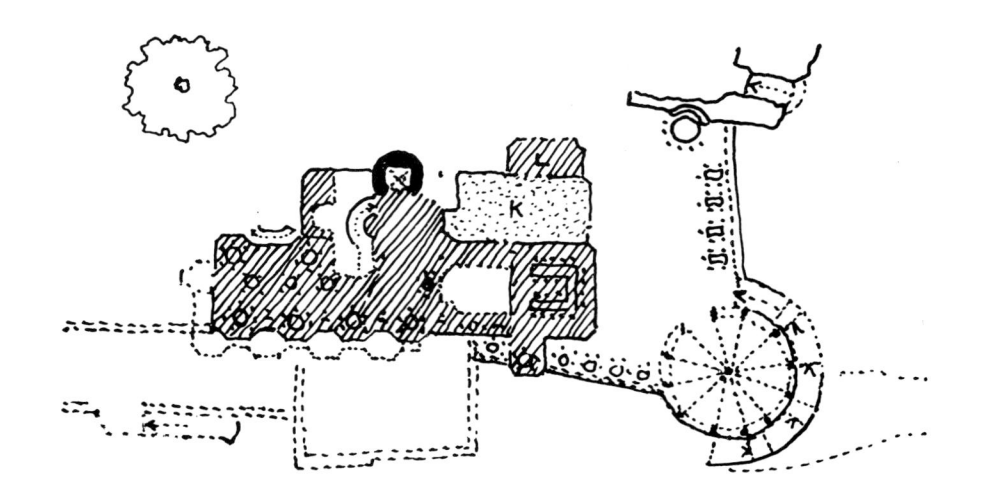

Bad Kreuznach — Restaurant

Bad Kreuznach — Ausbau einer Burgruine als Restaurant, 1969

Bad Kreuznach — Development of castle ruins into restaurant, 1969

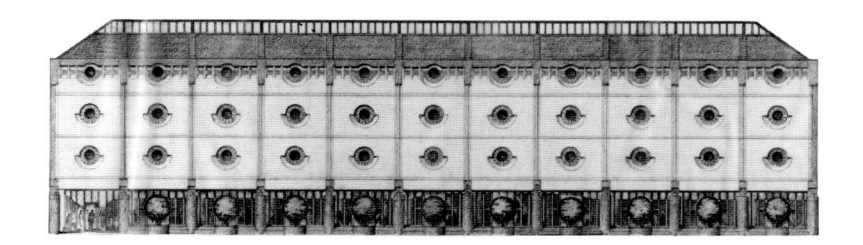

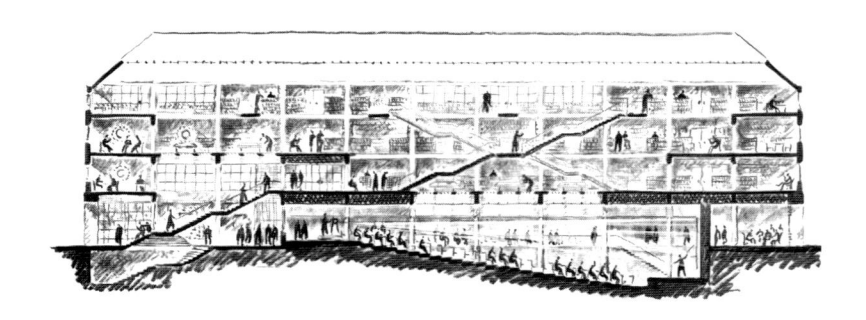

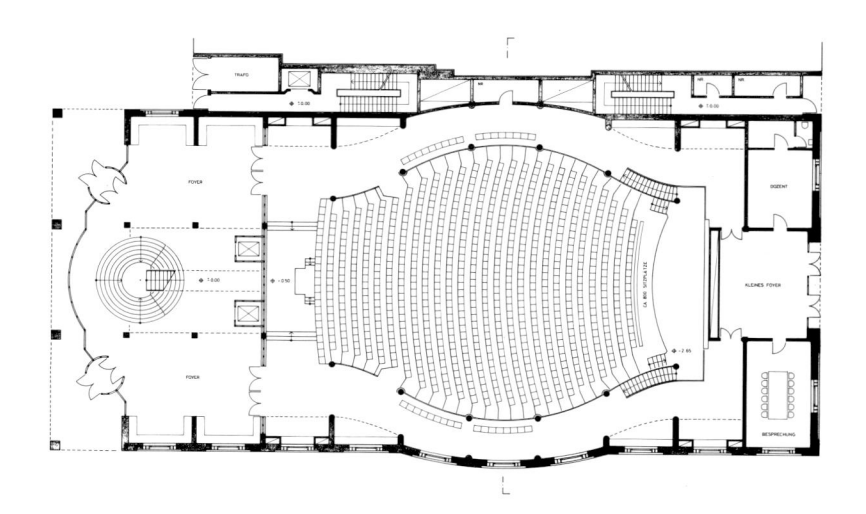

Mannheim, Universitätsbibliothek, 1987 — im Bau

Mannheim, University library, 1987 — under construction

Mannheim — Universitätsbibliothek

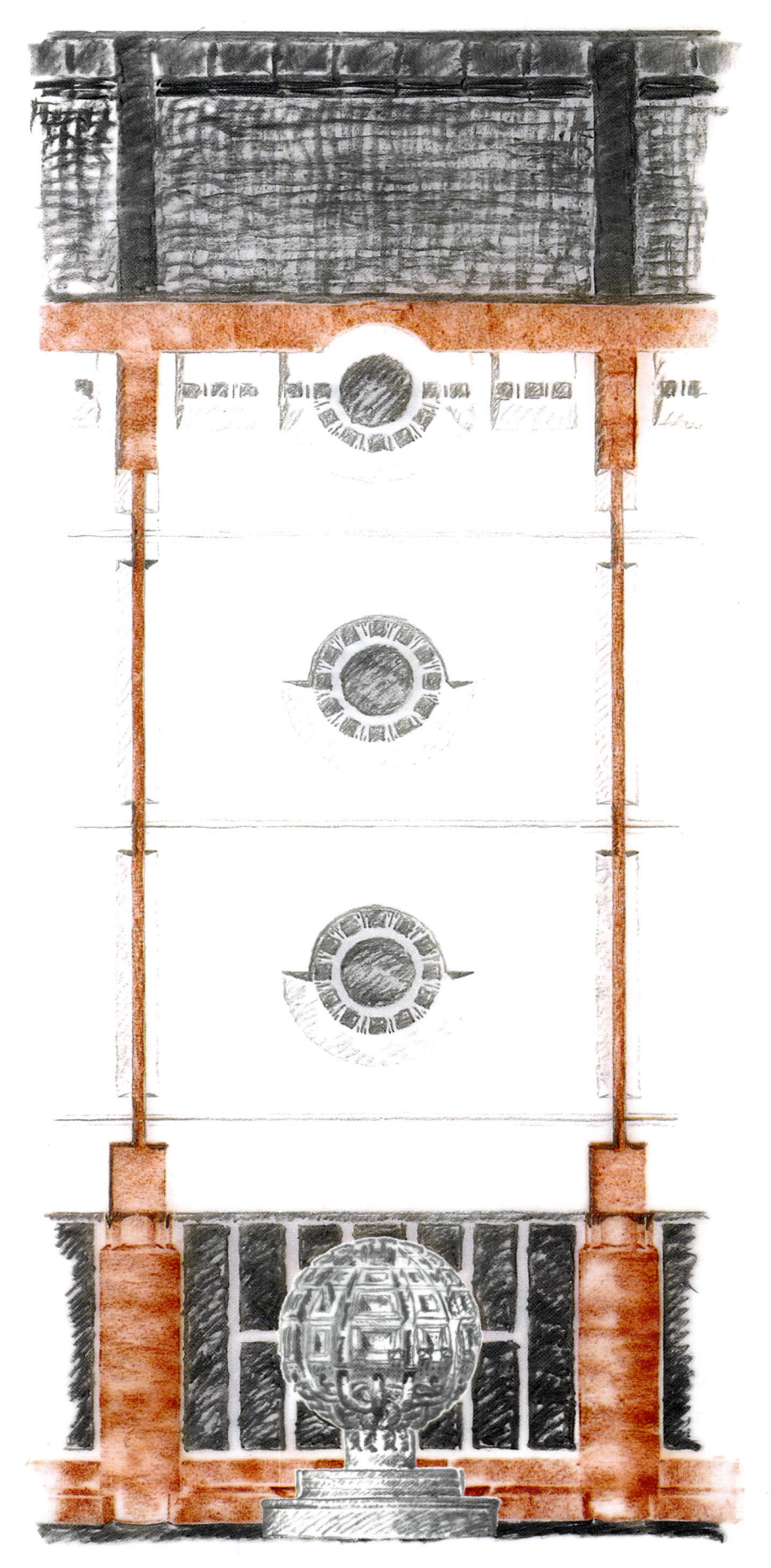

Mannheim — University library

Neulussheim | Brücke, 1986

Neulussheim | Bridge, 1986

Neulussheim — Brücke, 1986

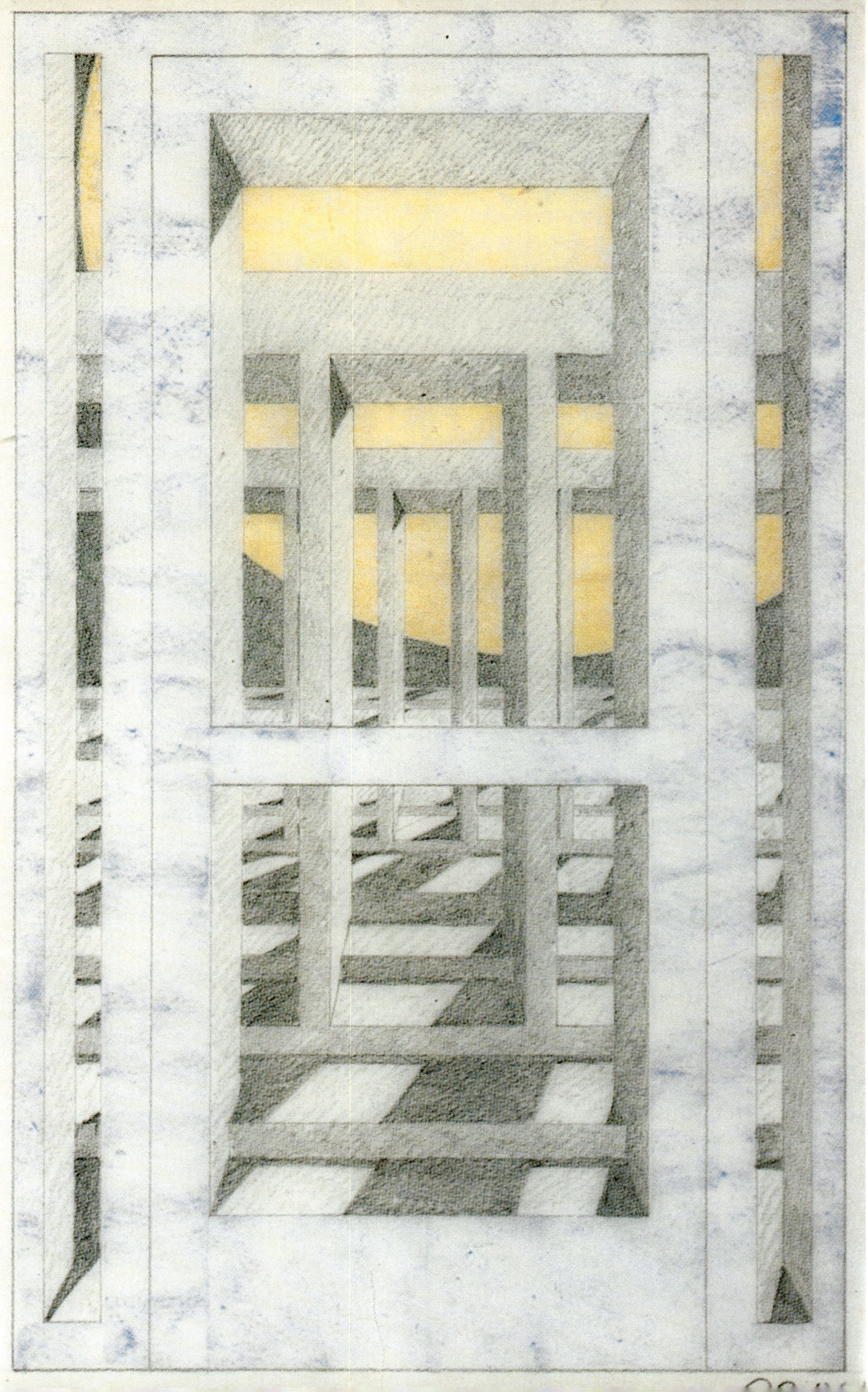

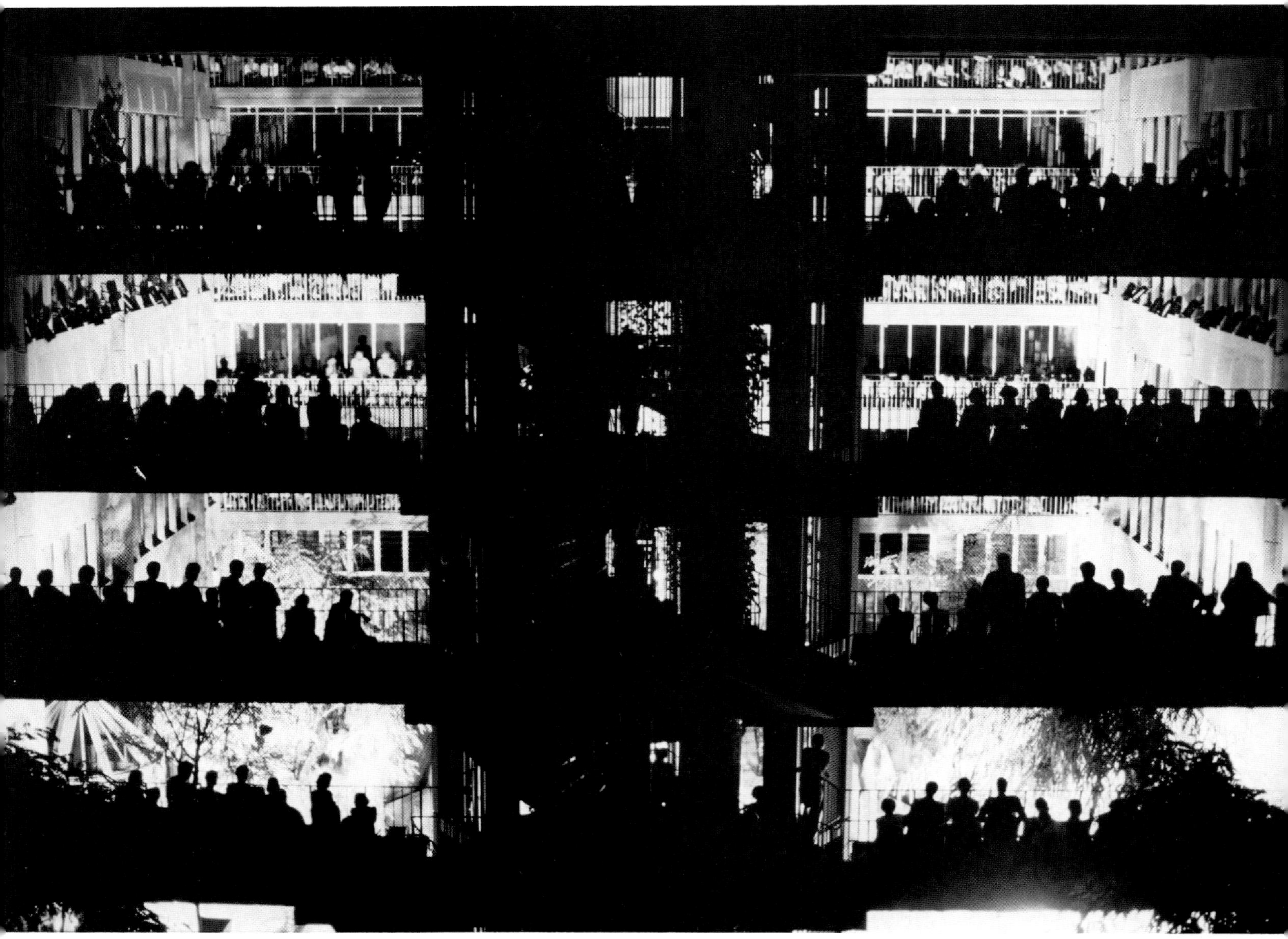

Verwaltungsbauten

Stuttgart Züblin-Haus, 1984, mit Dörte Gatermann, Jürgen Minkus, Federico Valda, Klaus Beckmannshagen. Ausführung mit der Architektengemeinschaft BFK, Stuttgart

Was erwartet man von einem Verwaltungsbau?
Der Bauherr will möglichst viel Bürofläche für möglichst wenig Geld, eine gute Ausnutzung, gute Belichtung usw. Das sind sicherlich wichtige Kriterien, aber darüber hinaus ist eine gute städtebauliche Einbindung notwendig, und zudem ist ein solches Gebäude der Lebensraum einer Gemeinschaft, die sich zusammenfindet und zusammen arbeitet. Das hätte man gern baulich ausgedrückt.
Verwaltungsbau Züblin. Der Standort für den Verwaltungsbau der Firma Züblin ist in einem Vorort von Stuttgart. Die Stadt ist umgeben von vielen kleineren Vororten, wie hier in diesem Fall Möhringen und Vaihingen, die beide ihren sehr eigenen Charakter haben. Diese Vororte wachsen mehr und mehr zusammen. Das Problem bei der Planung ist nun, wie man sie verknüpfen kann, ohne sie zu vermischen. Man möchte spüren, wo die eine Ortschaft anfängt und die andere aufhört, bzw. an welcher Stelle sie sich miteinander verbinden.

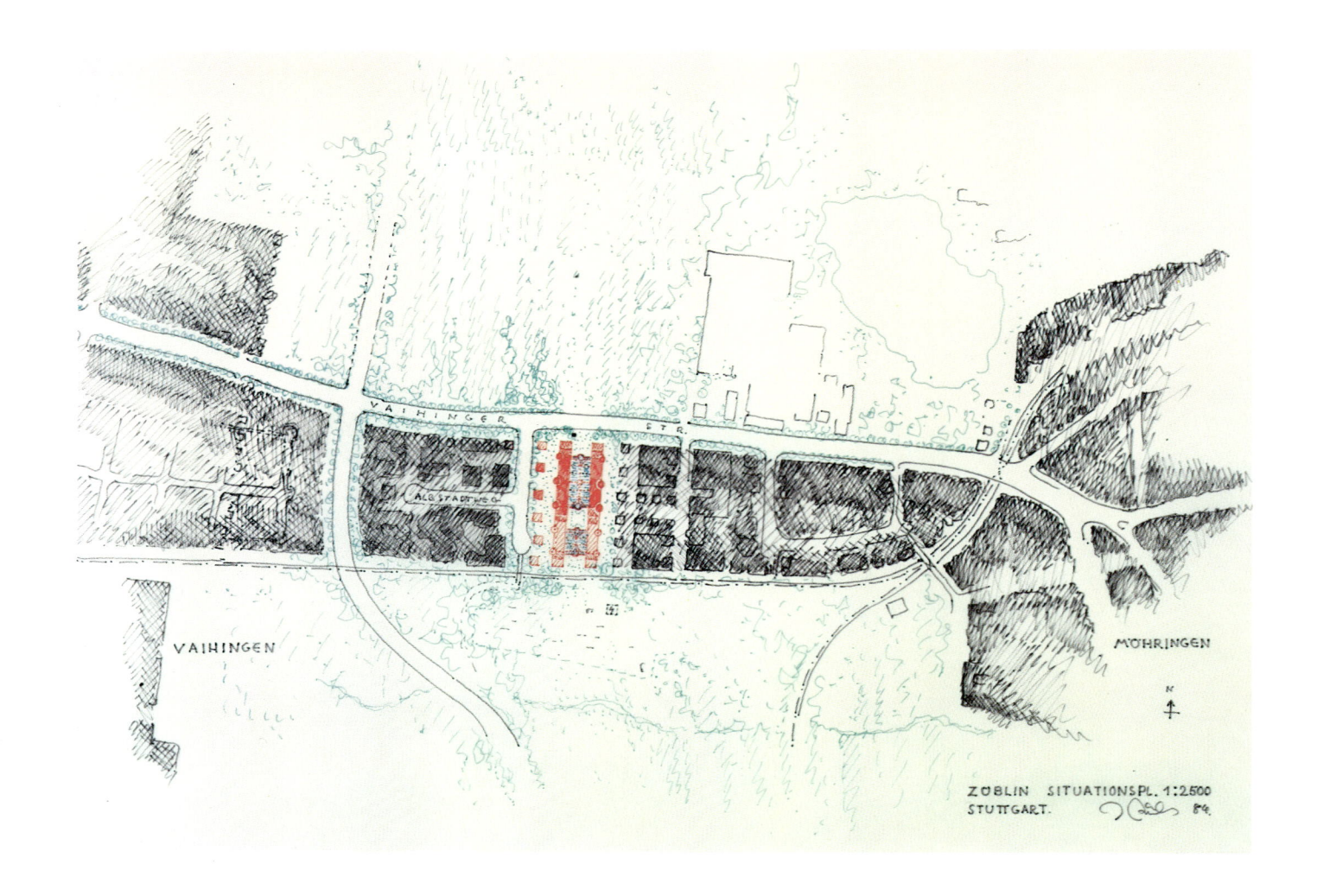

What does one look for in an administration building? The client usually demands a maximum of office space for a minimum of money, good exploitation of the site, good lighting, etc. These are certainly important criteria; but other factors also have to be taken into consideration: the qualitative integration of the structure into the existing urban fabric, for example. Furthermore, buildings of this kind represent a realm of life for a community of people who come together and work there; and one would wish to have this expressed in the built form.
Züblin Administration Building. The site for the administrative headquarters of the Züblin concern is in a suburb of Stuttgart. The city is surrounded by a great number of smaller suburbs, – in this case for example, Möhringen and Vaihingen, both of which have their own highly individual character. These suburbs are growing together more and more, however. So far as the planning is concerned, the problem is that of finding a way to connect them without blurring the distinctions. One would like to be able to tell where one place begins and another ends, or at what point they are linked.

Das Baugelände hat die Besonderheit, daß nur nach Westen und Osten eine Besiedelung angrenzt, während die Süd- und Nordseite in eine relativ unverdorbene Landschaft übergeht.
Wir haben nun für den Züblin-Bau zwei Büroriegel mit einer Verbindungshalle so angeordnet, daß die bauliche Entwicklung von den Orten Möhringen und Vaihingen dort gleichsam aufgehalten und zugleich der Verbund gezeigt wird.
Die beiden Grünbereiche nördlich und südlich werden in der Querrichtung zusammengeführt durch eine platzartige Halle von durchlässiger Struktur, die die beiderseits angrenzende Landschaft auf ihre Art verknüpft.
Die geraden Baukörper bringen natürlich sehr günstige Nutzflächen. Auch die Verbindungswege und Treppen sind hierbei einfach anzuordnen. Am schönsten wäre es gewesen, alle Erschließungen von der Halle ausgehen zu lassen, damit die Halle als wirkliche Mitte, als zentraler Platz erscheint, an dem alle ankommen, um von dort zu den Büros zu gehen. Bei einem offenen Hof wäre dieses möglich gewesen, nicht jedoch bei einer geschlossenen Halle. Trotz der vorgesehenen

One of the special features of this site is that it is adjoined by other developments only to the east and west. To the north and south it borders on relatively unspoilt countryside.
In the Züblin project we created two linear office blocks with a linking hall spanned between them. The development is laid out in such a way that the urban structures of the suburbs of Möhringen and Vaihingen are brought to a halt at this point, but are also joined by a visible connecting link.
The two green zones to north and south of the site are also linked in the lateral direction by the hall, which is in the nature of a large transparent space that draws in the landscape from both sides and unites it in its own special way.
The linear form of the office block facilitates an extremely functional planning of the floor areas, of course. The layout of lines of communication and staircases is also simplified by such an arrangement. Ideally we wanted to have all lines of access radiating from the hall, so that it would really have represented the focal point of the scheme, the true centre, where

Rauchabzugsvorrichtung ließ die Baupolizei eine Erschließung einzig von der Mitte her nicht zu, sondern forderte zusätzliche Fluchttreppen an den Außenseiten.

Die Halle selbst kann Schauplatz für vielerlei Veranstaltungen sein. Ihr ebenerdig zugeordnet sind der Vortragssaal, die Bibliothek, die Kantine usw., also Räume mit Funktionen, die in die Halle eingreifen. Ansonsten gibt es dort Ausstellungen und natürlich auch Festlichkeiten, die man in Stuttgart zu feiern versteht. Auch kleinere Konzerte finden in der Halle statt, und eine Oper soll aufgeführt werden, was ich mir bei den vielfältigen Möglichkeiten in der Gesamtheit des Raumes sehr schön vorstelle.

Es lag uns sehr daran, daß man diesen großen Verwaltungsbau nicht isoliert beließ, sondern daß er auf beiden Seiten von Wohnhäusern begleitet wird. Davon sind zwei tatsächlich gebaut. Das ergibt natürlich noch keine echte Reihe, die für die Straßenbildung notwendig wäre. Bisher erscheinen die beiden Häuschen eher wie Kavaliershäuschen, dem Großbau vorgelagert. Es sollen aber noch weitere hinzukommen. Wir haben Vorschläge gemacht für unterschiedliche Nutzungen: als Ein- und Zweifamilienhaus, als Appartementhaus (Gästehaus) und als Haus mit Laden im Erdgeschoß, wo man außerhalb der Kantine, zum Beispiel auf dem Heimweg, etwas kaufen kann. Diese Reihe von Einzelhäusern wird die Straße betonen und im Maßstab auf die Straßen der alten Ortschaften Bezug nehmen. Es ist natürlich dabei wichtig, daß auch die dazugehörenden Gärten normale Hausgärten werden, so wie sie in der Gegend üblich sind mit Obstbäumen, Gemüse und Blumen.

Die Wahl des Materials spielte bei dem Züblin-Bau eine ganz besondere Rolle.

Was ist heute eigentlich das »richtige Material« bzw. die »richtige Bauweise«? Mauerwerk im herkömmlichen Sinn gibt es heute nicht mehr. Was wir heute mauern, das ist bestenfalls eine halbsteinstarke Schicht, die wir verblenden, dahinter kom-

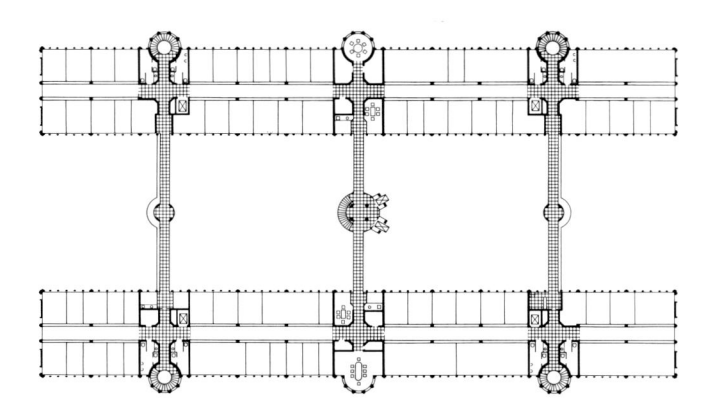

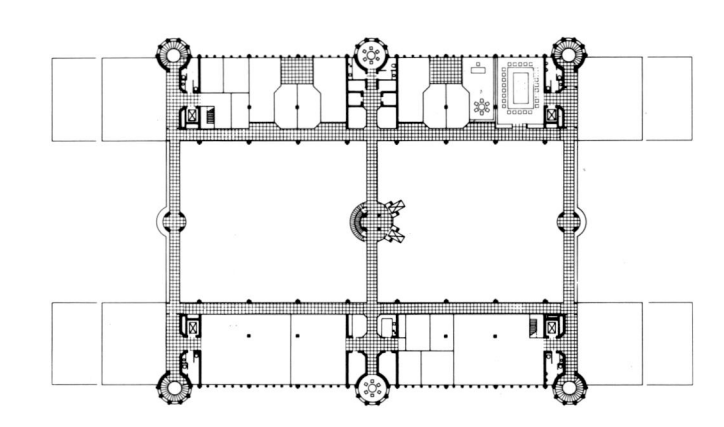

everyone arrives and goes off to the various offices. With an open courtyard this would have been possible, but not with a closed hall. In spite of the smoke extract plant that was planned, the local authorities would not permit access solely from this central area. They demanded additional escape staircases on the outer faces.

The hall itself can be the arena for many different kinds of activities. Linked to it at ground floor level are the lecture hall, library, canteen, and other facilities, including rooms for functions that can overflow into the hall. In addition, exhibitions can be held there and other festivities; for the people of Stuttgart know how to celebrate. Small concerts can be performed in this hall, and it is planned to stage an opera there, which I imagine could be an extremely beautiful occasion, in view of the wealth of possibilities that the space as a whole has to offer.

We were very much concerned that this large administrative complex should not remain isolated, that it should be flanked on both sides by housing. Two buildings have so far been erected. This is of course not enough to create a proper row, which would be necessary for the formation of a street. The two small houses built so far are more in the nature of little lodges set in front of this large complex. Further blocks are planned, however. We made proposals for different uses: as single-family and two-family houses, as blocks of apartments (a guest house), and as a block with shops on the ground floor, where it would be possible to do a bit of shopping (outside the canteen) on the way home. This row of detached houses will eventually define the street line here and take up the scale of the streets in the older settlement areas. As part and parcel of this it is of course important that the adjoining gardens become normal domestic gardens, just like the others in the area, with fruit trees, vegetable patches, flower beds, etc.

The choice of materials played a very important role in the Züblin development.

What does one mean by the »appropriate material« or the »appropriate form of construction« nowadays? Brickwork, in

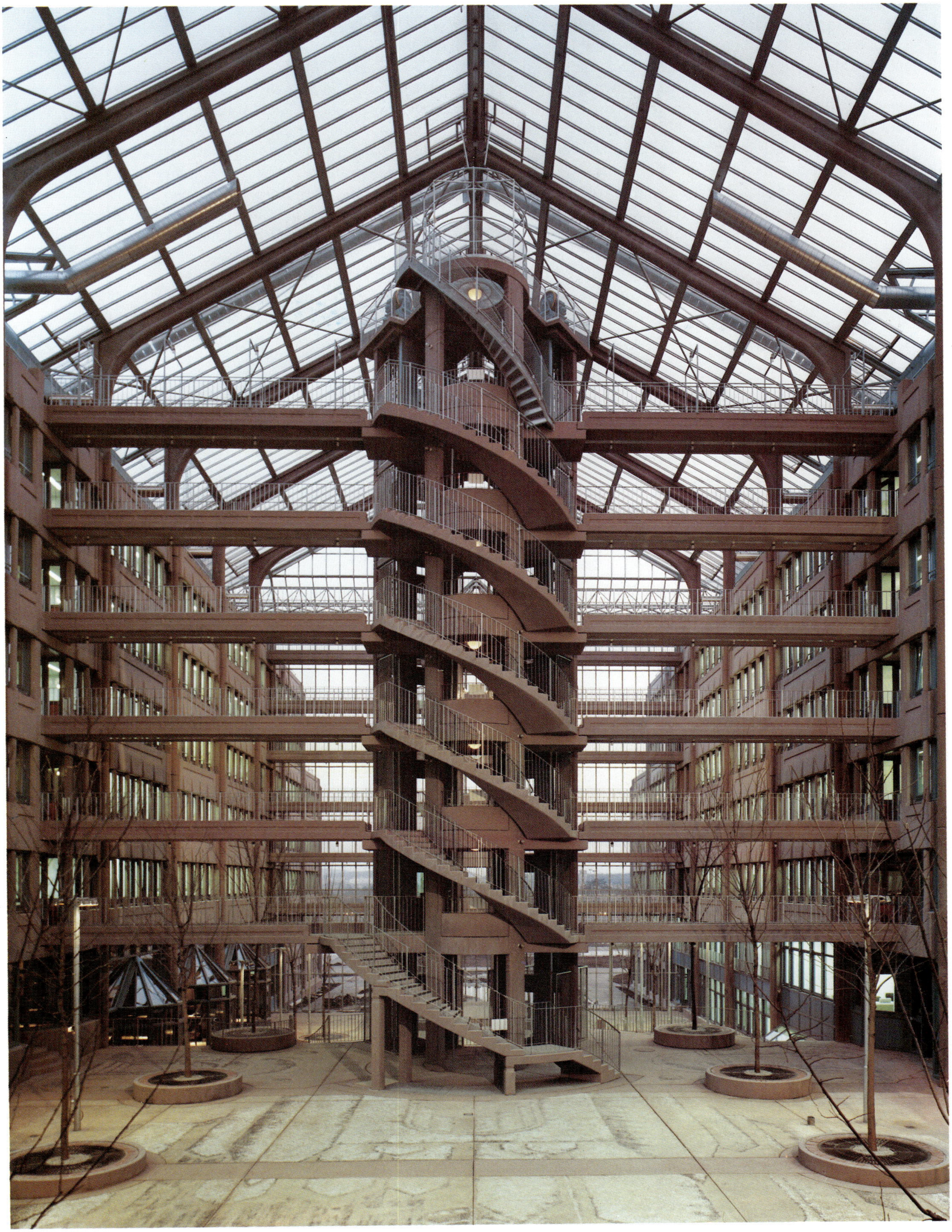

Züblin Staircase tower

men eine Wärmedämmung, Luft und Beton und hier und da vielleicht ein Ziegelstein. Aber es handelt sich eigentlich nur um eine Schale vor der Wand, die genauso gut aus Blech, Schiefer oder irgendeinem anderen Material sein könnte. Blech, Schiefer, Plattenverkleidung entsprechen eigentlich eher dem Charakter unserer konstruktiven Behandlung von Außenwänden. Selbst der Putz ist meistens nicht mehr das, was man vermutet, nämlich ein Material, das von seiner Eigenschaft her mit dem Mauerwerk und dessen Fugen zusammengeht. Putz ist heute meist millimeterdünnes Kunststoffmaterial auf Styropor aufgetragen, und dahinter verbirgt sich alles Mögliche. Alte Verfahren, wie Ziegelbau, kann man natürlich und wird man sinnvollerweise in bestimmten Fällen ausführen, wenn die Umgebung es erfordert. Man wird ja immer in der Wahl des Materials die Verbindung zur Nachbarschaft suchen, zumal wenn diese einigermaßen einheitlich gebaut ist.

Im Falle Züblin-Bau jedoch ist kein Material vorherrschend. In der Nachbarschaft ist alles vorhanden: Ziegelsteine, Beton, Putz und anderes mehr. Es schien uns daher richtig, das Material von der Konstruktion her zu bestimmen.

Relativ sauber im Hinblick auf die Sichtbarkeit der Konstruktion scheint mir der Stahlbetonbau zu sein. Da ist eine Stütze, die man sieht, auch wirklich die tragende Stütze. Und dieses Stützensystem, das sich im gesamten Bau wiederholt, ist zweckmäßig in Fertigteilen zu erstellen. Der Fertigbetonbau als Methode existiert zwar schon lange, aber er hat einen sehr

the conventional sense of that word, no longer exists. The brick walls we build today are at best a half-brick skin of facings, behind which are thermal insulation, a cavity and concrete; or occasionally a further layer of brickwork. But essentially all we see today in front of the actual wall is a relatively thin membrane that could just as well be of some other material such as metal sheeting, slating or panel cladding, — which would also be more in keeping with the character of our constructional treatment of outer walls nowadays. In most cases not even the external rendering is what one imagines it to be; i.e. a material whose properties match those of brickwork and its jointing. External rendering today is usually a plastic coating no more than a few millimetres thick and applied to expanded polystyrene, behind which all manner of things are concealed. Old techniques of building such as bricklaying can of course still be found and will be put to appropriate use in certain cases where the local environment calls for it. In the choice of materials one will always seek a point of reference in the immediate vicinity, especially when surrounding developments are of a more or less homogeneous construction.

In the case of the Züblin complex, however, no single material predominated in the area. In the neighbouring developments one can find all kinds of materials, — brickwork, concrete, rendering and many others. It therefore seemed sensible to us to allow the constructional constraints to determine the material.

Reinforced concrete seems to me to be a relatively clear cut material in terms of the legibility of the structure. One sees a column that is really a load-bearing column. A column system, such as the one used here, which recurs throughout the

schlechten Ruf bekommen wegen seiner durchweg lieblosen Ausführung. Es stellt sich nun die Frage, ob und wie man mit dieser Methode besser, das heißt schöner bauen kann. Wie können wir heute, da wir vom Funktionalismus geprägt sind, uns von einer falsch verstandenen Sachlichkeit befreien, die immer nur die technische Perfektion sucht und unsere Städte so steril und tot gemacht hat. Man glaubte, man dürfe Gebäude auf das billigste und pflegeleichteste sicher »verpacken«, ohne Rücksicht auf den Ausdruck von Inhalt und Konstruktion.

Die guten Bauten früherer Zeiten waren auch sachlich, aber nicht ärmlich. Die Fassaden Schinkelscher Häuser sind oft sehr schlichte Systeme. Er verstand es aber, sie zu bereichern, indem er auf Dinge, die aus der Funktion und der Konstruktion kommen, aufmerksam macht. Er hat die Fenster, die Türen, die Wandkanten betont und so ihre Funktionen zum Ereignis werden lassen. Oder er hat dort, wo das Dach auf der Wand ruht, die Verbindung durch Übertreibung betont. Die Betonung kann sehr, sehr zurückhaltend sein, aber etwas von dem Ereignis will man spüren. »Weniger ist« eben nicht von selbst gleich »mehr«; es muß zuerst eine Kraft vorhanden sein, die dann – in Zurückhaltung dargestellt – erst zum »Mehr« wird. Wer die Kraft zum Sündigen nicht hat, der braucht auch nicht die Kraft zur Beschränkung, der wird aber deshalb noch lange nicht zum Heiligen oder zum guten Architekten, sondern ist eher nur ein Langweiler.

building, lends itself to prefabrication. The use of prefabricated concrete elements is not a new method of construction, but it has acquired a bad reputation on account of its generally insensitive execution. One must therefore ask oneself, whether and in what way the method could be improved, in other words, how one could use it to build in a more attractive manner. Moulded by the philosophy of functionalism as we are today, how can we liberate ourselves from a false understanding of utility – as something that merely strives for technical perfection, – which has made our cities so sterile, indeed dead? For a long time people believed they could safely »pack« buildings in the cheapest and most simple to maintain forms, completely ignoring the question of giving expression to content and structure.

Fine buildings in earlier times were also functional, but they were not impoverished. The façades of Schinkel's buildings, for example, are often quite simple systems. But he knew how to enrich them by drawing attention to details that were derived from the function and construction. He accentuated the windows, the doors, the edges of walls, the quoins, and thus celebrated their function. Or he would articulate the function between roof and wall with a slight exaggeration. One can emphasize things in a very subtle, restrained manner; nevertheless one wishes to feel something of the event that is taking place. »Less« is not always in itself »more«. A certain innate strength has to exist in the first place. When this is presented in a restrained manner, then it can become »more«. Anyone who does not have the strength to sin, will not need the strength of restraint; nor will this necessarily make him a saint or a good architect, – more likely a bore.

Beim Züblin-Bau hatten wir zuerst die Vorstellung, jeweils für ein Geschoß ein Stützensystem mit Auskragungen zu konstruieren und die Brüstungsplatten dann einfach aufzulegen und einzuschieben. Aber wir haben uns belehren lassen, daß eine horizontale Fuge kaum machbar ist. Deswegen haben wir die Brüstungsplatten rückseitig aufgelegt und außen mit einer vertikalen Fuge versehen, wie sie eben für den Fertigbau und auch vom Ablauf des Bauens her richtig ist. Es erschien uns günstig, wenn die Teile dort verstärkt sind, wo sie aneinanderstoßen, weil sie beim Transport und Einbau doch leicht durch das Aneinanderschlagen beschädigt werden.

Im Innern kehrt natürlich das gleiche Stützensystem mit den Konsolen wieder. Es sind Omnia-Decken auf die längslaufenden Balken gelegt. Das sind dünne Platten, die die Decke glatt schließen. Mit einem Betonverguß und Estrich ist die ganze Decke fertig.

Wir haben die Brüstungsplatten über den Fenstern mit jeweils einer schrägen Fläche versehen, so daß sie wie kleine Dächer wirken, von denen das Wasser abtropft.

Die Schalung der Betonteile ist aus Stahlblech, eine relativ teure Schalung, die sich aber bei der hohen Stückzahl – alle Stützen und Brüstungsteile sind ja gleich – rentiert. Die Schalung wird mit einem Verzögerer bestrichen, der sich mit der obersten Betonschicht verbindet. Wenn das Schalungsteil ausgeschalt ist, wird diese oberste Schicht nach einigen Stunden abgespritzt, woraufhin die eigentliche Körnung und Farbe des Betons sichtbar wird. Farbe und Struktur werden mit der Zeit immer schöner; es gibt wenige Materialien, die so gut altern können.

Ein sehr wichtiges Element der Halle sind natürlich die Mitteltürme. Diese wurden in stockwerkshohen Teilen errichtet, die

With the Züblin scheme we initially had the idea of constructing a column system with cantilevered slabs for each floor and then simply setting the apron walls on top and sliding them into position. But we soon learned that a horizontal joint is scarcely possible or practical. For that reason we designed the balustrade elements for rear mounting with a vertical joint externally, as is the correct practice for prefabricated construction and indeed for the smooth running of the project. It seemed sensible to us to thicken the elements at those points where they abut, since they can be easily damaged by impact during transport or in the course of assembly.

In the interior the same column system with haunchings recurs from floor to floor. An Omnia floor system was used, comprising thin precast concrete planks laid between longitudinal beams. The planks abut to form a smooth surface. With a layer of concrete filling and a screed the floor slab is complete.

The apron walls above the windows were detailed with a splayed face, so that they would resemble small roofs from which the water simply drips off.

The formwork used for the concrete units was of sheet steel, – a relatively expensive kind of shuttering, which nevertheless proved economical due to the large numbers of elements. (All columns and apron walls were identical.) The formwork was coated with a retarding agent, which bound with the surface layer of the concrete. The formwork was struck and the surface was sprayed down after a number of hours, bringing out the true grain and colour of the concrete. The colour and texture become more and more attractive with time. There are few materials that age so well.

The central towers represent a major element of this hall. They were erected with storey-height units set on top of each other,

wie umgekehrte Tische aufeinandergesetzt wurden. Die Füße und die Platte sind ein Stück. Die Brücken liegen auf. Die oberste Brücke bildet zugleich das Zugband, das den Schub aufnimmt, der von den Dachbindern herleitet.

Als die Binder montiert wurden, waren drei Kräne notwendig, je einer für die beiden Binderteile und ein dritter, der die Gondel trug, von der aus die Arbeiter die beiden Teile oben mit dem Bolzen verbinden konnten. So wurde die gesamte Hallenkonstruktion ohne Gerüst montiert.

Die beiden Türme an den Hallenenden sollen von sehr geräumigen Pflanztrögen aus bewachsen werden. Die Hauptzentrale der Firma lag bisher an einem Weinberg. In Erinnerung daran haben wir die Tröge mit Weinstöcken bepflanzt. Wenn man von einem Riegel zum anderen geht, kommt man durch eine Weinlaube hindurch. Man kann sich dort mal ein wenig verkriechen oder es können sich auch zwei dort treffen. Das gehört ja doch auch zum Leben in einem Betrieb.

rather like upturned tables, the feet and top of which are in one piece. The bridging elements are simply laid on top. The uppermost bridge also forms the tie member that resists the thrust from the roof trusses.

Three cranes were needed to assemble the trusses; one for each of the two sections of the truss, and a third supporting the cradle from which the workers bolted the two sections together.

The entire hall was thus assembled without scaffolding. The two towers at the ends of the hall will be overgrown by plants from spacious planting boxes. The headquarters of the firm were hitherto situated near a vineyard, and in memory of this we planted these troughs with vines. In crossing from one strip of offices to the other, one passes through an arbour of vine leaves, where one can withdraw and find some peace and quiet, or where two people can meet. That is also part of life in a big firm.

Das Gebäude einschließlich der Glashalle ist nicht klimatisiert. Im Glasdach sind im oberen Teil viele Entlüftungsklappen und im unteren Öffnungsmöglichkeiten für die Zuluft angebracht.

Es hat sich gezeigt, daß die Halle selbst im Sommer an heißen, windstillen Tagen durch die natürliche Thermik sehr angenehm temperiert ist. Die überschüssige Wärme wird im First durch zwei Rohre abgesaugt und für die Warmwasserbereitung verwendet. Wenn die Sonne hereinscheint, dann ist das farblich schon eine tolle optische Musik. Normalerweise ist das Licht im Raum ruhiger.

Das oberste Geschoß beider Riegel haben wir in der Halle etwas zurückgesetzt, um die seitliche Belichtung für die unteren Geschosse zu verbessern.

Es ist auch nicht unwichtig, wie die Halle bei Abend und Nacht ausschaut. Leider habe ich nicht verhindern können, daß dann alle Stege beleuchtet sind. So sieht alles ein bißchen arg nach Weihnachten aus. Schöner wäre eine Beleuchtung nur

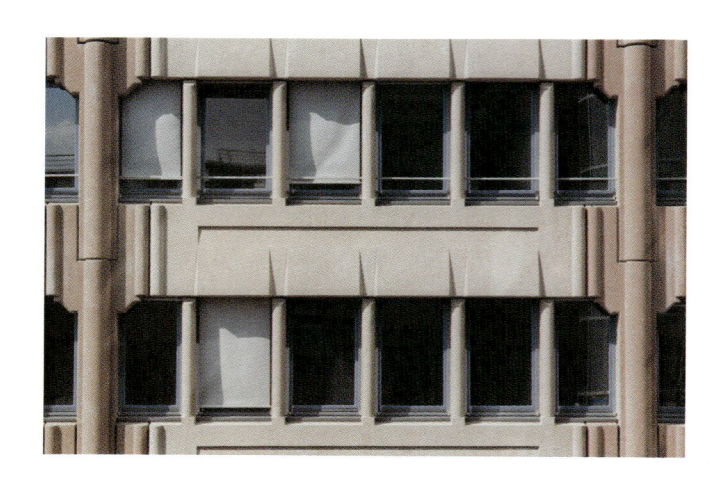

Neither the building nor the hall are air-conditioned. Built into the upper part of the glass roof are a large number of ventilation flaps. The openings lights in the lower section facilitate cross-ventilation.

Even in summer on hot, wind-still days, the natural thermal currents help to maintain a pleasant temperature within the hall. Excess heat is extracted at ridge level through two ducts and is used for heating the hot water supply. When the sun shines in, a marvellous visual music is set up in terms of colour tones. Normally, however, the lighting conditions are more subdued.

The topmost storey in both linear blocks is set back somewhat in the hall so as to improve lateral lighting conditions on the lower floors.

A further consideration that was of some importance was the appearance of the hall in the evening and at night. I was unfortunately unable to prevent all the internal galleries being illuminated. As a result it all looks a bit Christmassy. It would have been far more beautiful, if the illumination had been confined to the base – more in the form of street lighting perhaps –

unten wie ein Straßenlicht und oben nur von den Büroräumen her.
Das Glasdach kann man von oben mit einem fahrbaren Schlitten reinigen, der horizontal am Dach entlang fährt. Von innen wird das nur alle 10 oder 20 Jahre vom Steiger aus gemacht. Das war auch eines unserer Probleme: Die Halle mußte so beschaffen sein, daß der Steiger, ein Gefährt mit einem langen Arm und Arbeitskorb, alle Stellen erreichen kann.
Die Akustik der Halle ändert sich natürlich, je nachdem wieviel Leute darin sind. Zur Dämpfung des Schalls haben wir die

and the upper levels had been lighted purely from within the offices.
The glass roof can be cleaned on the outside from a cradle travelling horizontally along the roof. The underside of the glass will only be cleaned every 10 to 20 years from a hoist. That was one of the problems we had to overcome: the hall had to be designed in such a way that the hoist, a travelling mechanism with a long arm and working cradle, could reach every point.
The acoustics within the hall change according to the number of persons present. To reduce the noise level the undersides

Stege an der Unterseite mit schallschluckendem Beton versehen, ebenfalls den zurückliegenden Randbalken. Gerade die Raumkanten sind für die Schalldämpfung sehr wirkungsvoll. So scheint mir der Schall relativ gut erträglich. Der kleine Wasserlauf, der über den terrassierten Hallenboden plätschert, verschafft ein wenig Geräuschkulisse.

Ursprünglich hatten wir einen Hallenboden aus Naturstein vorgesehen. Das war aber zu teuer. Am Ende geht es ja immer ums Sparen. In diesem Fall muß ich sagen: Gott sei Dank. Wir haben uns dann zu einem Betonestrich entschlossen. Die Betonwände waren durch das Abwaschen am Ende so schön geworden, warum sollte das gleiche nicht auch beim Estrich möglich sein. Über ein gutes Jahr wurden Versuche angestellt. Schließlich gingen wir folgendermaßen vor: Nach der Vorlage eines Bildentwurfes wurden rote Betonbänder quer durch den Raum gezogen, um das Stützsystem der Wände optisch zu verbinden. Nachdem dann ein erdfarbener Estrich in die Zwischenfelder eingebracht wurde, mußte alles rasend schnell gehen. Noch vor dem Abbinden des Estrichs nämlich streuten wir schwarze und weiße Marmorstückchen ein, die wir dann noch einklopfen und einreiben mußten, damit sie ganz fest mit dem Estrich verbunden werden.

Beim Einreiben sollten eigentlich die Kanten nicht so sehr verwischen, das ganze hat jetzt die Unschärfe eines Aquarells. Der wieder völlig verriebene Estrich wurde mit einer grünen Brühe besprizt, die den Abbindevorgang in der obersten Schicht verzögert.

Das ist dieselbe Emulsion, die auch in die Betonschalung der Wände eingestrichen wurde. Sie kann nach einer gewissen Zeit mit der obersten Betonschicht abgespritzt werden, so daß die kleinen Steine wieder zum Vorschein kommen. Auf der einen Seite der Halle zeigt das Bild im Estrich die Charakteristik einer »Alten Stadt«, auf der anderen die einer »Neuen Stadt« mit der Kirche von Neviges, die 20 Jahre früher von der gleichen Baufirma gebaut wurde.

of the bridges were executed in sound-absorbing concrete, as were the setback edge beams. The edges of a space are extremely critical in terms of sound absorption. The noise level seems to me to be quite tolerable. The small stream of water rippling across the terraced floor of the hall also helps to create a pleasant background sound.

Originally we had intended the floor of the hall to be of natural stone. This proved too expensive, however. Towards the end of a project one is always on the lookout for savings, and I must say I am glad we made one in this case. We finally opted for a cement and sand screed. The concrete walls had turned out so well after the washing down process at the end that we asked ourselves why it should not be possible to do the same with the screed. The various trials that were made went on for over a year. In the end we decided on the following method. A picture design was made. In accordance with this model, red concrete strips were laid across the floor, creating a series of visual links between the wall columns. After an earth-coloured screed had been laid in the intermediate bays, everything had to be done at top speed. Before the screed had set, we strewed small pieces of black and white marble over the surface, which then had to be knocked in and rubbed down so that the whole would bind in smoothly with the screed.

In this rubbing down process we did not want the edges to be obscured too much. The floor now has the smudged quality of a watercolour. The screed, trowelled smooth again, was sprayed with a green fluid that retarded the setting process on the surface.

This was the same emulsion as was applied to the shuttering to the concrete wall units. After a certain time it can be sprayed off together with the surface layer of concrete, revealing the small stones and grain of the mix.

On one side of the hall the picture in the screed has the characteristics of an »old city«, and on the other side, those of a »new city« with the church of Neviges, erected twenty years previously by the same construction company.

Züblin — Nördliche Giebelwand der Halle

Züblin — Northern end gable wall to hall

Züblin

Giebelwand der Halle

End gable wall to hall

243

Städtebauliche Zusammenhänge

Frankfurt a. M.	Messehallen und Verwaltung, Wettbewerb, 1985, mit Hans Linder, Fritz Steinigeweg, Hasso Breuer, H. Huppert, Wolfgang Jung, Franz Kilian, Jürgen Minkus, Günter Kaintoch
Stuttgart	Mercedes Hauptverwaltung, Wettbewerb, 1982, mit Georg F. Adolphi, Bernd Hellriegel, Günther Kaesbach, Federico Valda, Klaus Beckmannshagen
Kassel	Friedrichsplatz, Wettbewerb, 1978, mit Markku Kari
Hannover	Das neue Steintor, Wettbewerb, 1984, im Bau, mit Bernd Hellriegel, Monika Adolphi, Gito Sugianto, Fritz Steinigeweg
Köln	Heumarkt, Sassenhof – Hotel Maritim, im Bau 1987, in Zusammenarbeit mit Krämer, Sieverts und Partner (KSP), mit Stefan Schmitz
Köln	Museum, Wettbewerb, 1979, mit Georg Feinhals, Werner Finke, J. Pieper, F. Popp, Konrad Schalhorn, Hans Schmalscheidt
Köln	Dombereich, Sanierungsvorschlag 1984, mit Lehrstuhl für Stadtbereichsplanung der RWTH Aachen
Dudweiler	Stadtmitte-Bebauung, 1979, mit Katja Hrankovicova, Miroslav Volf, Bernd Hellriegel, Jürgen Koch, Gerhard Loew, Petra Petschke, Federico Valda, Gudrun Wurlitzer, Georg F. Adolphi
Bremerhaven	Hochschule, 1. Bauabschnitt 1985, 2. Bauabschnitt in Planung, mit Georg F. Adolphi, Günther Kaesbach, Bernd Hellriegel, Hermann Neuerburg
Peking	Lufthansa German Center, Wettbewerb, 1986, mit Jürgen Minkus, Hasso Breuer, Federico Valda
Hannover	Messe, Wettbewerb, 1986, mit Georg F. Adolphi, Günther Kaesbach, Maria Mocanu, Federico Valda, Corinna Schaade, Sunsik Myeong
Boston	Stadtzentrum, Seminararbeit am Massachusetts Institute of Technology, Cambridge, 1983
Philadelphia	Vorschläge für die Bindung von Stadtzentrum und Universitätscampus, Seminararbeit an der University of Pennsylvania, Philadelphia, 1985
Starnberg	Seeanbindung, Städtebauliches Gutachten, 1986, mit Günther Kaesbach

Bei der Darstellung des Verwaltungsgebäudes Züblin habe ich darauf hingewiesen, was uns zu den plastischen Formen der Betonfassaden geführt hat. Aber etwas ist übrig geblieben, das ich gerade an dieser Stelle erläutern möchte, weil es letzten Endes auch die städtebauliche Problematik betrifft.

Die zwanziger Jahre und vor allem die Zeit von Mies van der Rohe hat uns gelehrt, das Elementare wichtig oder sogar absolut zu nehmen. Bei Mies ist eine Wand ein Element für sich, das eine Trennung markiert, auch der Boden oder die Decke sind Elemente, die für sich und in sich abgeschlossen sind. Das gleiche gilt für die Stütze. Jedes Element hat seinen eigenen Charakter und scheint weder auf das andere angewiesen zu sein, noch sich gar mit ihm verbinden zu wollen. Die Verbindungen sind fast zufällig, und möglichst unsichtbar verbergen sie sich hinter Schattenkanten und dergleichen, als ob es peinlich wäre, daß man sie benötigt. In der klassischen Architektur war das anders. Eine griechische Säule stellt auch das Elementare einer Stütze dar, aber zugleich sucht sie das Verbindende. Sie steht richtig auf, die Verbindung zum Boden ist sehr stark markiert durch die Basis. Das gleiche trifft für das Kapitell zu, es bildet die Verknüpfung mit dem Balken als besonderes Ereignis aus. Ja auch der Säulenschaft selbst mit seiner Schwellung ist wie ein angestrengter Muskel, ganz auf das Tragen eines anderen Bauteiles hin gerichtet. Die Säule scheint etwas zu tragen, selbst wenn der Balken gar nicht mehr daraufliegt.

Die Vorstellung der zwanziger Jahre von der Reinheit der Elemente gab es ja nicht nur in der Architektur, sondern auch in der Malerei, der Musik und natürlich vor allem auch im Städtebau, wo sie sich zum Positiven, aber auch zum Negativen

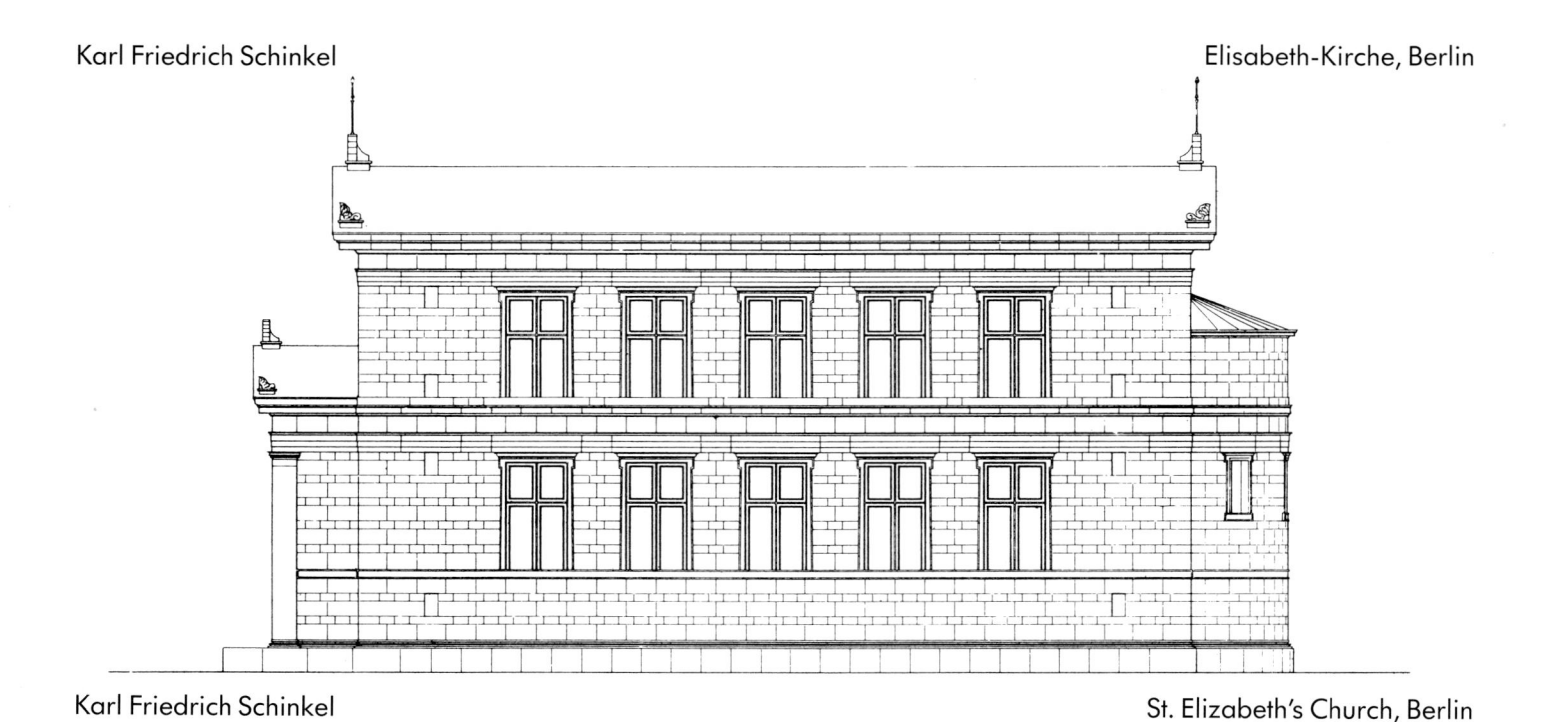

Karl Friedrich Schinkel　　　　　　　　　　　　　　　　　　　　　　　　　　　　　　　　Elisabeth-Kirche, Berlin

Karl Friedrich Schinkel　　　　　　　　　　　　　　　　　　　　　　　　　　　　　　　　St. Elizabeth's Church, Berlin

In my description of the Züblin administration building I mentioned the factors that led to the sculptural quality of the concrete façades. There is, however, a further aspect, which I should like to discuss at this point, since it is something that concerns the subject of urban planning in general.

The 1920s and in particular the age of Mies van der Rohe taught us to regard elemental things as something important, if not absolute. In Mies's case a wall is an element in itself, one that marks a division. The floor and the ceiling are also self-contained elements in their own rights; so too is a column. Every element has its own character and would seem neither to be dependent on the others, nor to wish to enter into a relationship with them. The connections are almost coincidental; and they are hidden from sight as far as possible behind shadow joints and the like, as if it were somehow embarrassing that they were necessary at all. In Classical architecture this was different. A Greek column also represents an elemental component of support. At the same time it seeks a linking role, a context. It stands boldly upright. The link with the ground is strongly underlined by the base. The same applies to the capital: the connection with the entablature is celebrated as a special event.

Even the shaft of the column with its entasis is like a straining, bulging muscle, concentrating its entire effort on supporting another element of the structure. The column seems to bear a load, even when the entablature has been removed.

The concept of the purity of elements that prevailed in the 1920s was not confined to architecture alone. One also finds it in painting, in music, and above all in urban planning, where it had both very positive and very negative effects.

besonders stark ausgewirkt hat.

Denken wir nur zum Beispiel an die gerade in letzter Zeit so oft praktizierte völlige Trennung von Fußgänger- und Verkehrsstraßen. Man kann wohl sagen, daß dies in den meisten Fällen verhängnisvolle Folgen hatte, und zwar nicht nur für die zu »Anlieferstraßen« degradierten Verkehrswege, sondern gerade auch für die »bevorzugten« Fußgängerzonen selbst, für die Art ihrer Nutzung, für ihr Niveau sowie für den Zusammenhang der städtischen Gesamtstruktur.

Aber das ist nur ein Beispiel von unzähligen im städtebaulichen Bereich, wo »reinliche« Trennung der Elemente neben Vorteilen eben sehr viele Nachteile für die städtische Gesamtheit mit sich brachte.

Ich sehe den ungeheuren Wert, die Elemente sehr rein darstellen zu wollen – und wenn ich dieses Thema über das verbindende Detail nochmals anspreche, dann deswegen, weil ich meine, wir sollten uns zwar den Sinn für das Elementare auf alle Fälle erhalten und dennoch auch im Verbindenden einen Wert sehen, den wir nicht zu verbergen brauchen. Das Problem scheint mir zu sein: Wenn man zu sehr nach dem Sichtbarmachen des Details sucht, läuft man Gefahr, scheinbare Notwendigkeiten zu erfinden, die man dann natürlich auch nicht ganz glaubhaft architektonisch darstellen kann und die damit die Kraft des Elementaren schwächen. Es geht eben nicht so sehr darum, die Bauten nur reicher zu machen (das wird ja heute auf mancherlei Weise unter teils sinnloser Anwendung historischer Motive versucht), sondern es geht vielmehr darum, das Aufregende der Verknüpfungen zum Ereignis werden zu lassen. Das gilt für das kleine Detail ebenso wie für die großen Zusammenhänge in der Stadt.

One merely has to think of the total segregation of pedestrian and vehicular traffic so widely implemented in recent times. In most cases this has had disastrous results, not only for the vehicular routes that have been relegated to mere »delivery streets«, but in particular for the pedestrian zones themselves, – despite the »preferential treatment« one believed one was giving them – in terms of the manner in which they are used, their quality and indeed the cohesion of the urban fabric as a whole.

That is simply one example amongst countless others in the realm of urban planning, where a »clean« separation of elements has brought not merely advantages but a great many disadvantages for the urban environment.

I recognize the tremendous virtue in wishing to represent basic elements in a pure form; – and in returning to this subject in the context of the connecting detail, it is because I think we should retain our feeling for elementary things at all costs. Nevertheless, we should also see the value of creating connections that we do not need to hide. The problem seems to me to be that, if one tries too hard to make the details visible, one is in danger of inventing things that are seemingly essential, but to which one is not in a position to give an entirely convincing architectural form, and this in turn results in a reduction of the force of the elemental qualities. It is not important simply to make buildings richer in detail. (Various attempts in this direction can be found nowadays, including the meaningless use of historical motifs.) What is of relevance today, is to allow the stimulating quality of connections, of combinations to become an event in itself. That applies as much to small details as to the general context in our cities.

Erweiterung der Messe in Frankfurt. Die Messe in Frankfurt ist bekannt durch die Festhalle von Thiersch und durch die schöne Galerie von Ungers, der auch ein Verwaltungshochhaus im Zwickel zwischen Bahn und Straße gebaut hat. Dieses Hochhaus stellt für das ganze Gelände einen Mittelpunkt dar und prägt gleichsam die Achse Messe-Stadt.
In der Umgebung existieren schon mehrere Hochhäuser; es war auch im Wettbewerb geradezu zur Aufgabe gestellt, die Messeerweiterung ebenfalls in einem Hochhaus unterzubringen. Standortuntersuchungen zeigten Möglichkeiten, wie und mit welchen Konsequenzen es plaziert werden könnte.

Frankfurt Trade Fair Extension. Amongst the well-known structures in the trade fair complex in Frankfurt are the Festival Hall by Friedrich von Thiersch and the fine gallery by O. M. Ungers, who also designed an administration tower block on a piece of land between the railway line and the road. This high-rise block creates a focal point for the entire site and establishes an axis between the trade fair area and the city. There are a number of other tall blocks in the vicinity; indeed it was one of the requirements of the competition brief to accommodate the trade fair extension in a tower block. Investigations of the site revealed various possible locations for this building and the consequences these would involve.

Wir haben jedoch in einem Gegenvorschlag die geforderten Hallen und Bürobauten in Höhe der schon vorhandenen Messehallen so angeordnet, daß sie für den großartigen Thiersch-Bau eine gebührende Umrahmung bilden. Ein Hochhaus an dieser Stelle würde sicher diese Architektur sehr beeinträchtigen und abwerten. Eine flächige Anlage würde das Messegelände sinnvoll vervollständigen, sich mit den vorhandenen Hallen verbinden und den Thiersch-Bau in einen städtischen Rahmen fassen.
Die Einrichtungen, die für den Zugang zur Festhalle, zu den Ausstellungshallen und dem gesamten Messegelände nötig

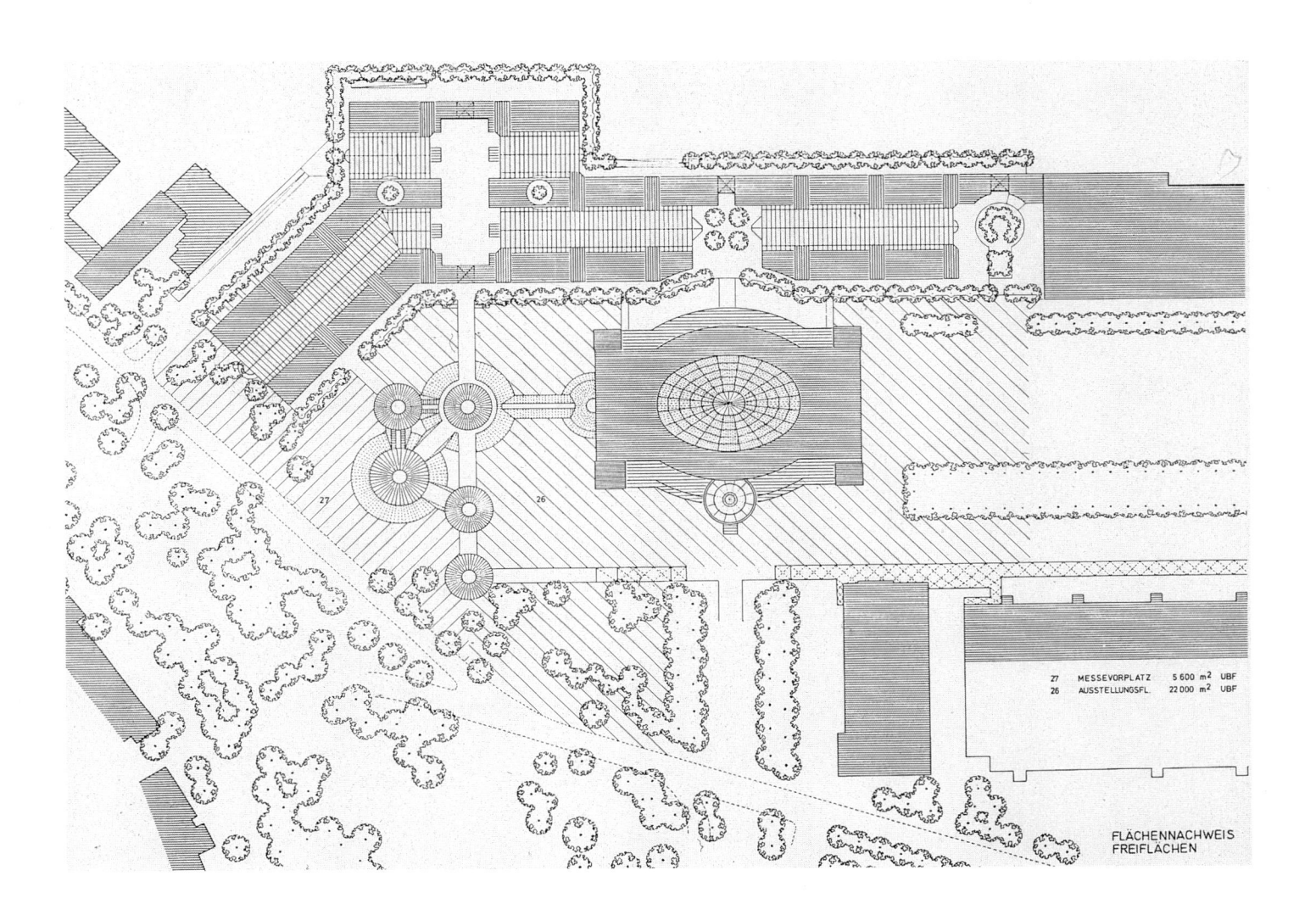

We nevertheless made our own counter-proposals, in which the requisite halls and office buildings were to be erected to a height conforming to that of the existing exhibition halls and laid out in such a way that they would form a fitting context for the splendid Thiersch building. A high-rise block at this point would without doubt seriously impair and devalue this piece of architecture. A lower-rise development, on the other hand, could meaningfully complement the trade fair site and would tie the existing halls and the Thiersch building into a unified urban complex.
We designed the facilities required for access to the Festival Hall, to the exhibition halls and the site as a whole in the form

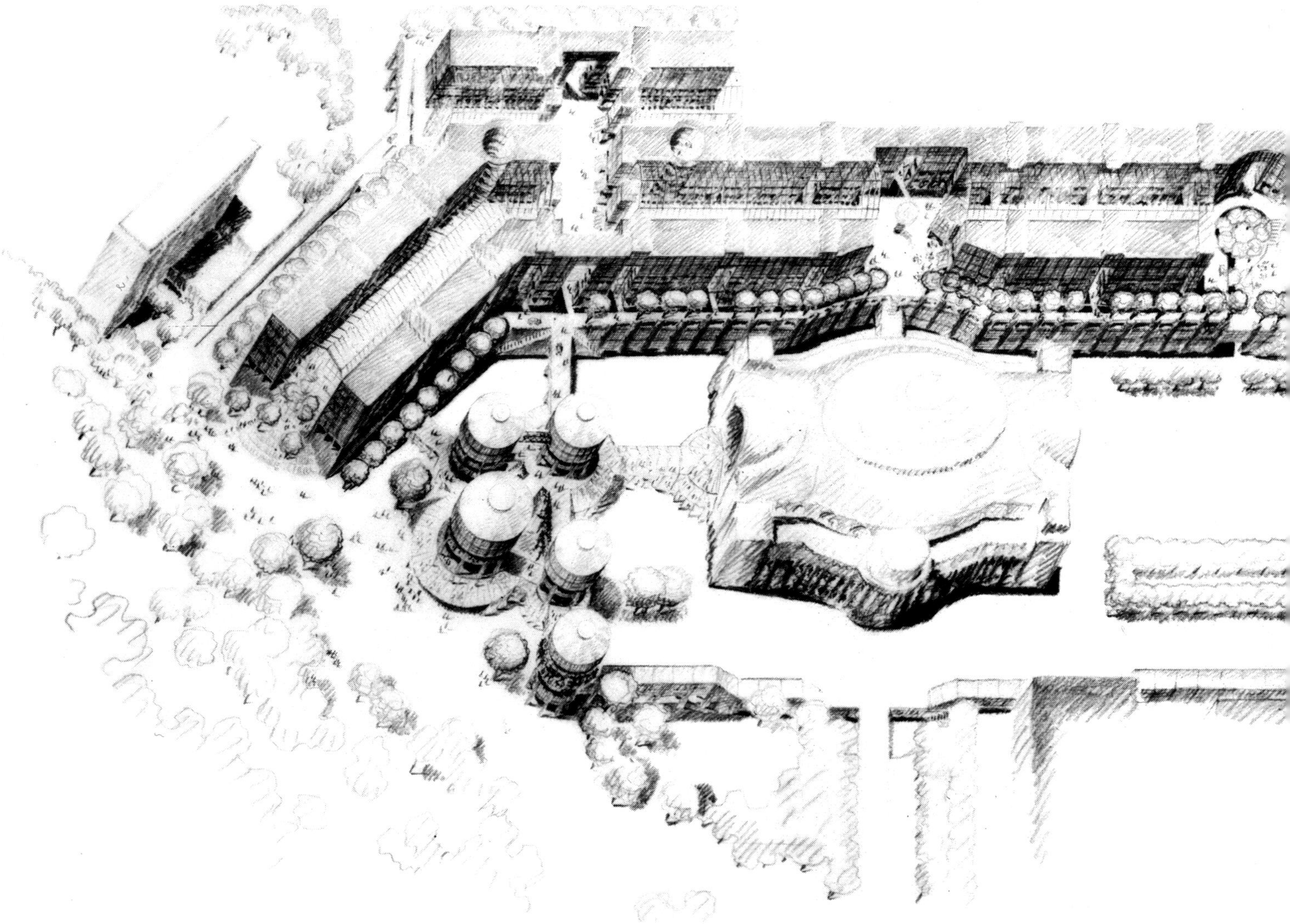

Messe

Trade Fair Complex

sind, haben wir in Einzelbauten geplant, die zusammen mit den Bäumen des Parks zwischen Stadt und Messe vermitteln. Diese Einzelbaukörper sind untereinander und mit dem ganzen Messegelände durch ein Fußgängerförderband verbunden.

Die gewaltige Menge der Büros, die in einem Hochhaus untergebracht werden sollte, haben wir stattdessen wie auf einem Hügel oberhalb der großen Ausstellungshallen als »Bürostadt« geplant, die über eine breite ansteigende Autostraße erreichbar ist. (Dabei denke ich etwa an Bergstädte wie Orvieto, durch die man bergan fährt mit vielen Einblicken in Gassen und Plätze, bis man in ihr eigentliches Zentrum eindringt.) Diese Straße ist direkt dem städtischen Straßennetz angeschlos-

of individual buildings that, together with the trees in the park, are meant to mediate between the city and the trade fair complex. These individual structures are linked to each other and to the other site facilities by a moving walkway.

The enormous amount of office space that was to be provided in the tower block is located in our proposals as if on a hill above the large exhibition halls, in the form of an »office city«, reached via a broad, rising vehicular road. (In this context I am reminded of hill cities like Orvieto, through which one drives up a hill, with innumerable views and glimpses into alleyways and piazze, before finally arriving at the actual centre.) This route is directly connected to the urban road network.

sen. Zwischen Ausstellungshallen und »Bürostadt« liegt ein ganzes Garagengeschoß mit Verbindungen nach unten in die Ausstellungshallen und nach oben zu den Büros, so daß dem Parkenden kurze Wege zu dem gewünschten Ziel möglich sind.

Die Straßen und Plätze der »Bürostadt« sind größtenteils mit Glas überdacht und können daher auch für Ausstellungen genutzt werden. Die Zufahrtsmöglichkeiten an den offenen Plätzen und die Anordnung öffentlicher Einrichtungen (Restaurants, Läden usw.) betonen den Charakter eines städtischen Gebildes. Eine Autostraße führt von hier aus über Brücken hinweg zu den Obergeschossen der Eingangsbauten bis zu dem Turmrestaurant.

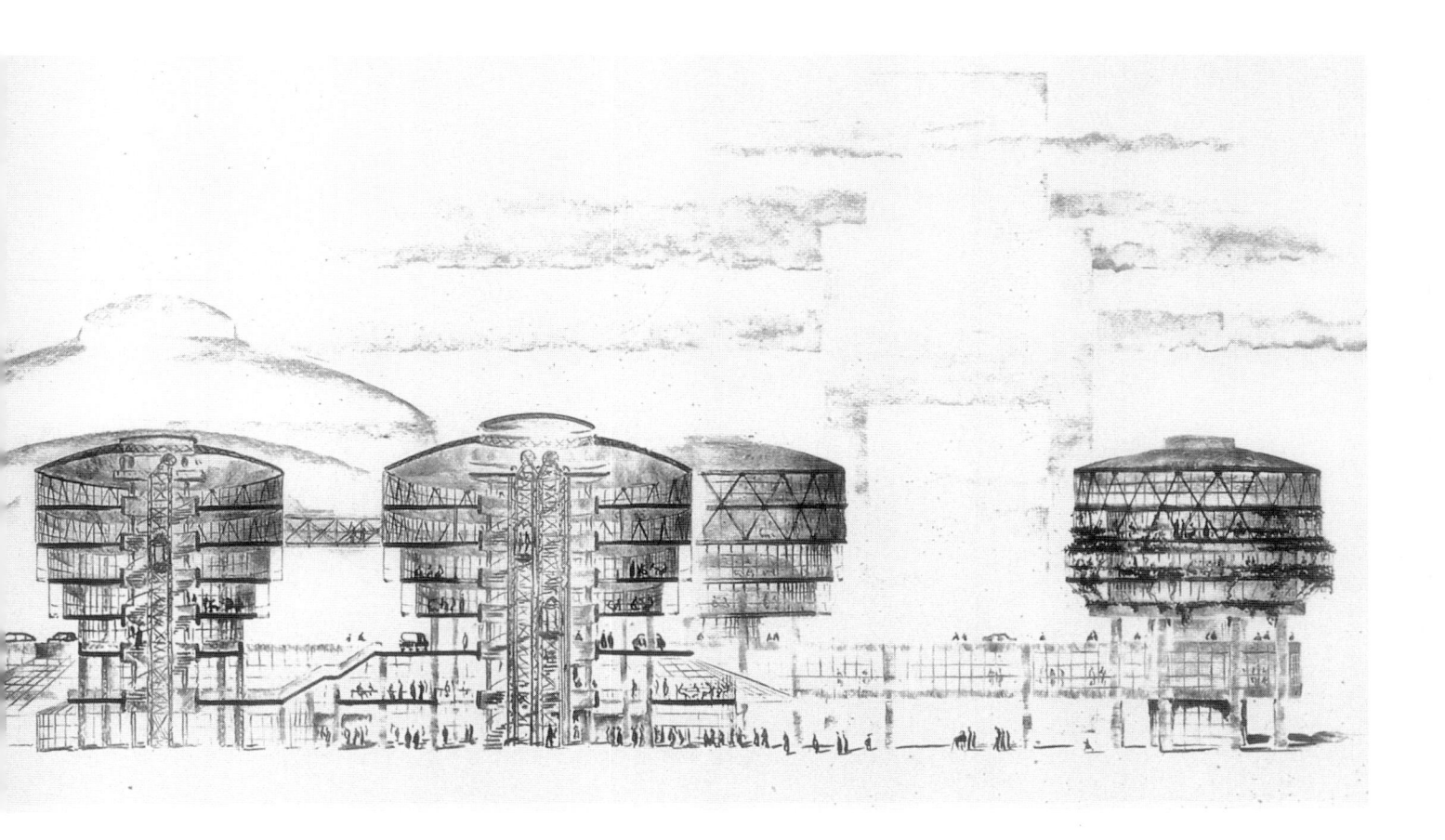

An entire storey, situated between the exhibition halls and this »office city«, is designated as parking space, with connections down to the exhibition halls and up to the offices. People parking cars here thus have short routes to their various destinations. The streets and squares in this »office city« are, for the most part, covered with glass and can thus be used for exhibitions as well. Vehicular access to the public open spaces, and the location of public amenities (restaurants, shops, etc.) help underline the urban character of this complex. A vehicular route also leads from this part of the fairs area over a series of bridges to the upper floors of the entrance buildings and the tower restaurant.

Verwaltung Mercedes in Stuttgart. Wie für den Wettbewerb Messe Frankfurt sollte auch für den Wettbewerb Mercedes Stuttgart ein sehr großer Verwaltungsbau mit Ausstellungshallen, Restaurants, Cafés usw. geplant werden. In diesem Fall war das Programm noch erweitert durch ein Museum, ein Auditorium und Lehrräume für die Angestellten.
Das Baugelände liegt in einer schönen Obst-Wiesen-Landschaft am Rande eines Vororts von Stuttgart. In solchen Situationen erscheinen uns die kompakten, voluminösen Baukomplexe, in denen Großverwaltungen meistens untergebracht sind, besonders fremd und störend. Deshalb haben wir das Bauvolumen so gegliedert, daß eine Art Bürostadt mit Straßen und

Mercedes Headquarters, Stuttgart. As in the case of the Frankfurt Trade Fair competition, the Mercedes Stuttgart competition called for the design of a very large administration building with exhibition halls, restaurants, cafés, etc. In this case the brief was even more comprehensive and also included a museum, an auditorium and staff training rooms.
The site is located in a beautiful landscape of orchards and meadows on the edge of a Stuttgart suburb. The dense, bulky complexes in which large-scale administrations are usually housed would be particularly alien and disturbing in a situation like this. For that reason we articulated the development into a number of volumes, so as to create a kind of office city

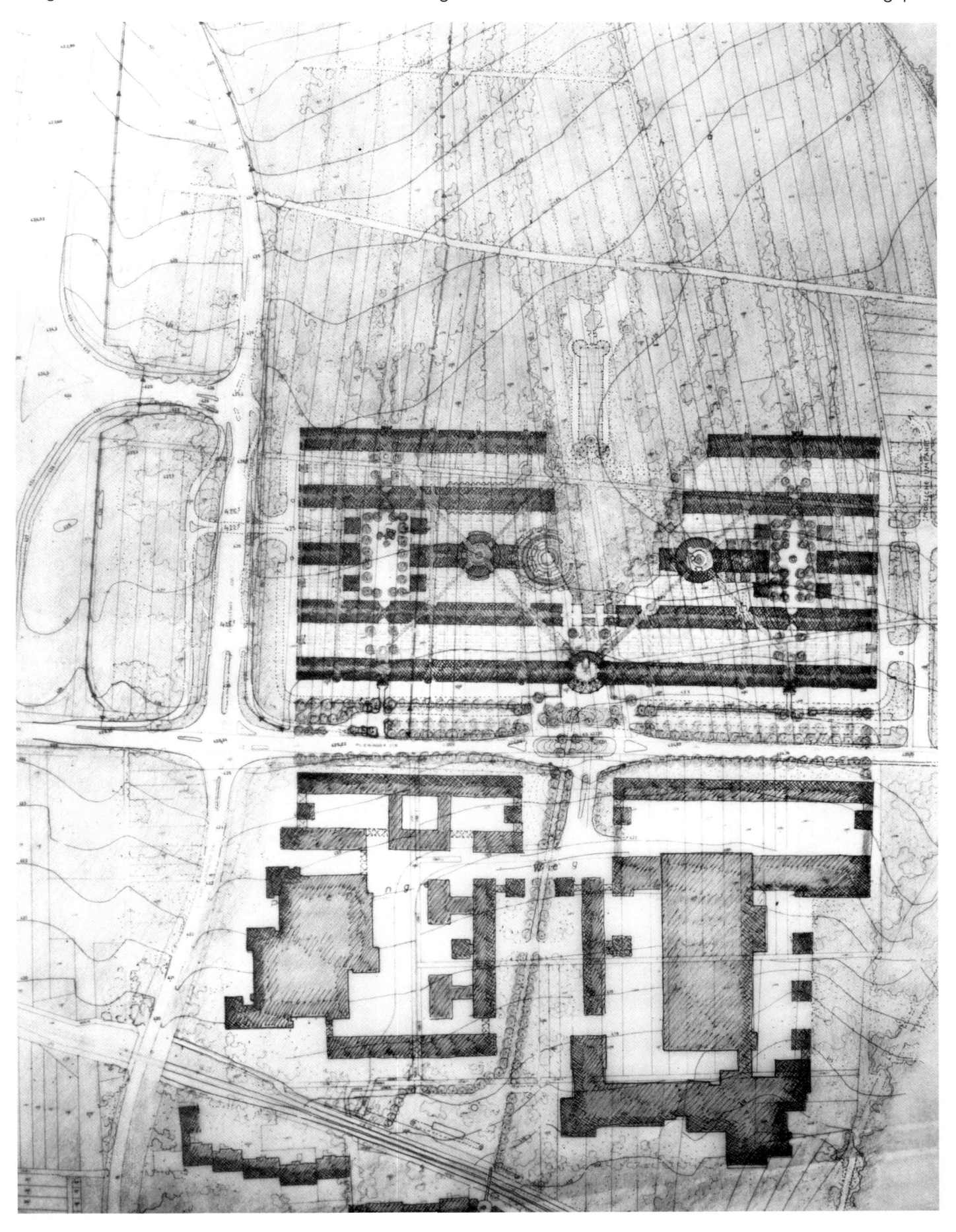

Stuttgart — Verwaltung Daimler-Benz AG — Lageplan

Plätzen entsteht, die in ihrer Maßstäblichkeit dem Charakter der dortigen gewachsenen Stadtstrukturen entspricht. Für eine solche Lösung war natürlich die Vielfalt der gewünschten Nutzungen günstig. Als Ausstellungshallen dienen zum Beispiel die mit Glas überdachten Straßen. So werden Oldtimer aus dem Museumsbestand ebenso wie neue Automobile, die zum Verkauf stehen, in einer für sie typischen Situation präsentiert. Überhaupt scheint mir das Arbeiten in so einer Bürostadt gegenüber einem üblichen großen Verwaltungsbau mit sterilen Fluren und Aufzugsverbindungen sehr viel lebendiger zu sein. Die Vielfalt an Verbindungswegen über Straßen, Plätze und Brücken bringt auch immer neue Situationen, wobei man auch mit all den unterschiedlichen Nutzungen immer wieder in Kontakt kommt.

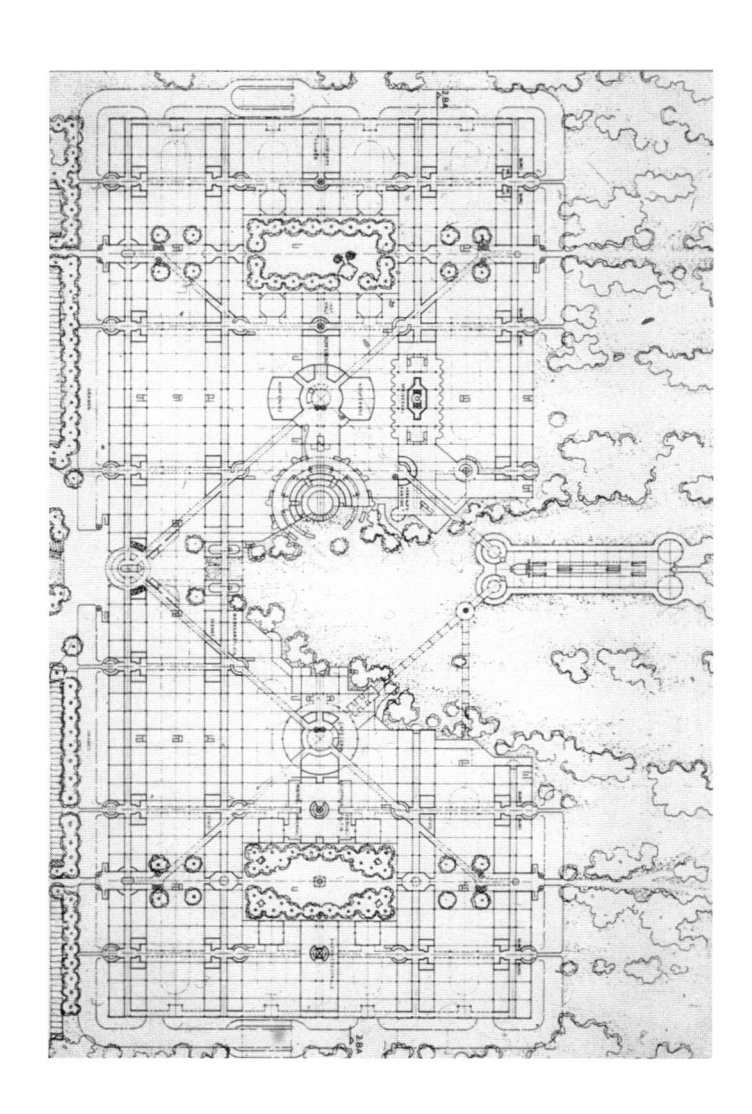

with streets and squares that would correspond in scale to the character of other old, established, local urban structures. The variety of functions to be accommodated was of course an advantage in proposing such a solution. The glass-covered streets, for example, serve as exhibition spaces. Vintage cars from the museum and new sales models can thus be presented in an appropriate situation. Working in an office city of this kind seems to me to be altogether much more attractive than in the usual sort of administration buildings with their sterile corridors and lifts. The variety of connecting routes — streets, open spaces, bridges, etc. — opens up ever new situations; what is more, one is constantly brought in contact with other departments and functions.

Um die neue Bauanlage an die übrige Bebauung anzuschließen, haben wir über den Wettbewerb hinaus den Vorschlag gemacht, die verstreut liegenden Gebäude an der Südseite des Geländes in gleicher Struktur einzufassen. Damit würde entlang der Hauptfront des Mercedes-Komplexes ein Straßenraum entstehen, dessen Charakter die Ortsmitte mit den beidseitigen Zugängen zu den jeweiligen Stadtteilen deutlich markiert.
Die Anlage ist zur Landschaft hin klar abgegrenzt, jedoch greift in der Mitte der Grünbereich mit Wiesen und Obstbäumen ins Innere der städtischen Anlage ein, so daß man aus den Straßen heraus auch immer wieder ins Grüne der Landschaft sieht.

In order to integrate the new development into the existing built fabric, we made the proposal (which went beyond the requirements of the brief) to link the scattered buildings to the south of the site with a uniform structure. This would mean that along the main front of the Mercedes complex a street space would be created that would have the character of an urban centre, from which the lines of access to both parts of the office city would extend.
The development is clearly demarcated from the open countryside. Nevertheless, at the centre the green surrounding landscape with its meadows and fruit trees reaches into the heart of this urban complex, so that one has constant views out into the countryside from the streets.

Der Friedrichplatz in Kassel ist ein rechteckiger Platz aus der Barockzeit. Drei seiner Seiten sind bebaut, während die vierte zur Landschaft hin offen blieb. Merkwürdigerweise wirkt auch diese Seite geschlossen. Dies erscheint wohl dadurch, weil das Gelände vom Platz zur Flußebene sehr stark fällt und so das sehr weit entfernt liegende Bild der Landschaft in den Platzausschnitt rückt. Diese Verschiebung des Maßstabes markiert die Raumbegrenzung.
Der Platz sieht heute ziemlich trostlos aus. Größtenteils wird er als Parkplatz benutzt und außerdem von einer verkehrsreichen Straße in der Mitte durchschnitten.

Friedrichplatz in Kassel is a rectangular open space dating from the Baroque age. It is built up on three sides; the fourth is open to the countryside beyond. Curiously enough, even this fourth side gives the impression of being closed, probably because the land falls away quite steeply from the square to the river valley, thus drawing the distant picture of the landscape into this section of the open space. It is the shift in scale that marks the edge of space.
Today the square looks rather desolate. It is used largely as a parking area and is, in addition, bisected by a busy road. If the square is to be experienced as a homogeneous whole again, the road would have to be laid underground. A depart-

Um den Platz wieder als einen Gesamtplatz erlebbar zu machen, müßte die Straße unter den Platz verlegt werden. Die Finanzierung wollte ein Warenhauskonzern teilweise übernehmen, falls ihm der Einbau eines Warenhauses unter der Platzfläche mit einem oberirdischen Eingangsgebäude zugesichert würde. Dies zu verwirklichen, ohne den Platz noch mehr zu zerstören, schien uns zunächst unmöglich. Es kam uns dann aber der Gedanke, ähnlich der früheren mit Bäumen eingefaßten Promenadenallee auf dem Platz einen neuen Weg zu schaffen, der sich wie ein Bach langsam in die Fläche eingräbt. Das heißt, er senkt sich von der Platzebene langsam ab, zunächst unter der Platzfläche eingeschossig, dann weiter abfal-

ment store concern was prepared to take over part of the costs, on the condition that permission were granted for a store beneath the square, with an entrance structure above ground level. Initially this seemed impossible without destroying the square even further. We then had the idea of creating a new route across this public open space, not unlike the promenade or avenue lined with trees that had once graced this square. This new route would cut its way deeper and deeper into the surface, rather like a stream. In other words, it would gradually sink below the level of the square, one storey deep at first, then dropping even further, until, at a depth of two storeys beneath the surface, it passes under the sunken lateral road and

lend bis er zweigeschossig unter der abgesenkten Querstraße durchführt und schließlich amphitheatralisch zum Park ausläuft.

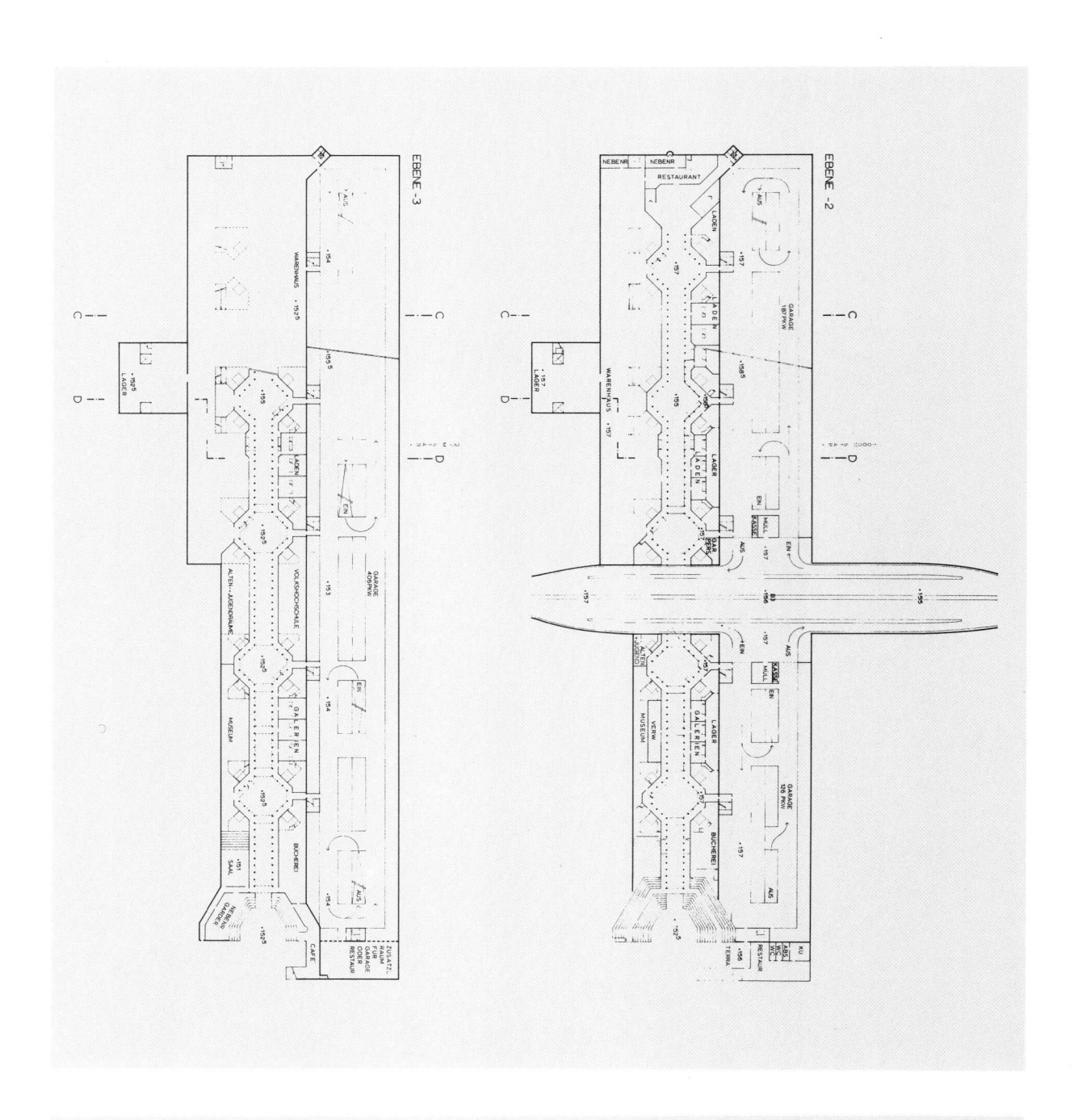

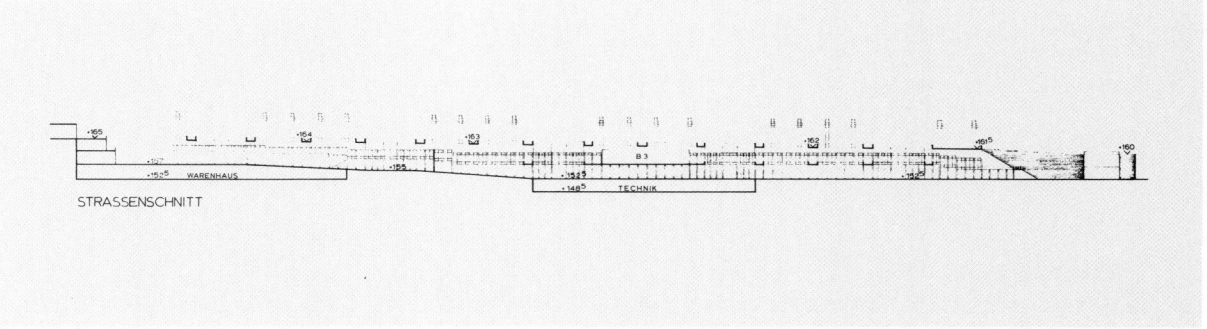

finally emerges in amphitheatrical form into the park at the end.
In the longitudinal section one can see the relative levels of this promenade together with those of the department store, the

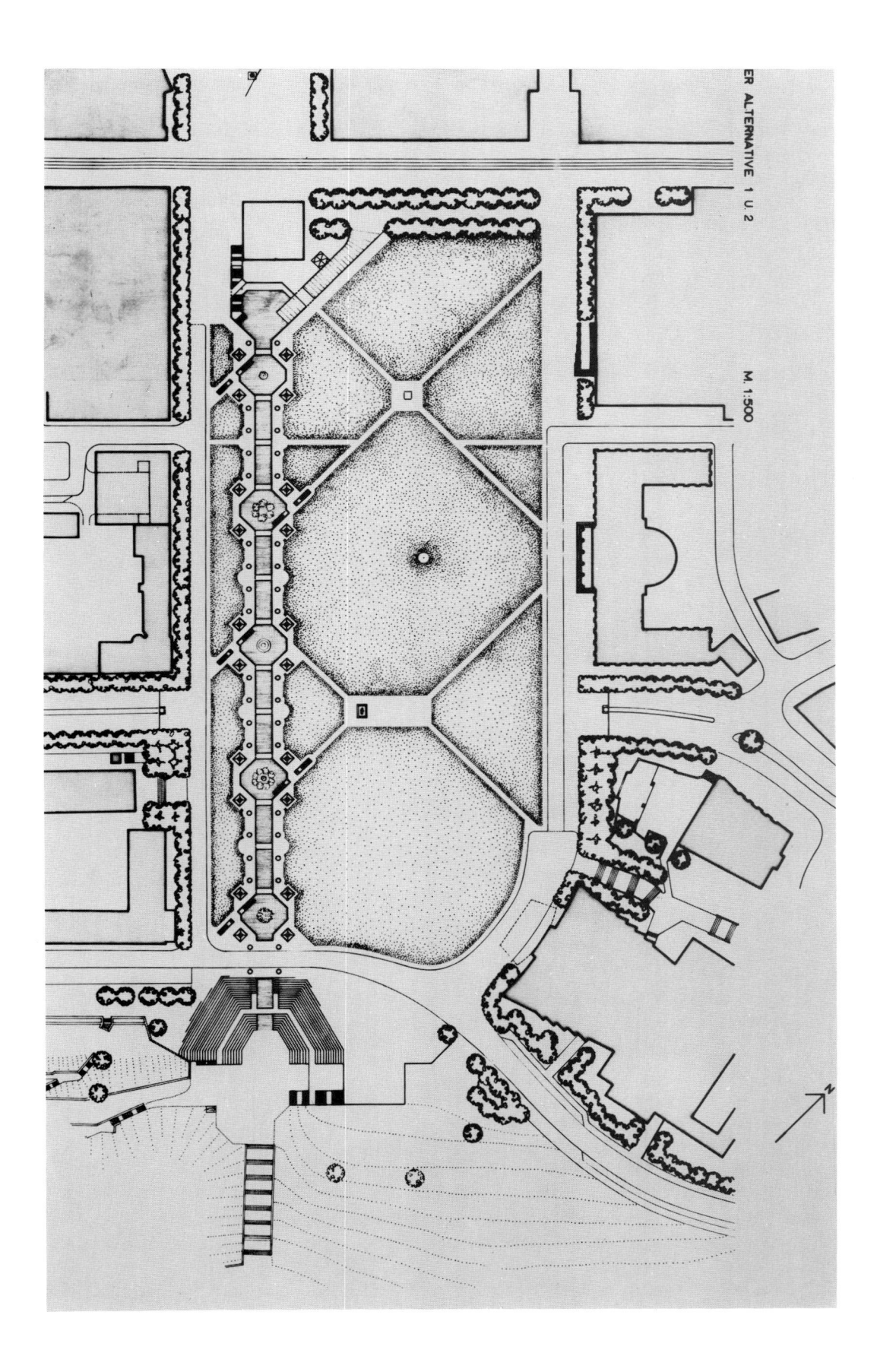

Im Schnitt ist der Höhenverlauf der Straße zu sehen mit dem Kaufhaus und Einzelläden sowie öffentlichen Einrichtungen.

individual shops and public amenities. Along the route are a series of smaller open spaces of differing character. The street

Die Straße bildet immer wieder kleine Plätze mit unterschiedlichem Charakter, bis sie am Ende den Ausblick in die freie Landschaft öffnet. Seitlich der Ladenzone sind unter dem Platz Parkflächen vorgesehen. Diese sind von der tiefgelegten Straße gut anzufahren, und das Rein- und Rausgehen ist schön, denn man geht ja ebenerdig gleich in den tiefliegenden Weg entlang der Schaufenster von Läden und Kaufhaus.

Die gesamten Räumlichkeiten, die unter der Platzebene liegen, müssen natürlich künstlich be- und entlüftet werden. Dafür haben wir eine doppelte Reihe von gläsernen Rohren vorgesehen, die durch ihre plastisch-abstrahierte Form an die ursprüngliche Promenadenallee auf der Platzoberfläche erinnert.

Die Errichtung einer solchen Gesamtanlage ist mit großen Kosten verbunden, aber das wäre zu finanzieren, weil eine ungeheure Fläche rentabel nutzbar gewonnen wird. Der Leitgedanke war, soviel Nutzfläche zu gewinnen, daß über die Rentabilität der Bebauung auch die Tieferlegung der Straße finanzierbar wäre. Ohne die besonders störende Schnellstraße wird der Platz so beschaffen sein, daß man sich gerne dort aufhält. Zudem wird die tieferliegende Kaufallee und vor allem die günstige Lage der Parkplätze viel mehr Menschen in das Gebiet und auf den Platz bringen.

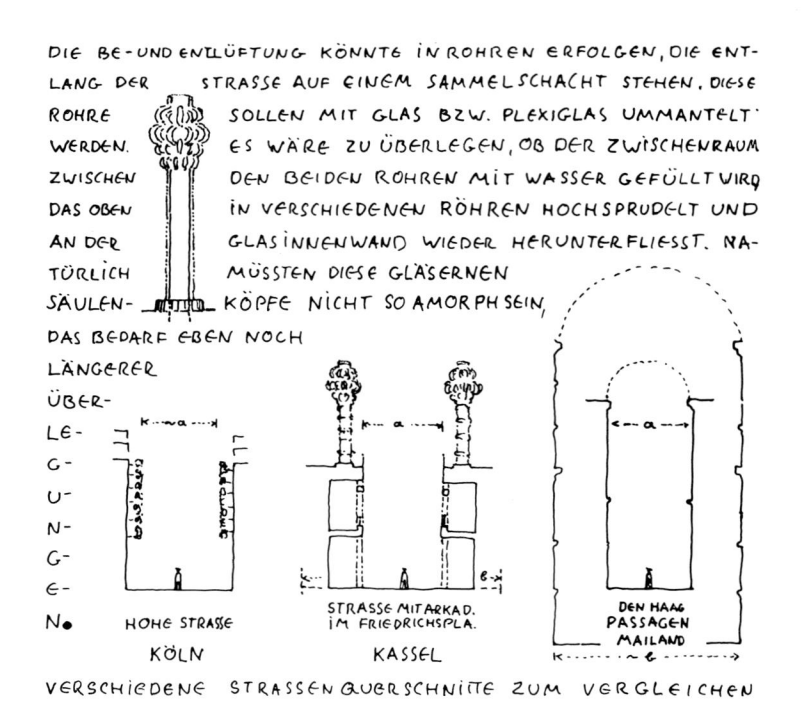

Die Be- und Entlüftung könnte in Rohren erfolgen, die entlang der Straße auf einem Sammelschacht stehen. Diese Rohre sollen mit Glas bzw. Plexiglas ummantelt werden. Es wäre zu überlegen, ob der Zwischenraum zwischen den beiden Rohren mit Wasser gefüllt wird, das oben in verschiedenen Röhren hochsprudelt und an der Glasinnenwand wieder herunterfließt. Natürlich müßten diese gläsernen Säulenköpfe nicht so amorph sein, das bedarf eben noch längerer Überlegungen.

HOHE STRASSE KÖLN — STRASSE MIT ARKAD. IM FRIEDRICHSPLA. KASSEL — DEN HAAG PASSAGEN MAILAND

VERSCHIEDENE STRASSENQUERSCHNITTE ZUM VERGLEICHEN

finally opens out at the end, affording a view to the landscape. Beneath the square to one side of the shopping zone two storeys of parking space are planned, which can be easily reached by car from the sunken road. Access to these areas on foot is also an agreeable sensation; for one walks from ground level straight down to the lower levels past shop windows and the department store.

All spaces beneath the level of the square will of course have to be artificially ventilated. For this purpose we have planned a double row of glass tubes, the abstract, sculptural form of which recalls the original avenue of trees along the promenade at ground level in the square.

The construction of a large-scale complex like this is an extremely costly undertaking. It would be possible to finance it, however, since there would be a tremendous gain in commercial floor area. The basic idea was to create so much exploitable floor area that the commercial viability of the development would pay the costs of lowering the level of the road. Relieved of this particularly disturbing fast traffic route across it, the square would be a place where people would happily congregate. In addition the sunken shopping mall and the optimal location of the parking spaces would attract many more people into the area, into this square.

Kassel — Friedrichplatz — vertiefte Arkadenstraße

Kassel — Friedrichplatz — Sunken arcade street

»Am Steintor«, Hannover. Obschon die Stadt sich mit der Pflasterung, der Bepflanzung mit Bäumen und überhaupt mit der Platzgestaltung sehr viel Mühe gegeben hat, ist der Platz am Steintor kein richtiger Platz geworden, da die heterogene Randbebauung keine wirkliche Raumbegrenzung ergibt. Ein Lichtblick in dem Durcheinander langweiliger Bauten ist lediglich das »Anzeiger-Haus« von Höger aus den zwanziger Jahren. Es ist, mit dunklen Ziegeln verblendet, ein monumentales Gebäude, am Rande der Platzwand gelegen.

»Am Steintor«, Hanover. Although the city has taken great pains with its pavings, its tree-planting and the general design of its squares, the public open space at the Steintor has no true sense of »place«; the heterogeneous peripheral developments do not represent a proper spatial demarcation. The only bright spot in this motley array of dull and boring developments is the »Anzeiger« building by Fritz Höger, dating from the 1920s, a monumental structure faced with dark-coloured bricks and standing at one edge of the open space.

Unser Bemühen ging nun dahin, an den Charakter des Högerschen Baues mit seiner turmartigen Betonung wie mit seinem Baumaterial anzuknüpfen, damit sich von dieser Randzone her zur Mitte der Platzrandbebauung ein Rhythmus entwickelt, der sich vielleicht später noch so fortsetzen läßt, daß dieser städtische Raum eine sehr ausgeprägte Platzwand erhält. So würde auch das Högersche Hochhaus mit eingebunden sein, gleichsam als Endpunkt dieser Bebauungskette.
Dies ergab für unsere Planung zwei erhöhte Baukörper, die einen niedrigeren Mittelteil mit dem Zugang zur Hofbebauung

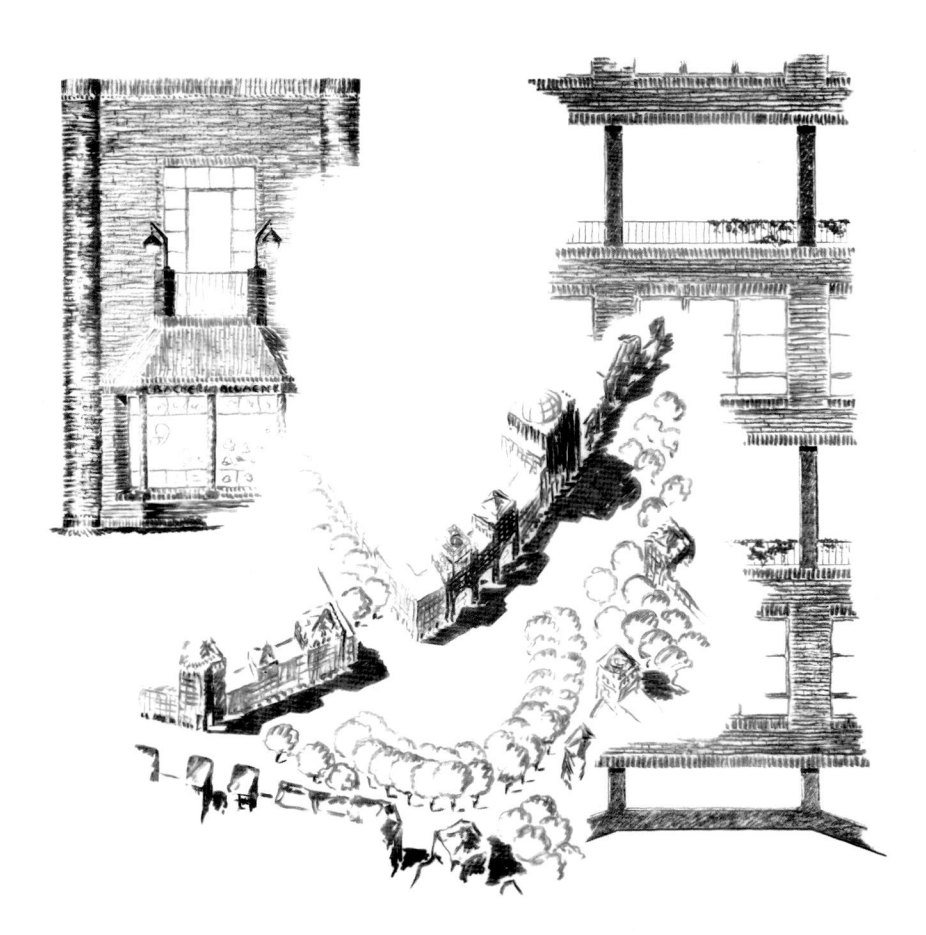

In our scheme we orientated ourselves to the tower-like accentuation and the materials of the Höger building, in order to establish a rhythm extending from the edge to the middle of this peripheral development, a rhythm that it would perhaps be possible to take up and continue again later and that would give the face of the square a distinctive appearance. In this way the Höger block would also be tied in as the culmination of this chain of buildings.
Our proposals took the form of two tower-like volumes flanking a lower middle section, through which access is provided

flankieren. Der Hof ist nur zum Teil mit Glas überdacht, so daß an den offenen Teilen Bäume gut gedeihen können. Die vielen kleinen Läden und Kioske, die um den Hof liegen, verleihen ihm den Charakter eines Marktes.

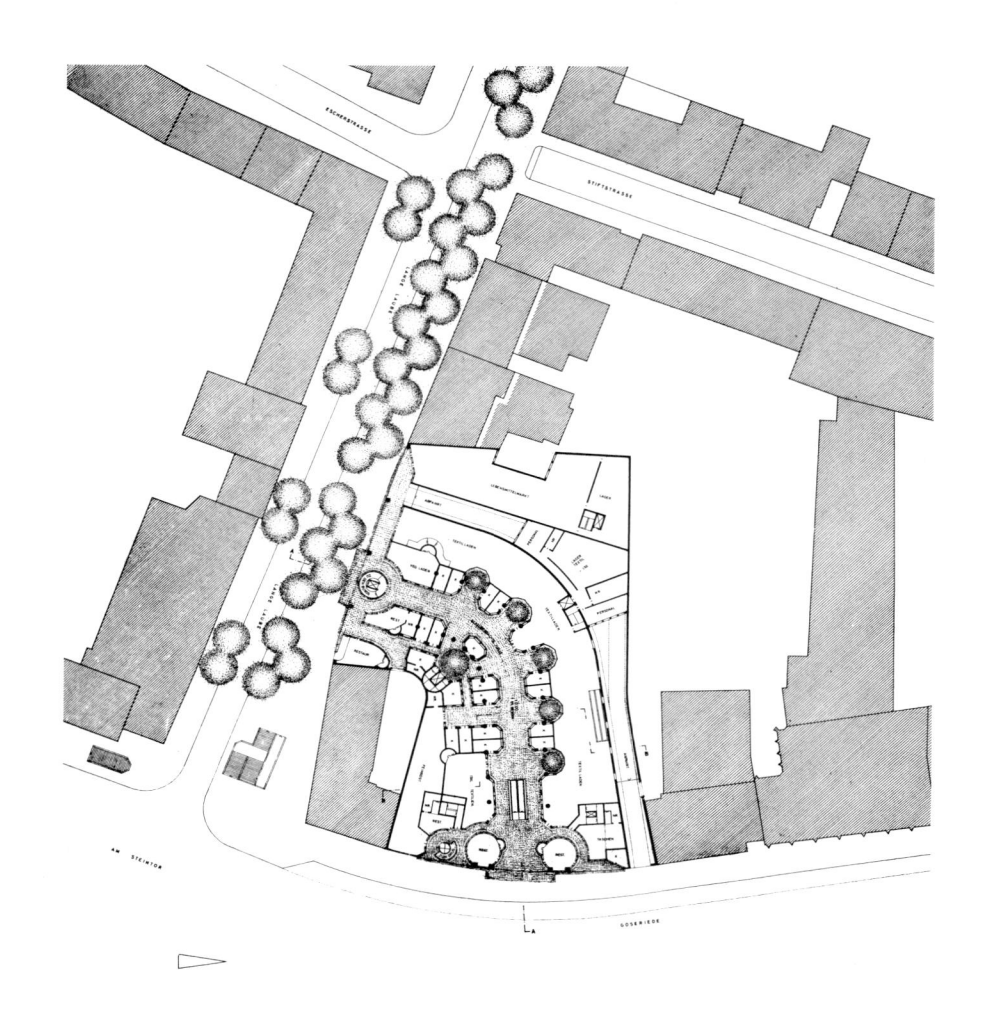

to the rear courtyard development. The courtyard is only partially covered with glass, enabling trees to be planted in the open areas between. The numerous little shops and kiosks about the courtyard give it something of the character of a market place.

Die Wahl des Materials war nicht schwer, wollten wir doch mit dem Bau von Höger einen Zusammenhang bilden. Wir haben allerdings vor, den Ziegel als Verblendung der Konstruktion offen zu zeigen, das heißt die Ziegel werden so um die Betonkonstruktion gefügt, daß diese immer wieder in Erscheinung tritt.

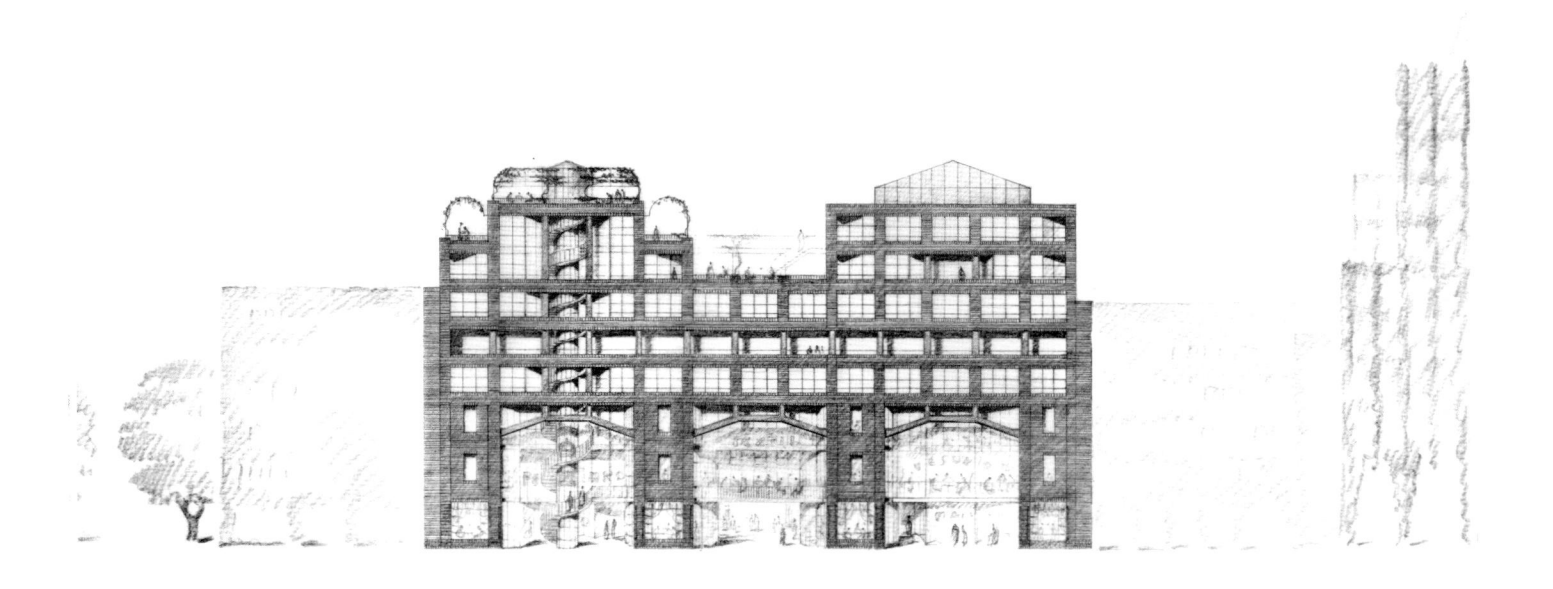

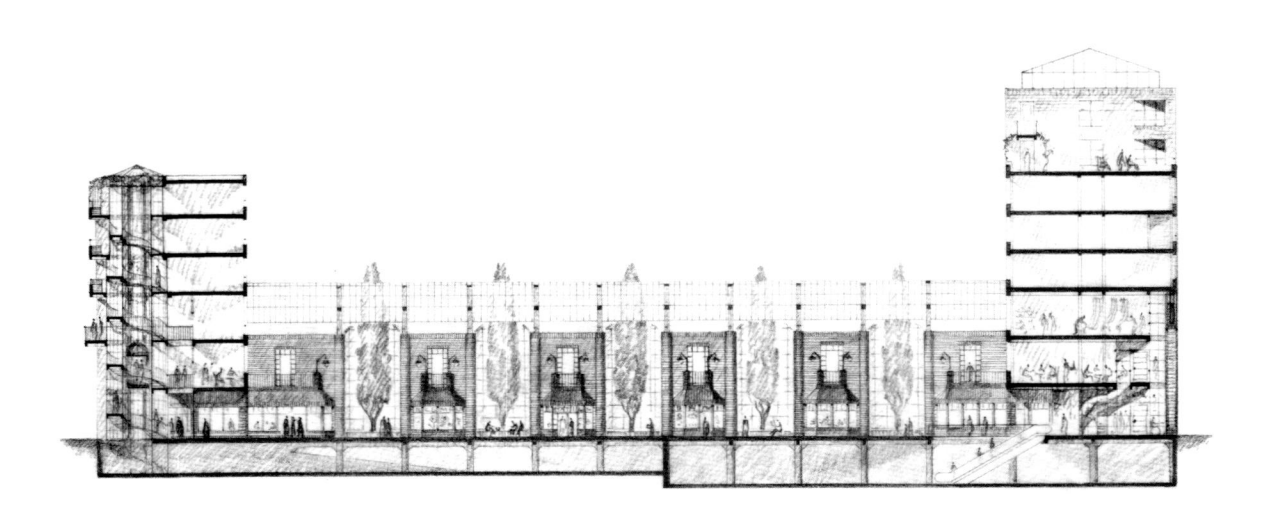

The choice of materials was not difficult, since we wished to establish a link with the building by Höger. We propose, however, to show the brickwork for what it is, namely a facing to the structure. In other words, the bricks will be laid about the concrete structure in a way that will allow the latter to show through.

Hannover

268 Hanover

»Am Steintor«

M. 1:100

Rheinuferbebauung in Köln. Wir haben in mehreren Seminararbeiten an der Hochschule das Gebiet Köln bearbeitet, das sich am Rheinufer entlang vom Ubierring bis nördlich des Domes erstreckt. Dieses Gebiet ist vor allem durch die Verkehrsführung nach dem Krieg besonders stark mitgenommen. Ich will hier nur auf die Schwerpunkte hinweisen: das Severinsviertel, den Heumarkt und den Bereich Dom/Bahnhof.
Überall wurden dort städtische Strukturen zerrissen, und es ging in dem Seminar darum, wie man wieder Zusammenhänge schaffen kann, ohne Vorteile wie die der neuen Verkehrsführung aufzugeben.
An allen drei städtischen Schwerpunktsituationen führen große Brücken den Verkehr von Osten her über den Rhein in die Stadt, aber keine der Brücken erreicht die Stadt in einer so markanten Weise, die das Erreichen des Ufers und das Eindringen durch die Uferbebauung in das Gefüge der Stadt richtig erleben läßt. Bei der Severinsbrücke fließt der Verkehr irgendwo weit innerhalb der Stadt in das Straßennetz. Bei der Deutzer Brücke verstreut sich der Verkehr quer über den einst großartigen Heumarkt und erst von dort kommt man eigentlich in die Stadt. Bei der Hohenzollernbrücke ist es erst der Bahnhof, an dem die Brücke in die Stadt eintaucht, und dieser liegt ja auch irgendwie hintendrin, schräg zum Dom verschoben.

Rhineside Development in Cologne. In a number of tutorial projects at the university we have examined the district in Cologne that stretches along the bank of the Rhine from the Ubierring to north of the cathedral. The area has suffered a great deal, mainly as a result of post-war transport planning. At this juncture I wish to refer merely to the main points under consideration: the Severin district, the Heumarkt (the old hay market), and the area round the cathedral and station.
Everywhere here old urban structures have been torn apart. In our seminar we were concerned with finding ways to create new connections, without sacrificing the advantages gained, such as the new lines of communication.
At each of these three urban nodes major bridges channel the traffic from the east over the Rhine into the city. None of these bridges, however, enters the city in such a manner that the act of reaching the shore, of penetrating the riverside developments and the urban fabric, is experienced as the event it should be. Traffic across the Severin Bridge flows somewhere deep inside the city into the urban road network. In the case of the Deutz Bridge the traffic is scattered all over the Heumarkt, which was once such a grand urban space; only subsequently does one enter the city proper. The Hohenzollern Bridge route only really becomes part of the city at the station, which is situated somewhere to the rear, pushed at an angle to the cathedral. We were therefore concerned with making the arrival at these bridgeheads and the entry into the fabric

Es geht darum, die Ankunft der Brücken und das Eindringen in das Stadtgefüge, was ja doch ein besonderes Ereignis sein könnte, sichtbar zu machen.

Für das Severinsviertel, das zur Zeit durch die Straßenführung so sehr durchschnitten ist, wurden Vorschläge erarbeitet, die zeigen, wie es möglich wäre, trotz der Verkehrsschneise dort wieder einen Zusammenhang zu schaffen. Das ist gar nicht so hoffnungslos wie man es leicht hinstellt und auch finanziell durchführbar, es müßte nur von der Stadt gewollt sein.

Auf dem Heumarkt, der heute vom Verkehr völlig zerrissen ist, sehen die Entwürfe Vorschläge vor, unter Beibehaltung der Verkehrsführung den Platz wieder zusammenzufügen und als Gesamtplatz erlebbar zu machen. Die meisten dieser Vorschläge erhöhen einen Teil des Platzniveaus, so daß der Fahrverkehr unter dem Platz hindurchgeführt werden kann. Mit der Höherlegung des Platzes entstehen viele neue und wertvolle Nutzflächen, die sicher bei der Finanzierung der Baumaßnahmen helfen können, so wie es auch im Falle des Kasseler Projektes Friedrichplatz vorgesehen war. Der Platzraum sollte baulich so geschlossen werden, daß man, über die Rheinbrücke kommend, die Stadt auch schon an der Uferfront erreicht, dort das Eintreten erlebt und dann erst vom großartigen Heumarkt empfangen wird.

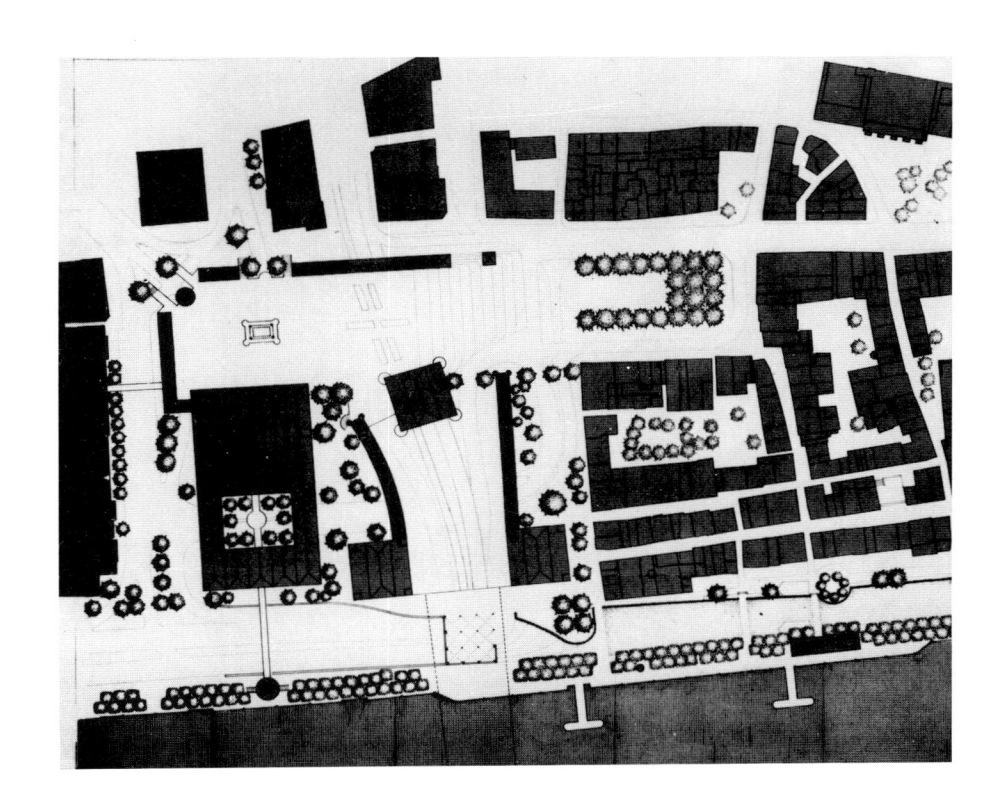

of the city the special perceptible events they should be.

The proposals put forward for the Severin district, which is at present badly cut up by traffic routes, show how it would be possible, in spite of the gash caused by the road, to establish new links at this point. The situation is not as hopeless as it is often described. The scheme would also be financially feasible. The city simply has to show the will to implement it.

For the Heumarkt, which is today completely carved up by traffic, the designs comprise proposals to retain the present transport routes and nevertheless to knit the area together again, so that it will be possible to experience it as a unified open space. Most of these proposals suggest raising the level of this space in part, so that vehicular traffic could be channelled through below the surface. As a result of this elevation of ground level, a great deal of new and valuable floor space would be created that would certainly help to finance the construction measures; (as in the Friedrichplatz scheme in Kassel). The public open space should be closed, so that when approaching across the Rhine bridge, one would already have the sensation of arrival on reaching the shore, from where one would enter the city and then be welcomed into the grand space of the Heumarkt.

Köln, Heumarkt, Vorschlag 1980

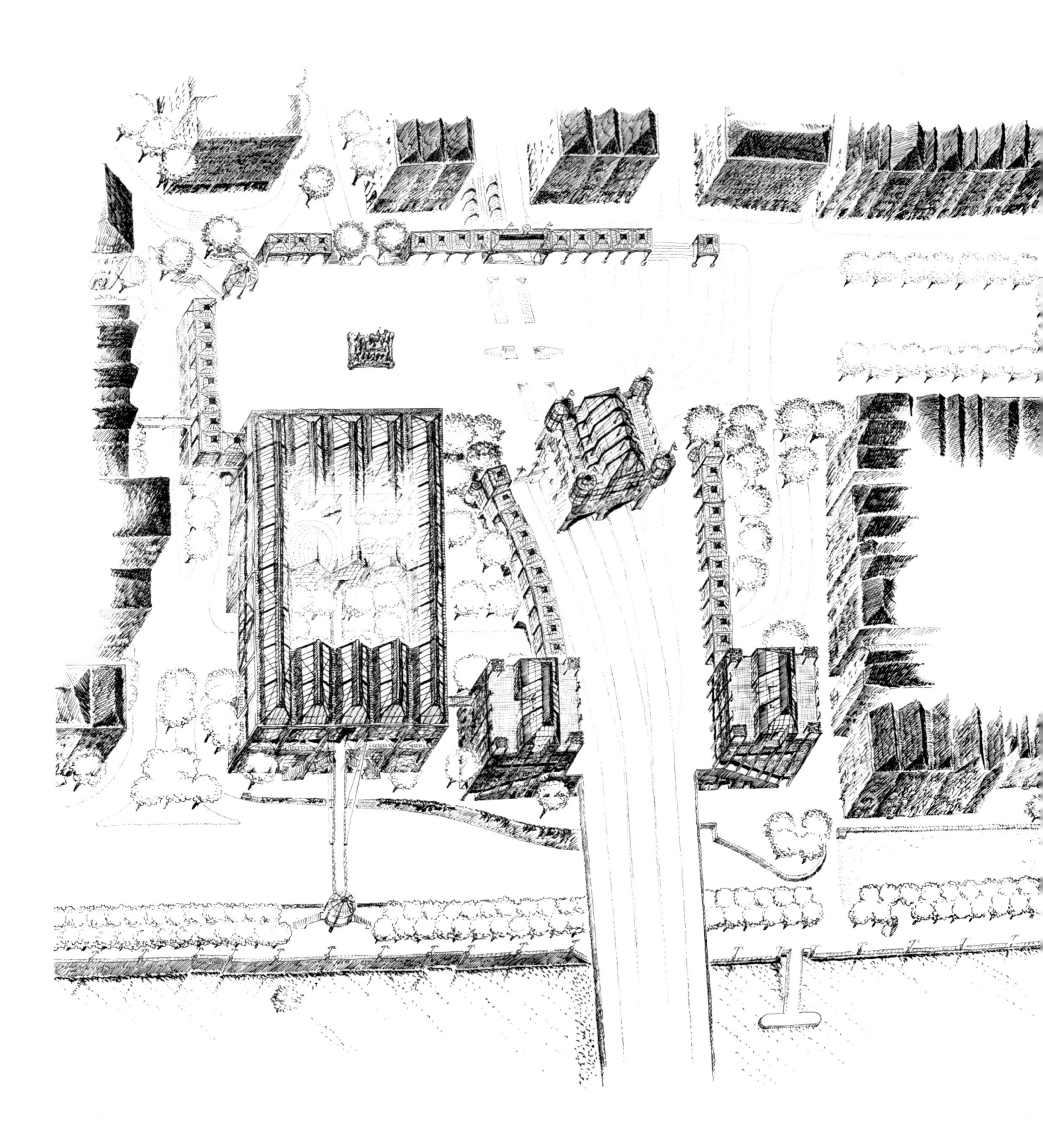

Cologne, Heumarkt, proposals 1980

Platzsanierung/Neubebauung

Public open space/Rehabilitation-Redevelopment

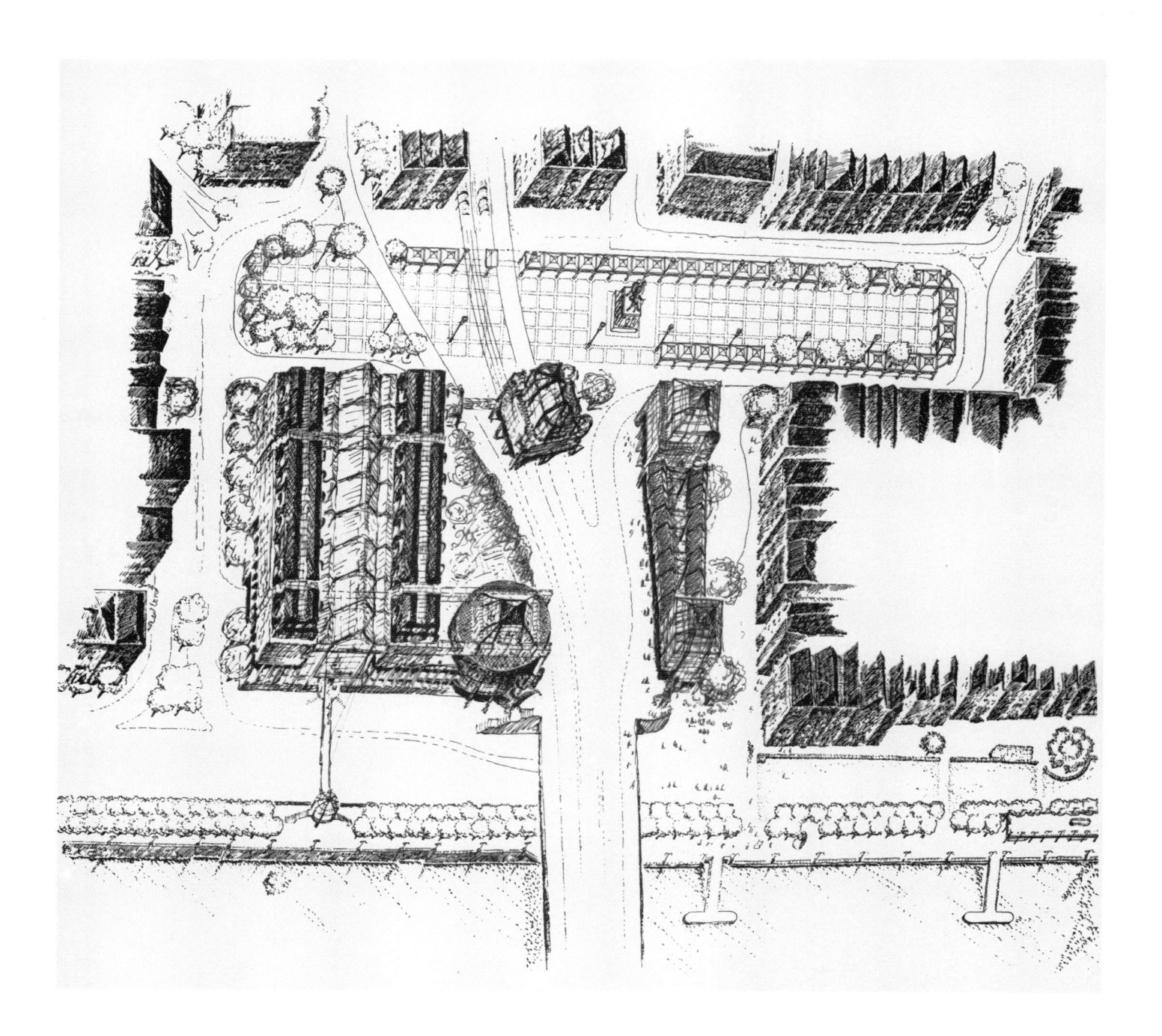

Köln, Heumarkt, Projekt 1987 — in Zusammenarbeit mit Kraemer, Sie[...]

Cologne, Heumarkt, project 1987 — in collaboration with Kraemer, Sie[...]

Sassenhof-Hotel Maritim

Köln, Heumarkt

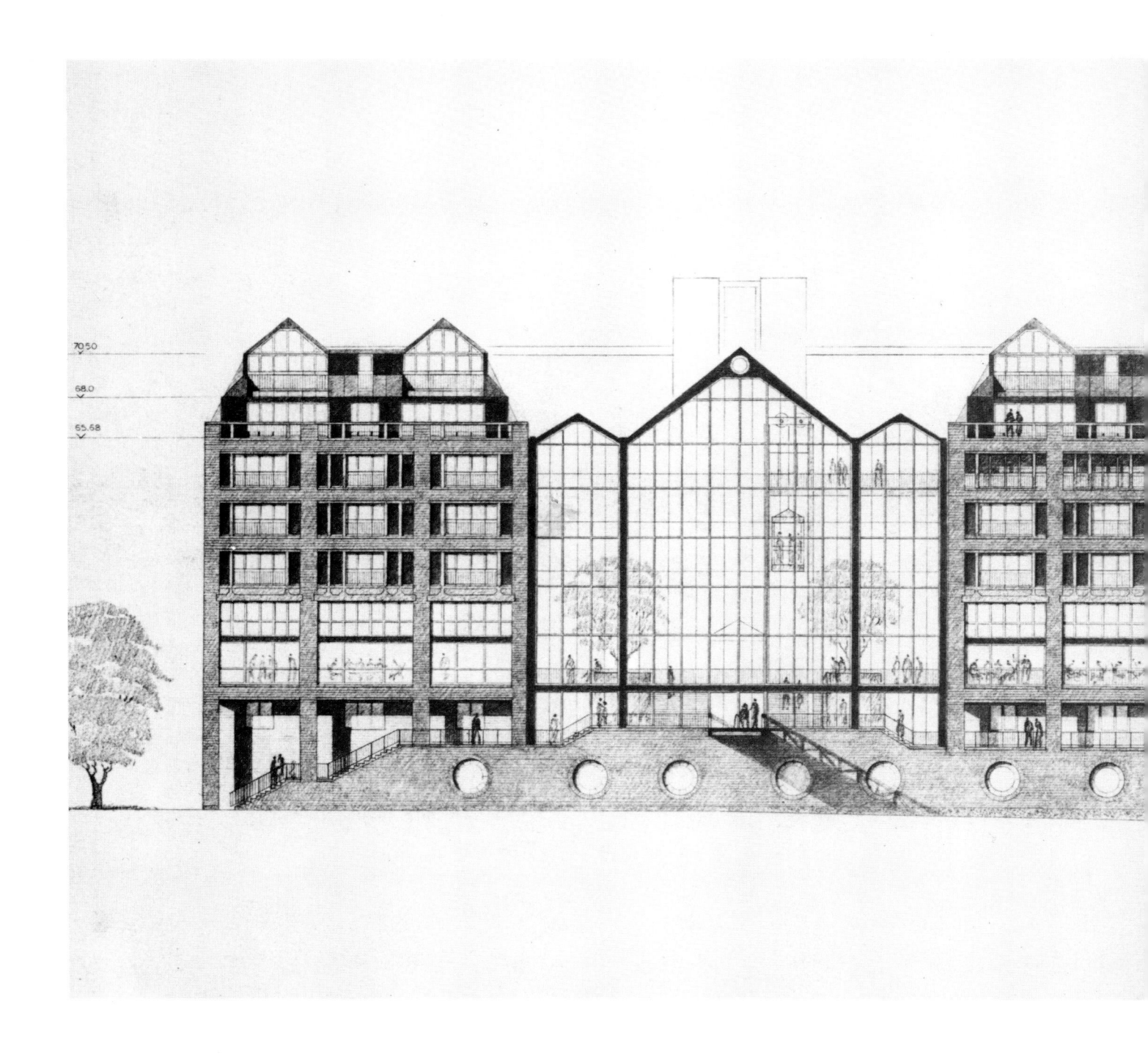

Cologne, Heumarkt

Sassenhof – Hotel Maritim

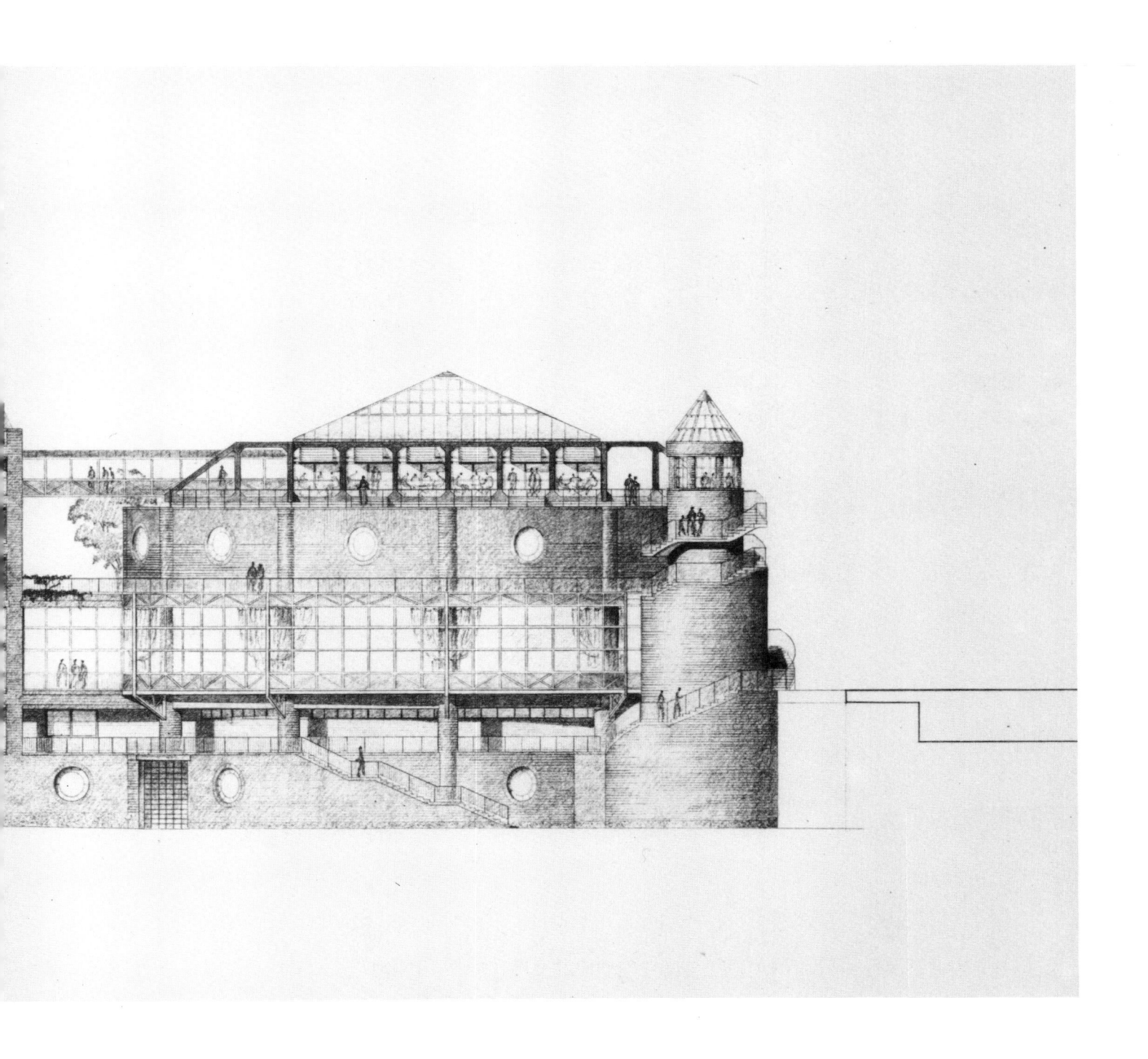

Im Bereich um den Dom ist die Stadtstruktur auch sehr zerrissen. Im Norden wurde sie schon zur Gründerzeit durch das Bahnhofsgelände brutal zerschnitten. Im Süden hat sich in der jüngsten Zeit ein überdimensionaler Museumsbereich ausgedehnt und somit das interne städtische Leben verdrängt. Wir haben deshalb im Museumswettbewerb (1979) mit unserem Lehrstuhlprojekt vorgeschlagen, das Museum mit anderen städtischen Einrichtungen, wie Wohnungen, Läden, Restaurants usw., gleichsam einzupacken und so an die Nutzungsvielfalt des südlichen Altstadtbereichs anzuknüpfen.

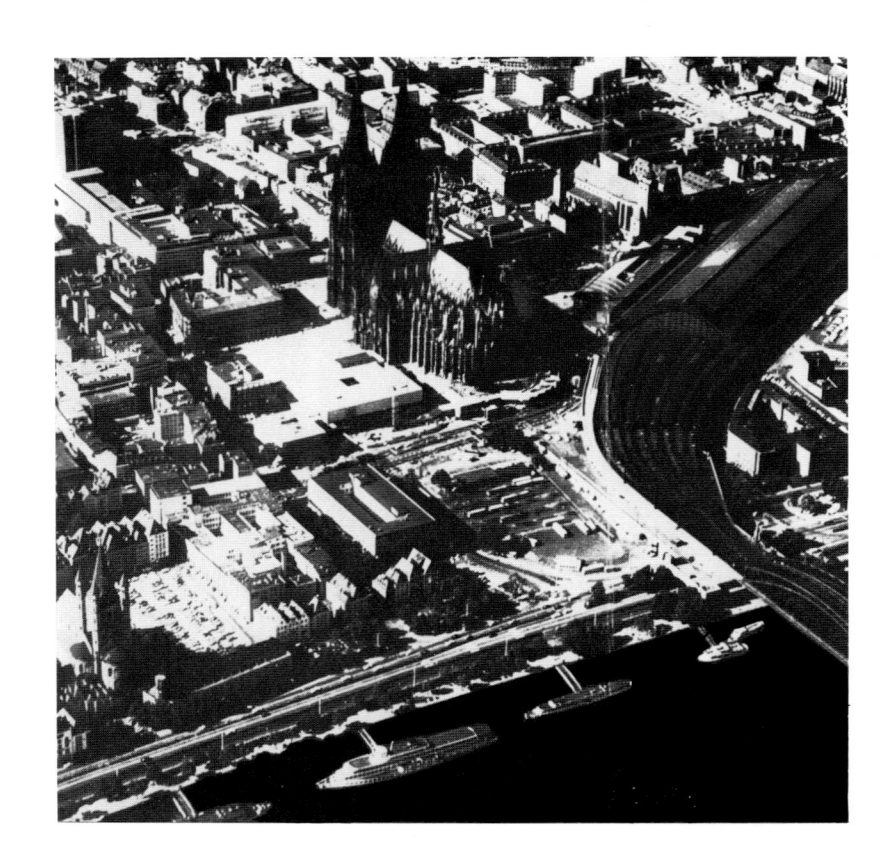

The urban structure in the area about the cathedral is also very fragmented. To the north it was already brutally dissected in the last century by the station development; and in recent times a mammoth museum complex has sprawled over the area to the south, squeezing out a great deal of inner urban life. In our faculty project for the museum competition (1979) we therefore proposed a mixed package comprising museum facilities and a variety of other urban amenities, such as housing, shops, restaurants, etc., which would be grafted on to the old southern part of the city with its diversity of functions.

Auch dem vorhandenen Römisch-Germanischen Museum und dem Diözesanmuseum wurden solche Nutzungen zugefügt, um eben normale Stadtstrukturen bis an den Dom zu führen, diesen aus den Klauen der Museen zu befreien und ihn als einen Bau erscheinen zu lassen, der Teil und Herz der Struktur ist, die zum internen Leben der Stadt gehört. Unser Vorschlag sah drei Gassen vor, die vom Dom zu einer breiten Treppenanlage am Rheinufer führen. Zwei davon sind offene, normale Gassen mit der für die Umgebung typischen Nutzungsmischung. Die dritte, in der Mitte liegend, führt wie eine Passage durch das Museum. Alle drei Gassen sind querverbunden mit Blickbeziehungen durch das Museum.

Uses of this kind were also added to the existing Roman-Germanic Museum and the Diocesan Museum, in an attempt to bring normal urban tissue right up to the cathedral. Our aim was to rescue the cathedral from the clutches of the museum buildings and to restore to it the appearance of an independent structure, – both part of and the very heart of the urban fabric that constitutes the life of the city centre. In our scheme we proposed creating three lanes that would lead from the cathedral to a grand flight of steps descending to the bank of the Rhine. Two of these paths would be normal, open routes,

So schön die Bahnhofshalle mit ihrer herrlichen Stahlkonstruktion ist, so ist doch das gesamte Bahngelände ein starker Eingriff in das Stadtgefüge. Die Bahntrasse schneidet wie ein sich ausbreitender und wieder verengender Fluß mit einer Windung vor dem Dom in die Stadt ein. Das ist nun so, und man sollte es erst gar nicht versuchen zu vertuschen. Es wäre besser, die eigentliche Stadtstruktur konsequent über den Verkehrsfluß hinweg durchzuführen, so daß sie auf beiden Ufern wieder in Erscheinung tritt. Somit wäre auch die Bahnhofsvorhalle so eingebunden, daß nur die Bahntrasse mit der Bahnsteigüberdachung in das System einschneidet.

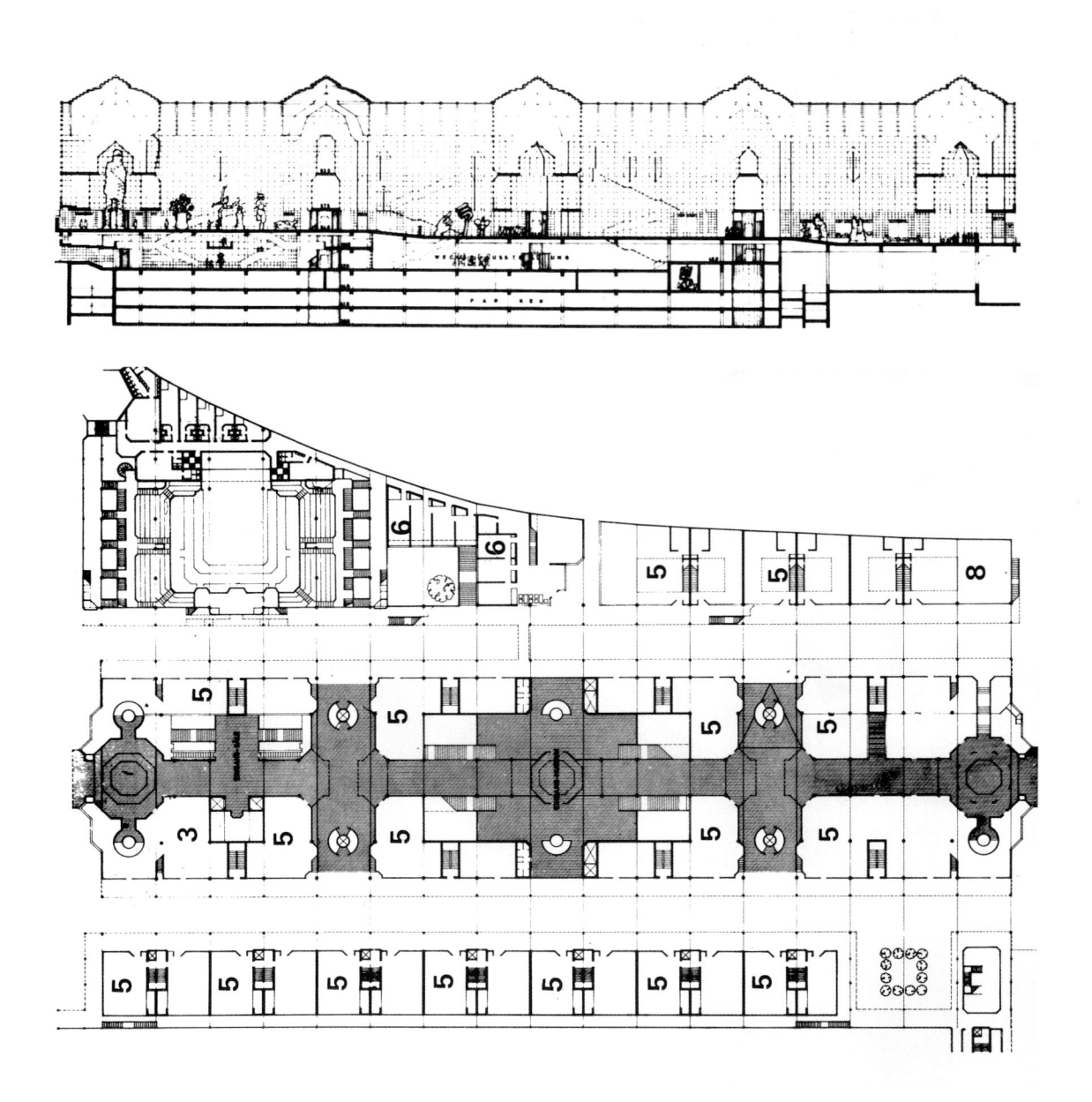

along which would be a mixture of uses typical of this area. The third lane, situated in the middle, would be in the form of an arcade leading through the museum. All three routes are connected laterally to each other and afford visual links through the museum.

However fine the station hall may be, with its superb steel structure, the entire station complex represents a major incision in the urban fabric. The railway tracks shear their path into the city, expanding and contracting in a broad curve in front of the cathedral rather like a river. No one can conceal this fact, nor should one try. It would be a better solution to continue the true urban structure systematically over the stream of traffic, so that the fabric of the city would be visible again on both banks of the river. It would then be possible to integrate the station vestibule into this structure, leaving only the area of the

In diesem Sinne ist die neu zu errichtende Bahnhofsvorhalle in unserem Vorschlag als ein großer überdachter Bereich in das Netz der städtischen Struktur eingeordnet und mit vielerlei Funktionen und Wegeverbindungen zu den Bahngleisen, zur U-Bahn, Bussen, Taxis usw. versehen.
Auch der Dom sollte mit diesem überdachten Platz durch eine Unterkirche verbunden sein. Der gesamte Platz mit seiner Glashülle gibt vielfältige, immer wieder wechselnde Durchblicke frei, vor allem natürlich zum Dom, wobei die vielen Einbauten und Wegeverbindungen durch ihre Kleinmaßstäblichkeit den Dom noch großartiger erscheinen lassen.

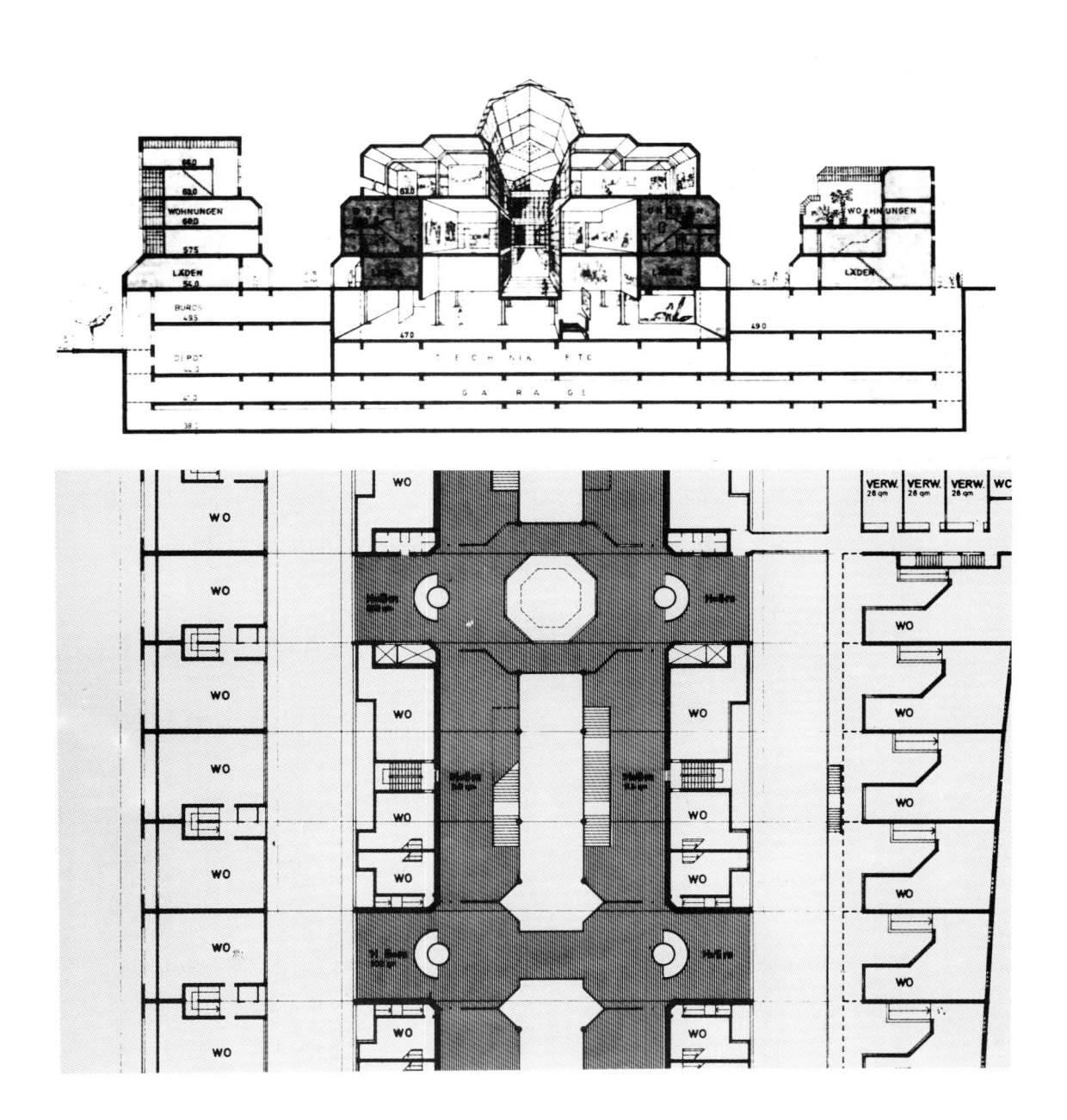

railway tracks and the roof over the platforms as intrusions in the system.
In accordance with this, the new station vestibule in our proposals would take the form of a large covered realm integrated into the fabric of the city, and containing a variety of functions and routes that link up with the platforms of the main station, with the underground railway, buses, taxis, etc.
The cathedral would also be linked to this covered space by an ancillary church. The entire space with its glass skin would afford manifold and constantly changing views, especially to the cathedral. The microcosmic scale of the many small structures and linking routes would accentuate the grandeur of the cathedral even more.

Köln, Museumsneubau, Wettbewerbsentwurf

Cologne, New museum, Competition design

Gesamtansicht, unten Ausschnitte

Overall view; below, details

Köln, Dombereich

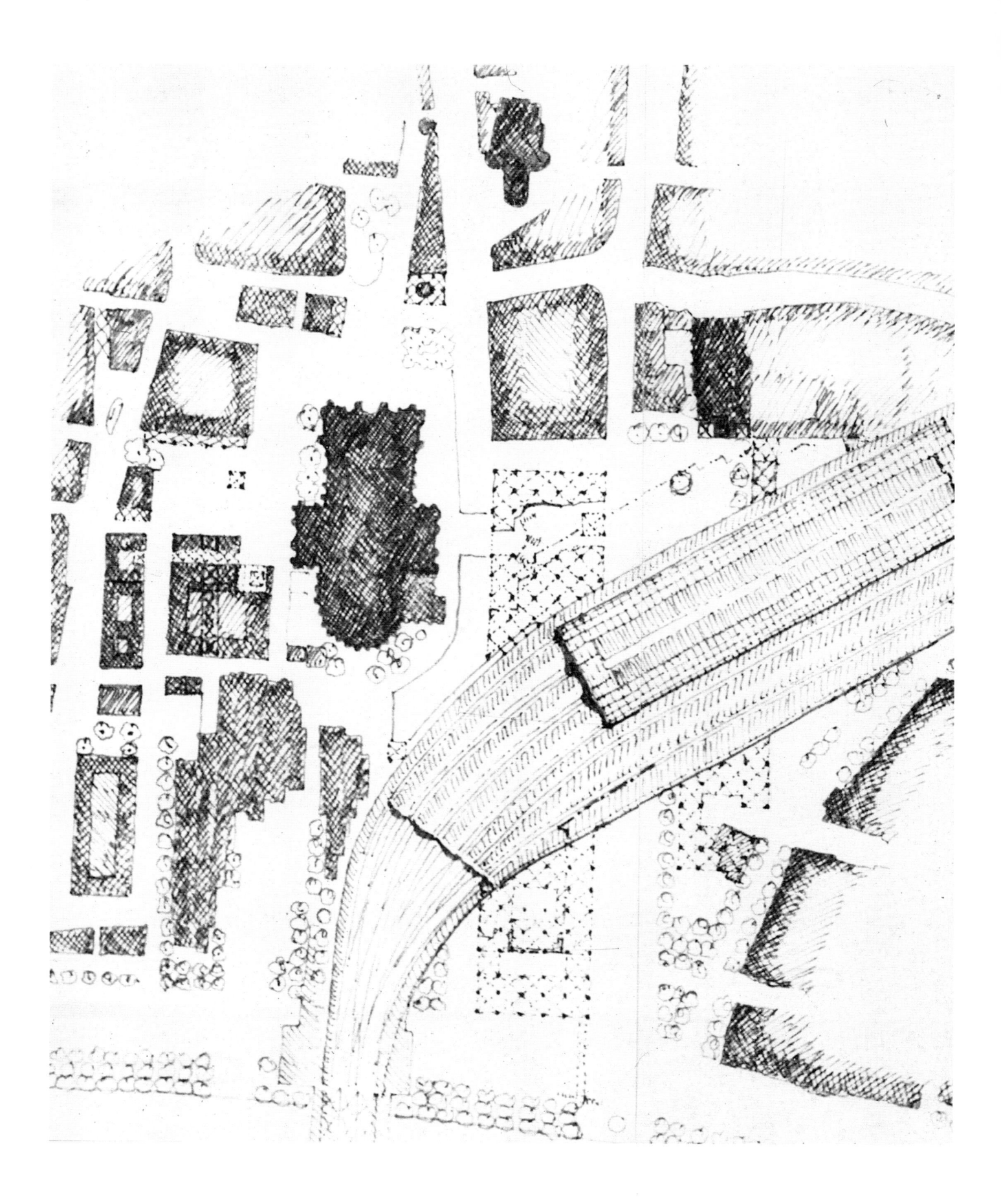

Cologne, Cathedral precinct

Sanierungsvorschlag, 1984

Rehabilitation proposals, 1984

Dudweiler ist eine Stadt in der Nähe von Saarbrücken, die sich überwiegend entlang der Hauptstraße in Nord-Südrichtung entwickelt hat. Die Neugründung der Saarbrücker Universität östlich des Ortes legt es nahe, die weitere Entwicklung in der Querrichtung zu planen. Dazu bot sich eine ungenutzte Freifläche gleich im Anschluß an die Hauptstraße an. Die Stadt, die bisher keine eigene Mitte hatte, erhielt durch unsere Planung an diesem Knotenpunkt der beiden Richtungen einen Marktplatz mit Kaufhaus, Läden, Restaurants usw. Eine Passage führt von hier aus in einen begrünten, verkehrsfreien

Dudweiler is a town near Saarbrücken that has developed largely in a north-south direction along the main road. The new foundation of Saarbrücken University to the east of the town suggested the idea of planning a further, lateral development in an east-west direction. An undeveloped area immediately adjoining the main road presented an obvious starting point for this.
Hitherto the town had not had a proper centre. As a result of our planning proposals it suddenly acquired a market place

Stadtanger. Dieser ist seitlich gefaßt von einer Wohnbebauung, die zur Straße eine relativ geschlossene Front bildet und nach innen mit Terrassen, Lauben, Außentreppen zum grünen Anger hin überleitet. Im Osten wird die gesamte Anlage durch ein Bürgerhaus abgeschlossen. Zugleich markiert dieses Gebäude den Zugang zur Stadt von Osten her. Das Bürgerhaus selbst ist auf Seite 154 bei den Theaterbauten besprochen.

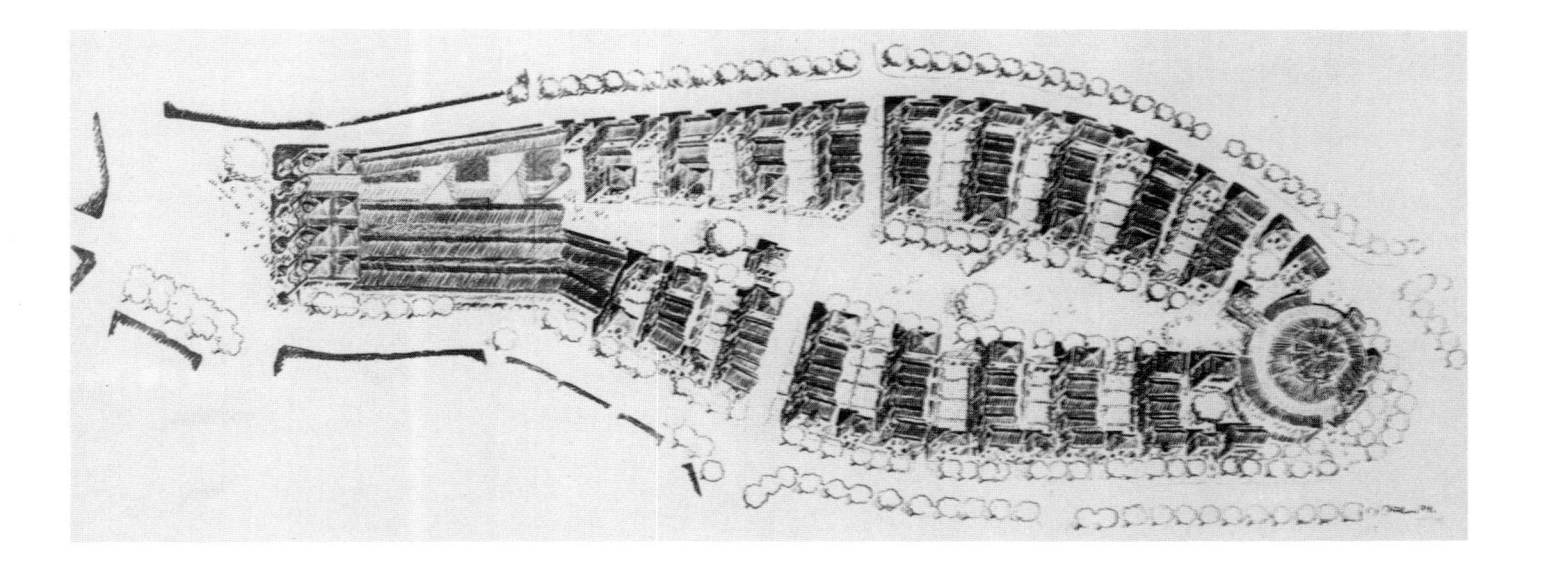

with a department store, shops, restaurants, etc. at the junction of the two directional axes. A covered arcade leads out to a green town common, which is free of vehicular traffic. It is flanked by a housing development with a relatively closed street face. On the inside the transition to the common is via a series of terraces, summer houses, pergolas, and external stairs. The entire development is closed at the eastern end by a civic hall. This building also marks the point of access for the town from the east. The civic hall itself is described on p. 154 under the theatre projects.

Dudweiler

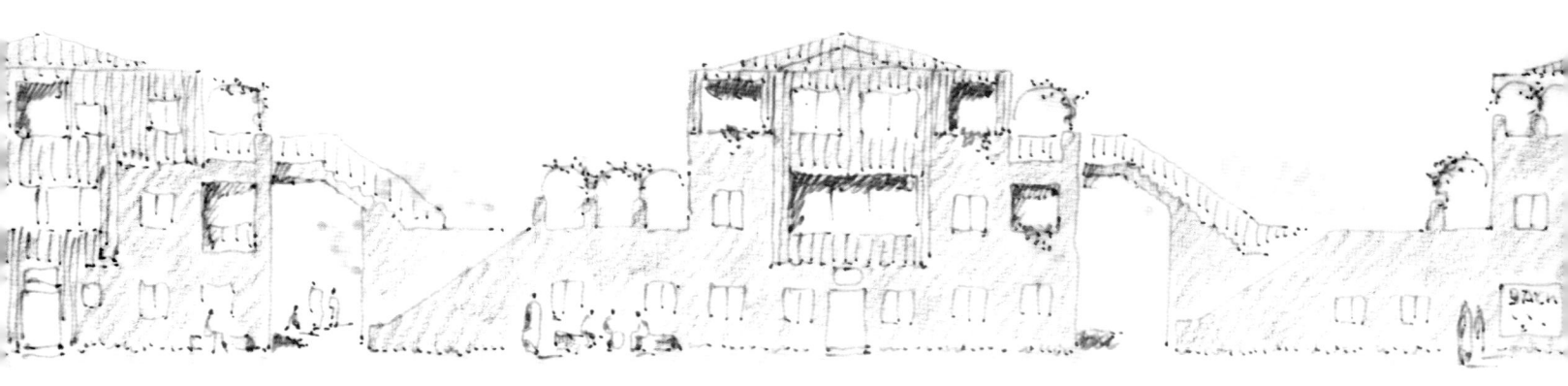

Stadtmitte

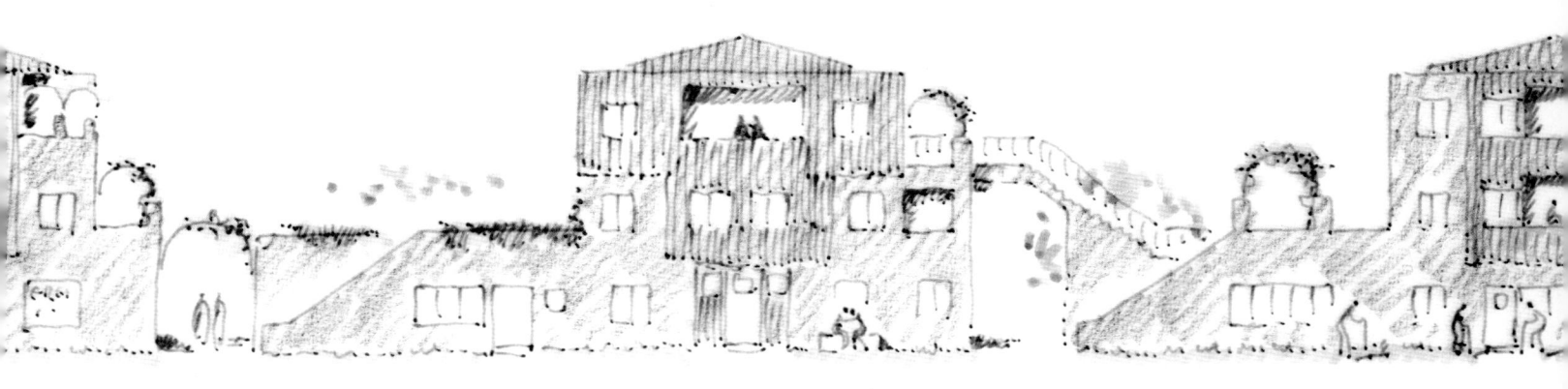

Town centre

Hochschule Bremerhaven. Bremerhaven, einstmals sehr einheitlich, kleinmaßstäblich, drei- bis viergeschossig gebaut, wurde in den sechziger und siebziger Jahren an seiner Westseite durch eine sehr hohe und maßstäblich gröbere Bebauung in zwei verschiedene Teile zerrissen. Diese Situation erscheint uns erträglich nur, wenn es gelingt, die dort entstehende Bebauung mehr und mehr in die Kleinmaßstäblichkeit der Altstadt einzubinden und auf diese Weise wieder eine Einheit herzustellen.

In diesem Rahmen haben wir unsere Aufgabe bei der Erweiterung der Hochschule Carlsberg gesehen. Daher haben wir

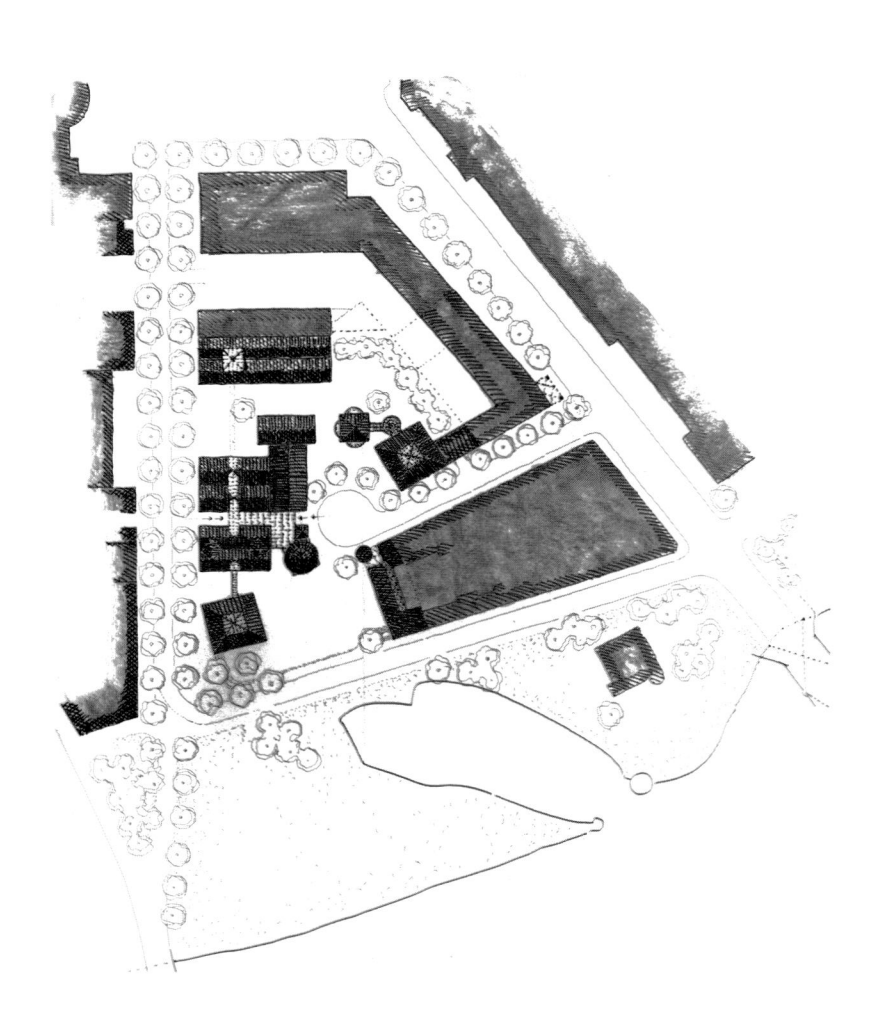

Bremerhaven University. Bremerhaven was once a very homogeneous town with a small-scale structure of 3 to 4-storey buildings. In the 1960s and 70s it was torn into two distinct parts in the west by a very high development built to a much coarser scale. The only way to make this situation more acceptable, it seemed to us, was to integrate the high-rise development going up there into the small-scale structure of the old part of the city and to re-establish a unity in this way.

These were the parameters within which we approached our scheme for the extension of Carlsberg University. We therefore designed an ensemble of buildings that, through the actual scale of the volumes and the creation of streets and other

eine Baugruppe geplant, die in den Baumassen wie in der Straßen-Platzbildung Übergänge von der alten in die neue Struktur herstellt.
Ein Straßenweg führt teilweise als Passage durch die Gebäudegruppe und erweitert sich zu einer Halle mit Treppen, Brücken und Erschließungswegen. Ich muß da vielleicht noch erwähnen, daß auf dem Baugelände ein altes Gebäude vorhanden war, eine ehemalige Brauerei, die auch einmal als Asyl für Auswanderer nach Amerika diente. Der Bau war verkommen und sollte eigentlich abgerissen werden. Er entpuppte sich jedoch bei weiterer Untersuchung und Behandlung als eine

open spaces, would represent a transition between the old and new structures.
A pedestrian route leads through the group of buildings. For part of its length it is in the form of a covered arcade. It widens out into a hall with stairs, bridges and various access routes. In the meantime this has established itself as a popular meeting place for students and citizens. I should perhaps mention that there was an old building on this site, — an ex-brewery that had also served for a time as a home for emigrants bound for America. This building was very dilapidated and was actually due for demolition. On closer investigation and after further treatment, it revealed itself to be a fine piece of

recht großartige Architektur von historischer Bedeutung. Außer diesem Gebäude wurde auch noch ein Betonskelett, Reste der Brauerei aus den zwanziger Jahren, integriert und zu Seminarräumen ausgebaut.
Der neue runde Turm enthält im Erdgeschoß ein Auditorium, und darüber wurden Räume für Studenten und Dozenten eingerichtet.

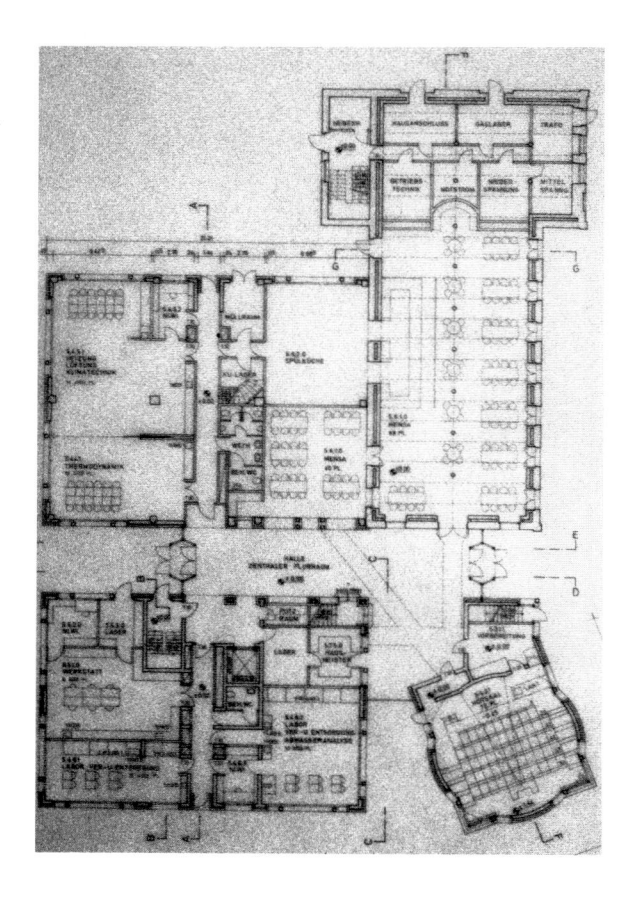

architecture and a building of historic importance. In addition to this building, a concrete skeleton structure, also part of the brewery, dating from the 1920s, was integrated into the new development and converted into seminar rooms.
The new round tower houses an auditorium on the ground floor and rooms for students and lecturers above this.

Bremerhaven — Hochschule

Bremerhaven — University

Lufthansa German Center, Beijing. Das vorgesehene Baugelände für das German Center befindet sich in einer durchgrünten Stadtrandzone Pekings. Im Anschluß soll ein großer Park entstehen, so daß der Charakter dieses Stadtgebietes festgelegt ist. In der näheren Umgebung stehen einige punktartig situierte Hochhaustürme und aller Wahrscheinlichkeit nach wird die Bebauung auf diese Weise fortgesetzt.

Wir haben deshalb das Bauvolumen für das Hotel, für die Restaurants, Appartements und Büros in kleinstflächige aber

Lufthansa German Centre, Beijing. The site foreseen for the German Centre is located in a continuous green zone on the outskirts of Peking. A large park is planned for the area adjoining the site. The character of this district is thus already determined. In the immediate vicinity are a number of high-rise point blocks, and in all probability future developments in this area will take the same form.

We therefore divided up the overall volume for the hotel, the restaurants, the apartment dwellings and offices into tall,

turmartig hohe Baukörper aufgegliedert. Sie werden in den unteren Zonen mit dem Kaufhaus und den übrigen kleinförmigen Bauten durch einen Sockel zusammengefaßt, der die Einheit des Komplexes erkennbar macht. Es war uns wichtig, daß die Grünzonen außerhalb des Gebäudes durch große Öffnungen auch ins Innere der Anlage hereingezogen werden. Mit der terrassenartigen Staffelung und Begrünung des Sockels nimmt die Anlage Bezug auf traditionelle chinesische Gärten.

tower-like structures with a minimum ground area. In the lower zones they will be linked to the department store and the other smaller-scale buildings by a plinth base that demonstrates the unity of the complex. For us it was important that the landscaped areas surrounding the development should be drawn into the interior through broad openings. In the stepped down, landscaped terraces of the plinth we made reference to the traditional Chinese garden.

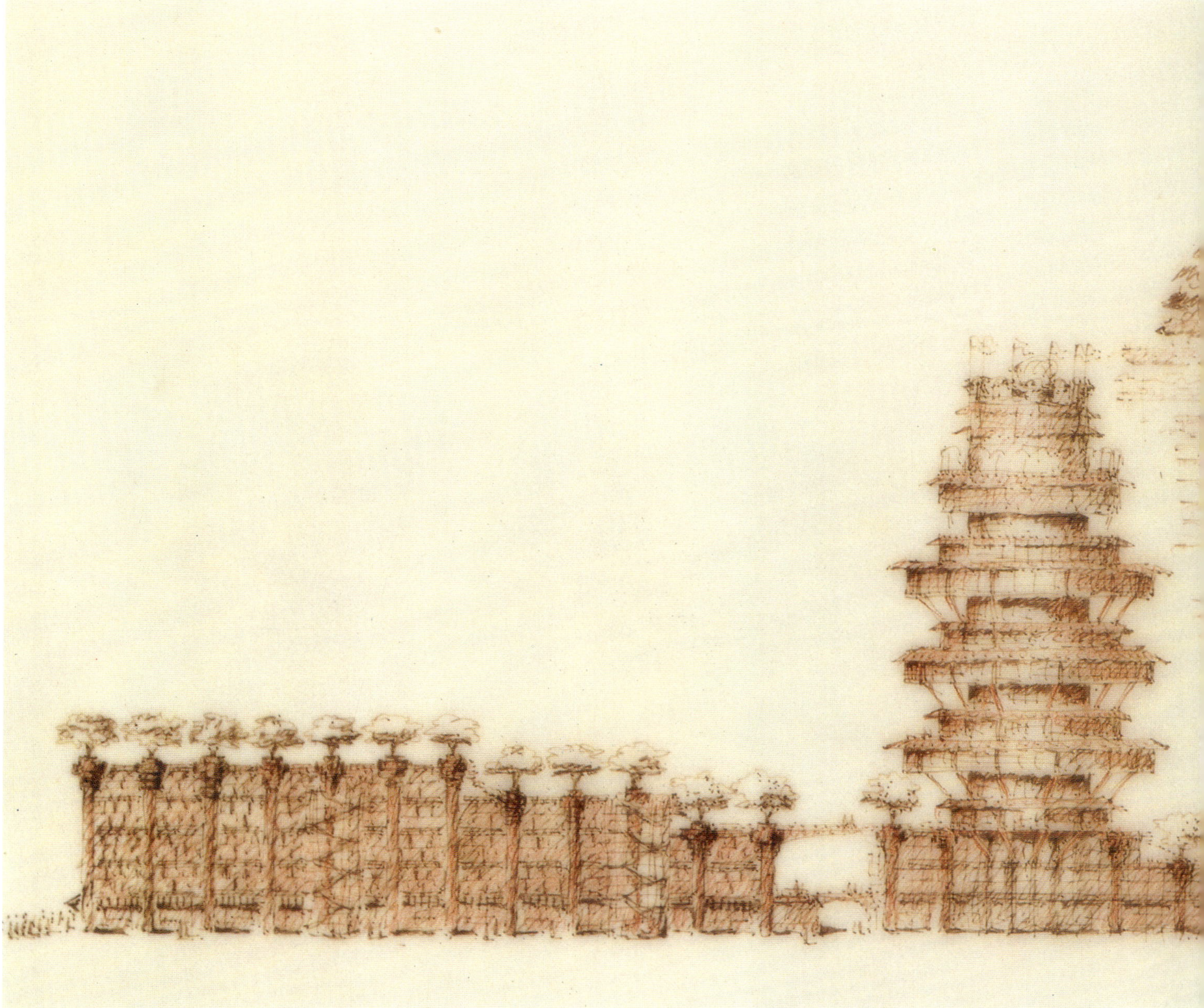

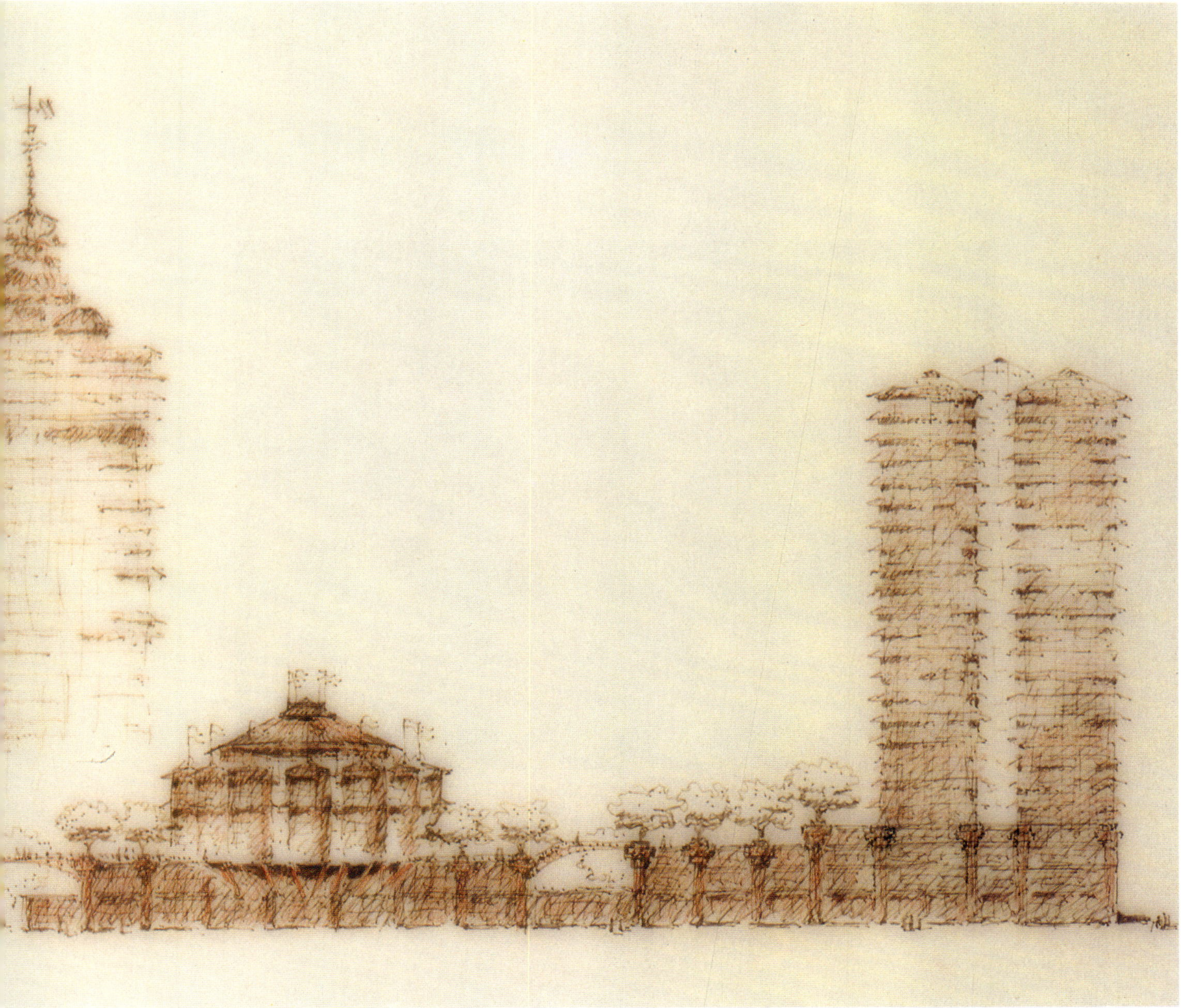

Messe Hannover. In der zentralen Grünzone des Messegeländes in Hannover soll ein neues Tagungs- und Ausstellungszentrum entstehen. Die die Grünzone umgebenden Messehallen haben den üblichen provisorischen Charakter solcher »Zweckbauten«.
Unser Gedanke war, in so einem Areal der steten baulichen Veränderung einen konstanten Kern zu schaffen, der durch Übernahme städtischer Elemente und Materialien Bezüge zur Stadt Hannover und zur Region herstellt. Es wäre für die Prä-

Hanover Trade Fair. A new daytime area and exhibition centre is planned in the landscaped area at the heart of the trade fair site in Hanover. The various exhibition halls surrounding this landscaped zone have the provisional character usually associated with functional buildings of this kind.
Our concept was to create a permanent core structure in an area that was subject to constant constructional change, and by incorporating urban elements and materials, to establish a relationship to the city of Hanover itself and to the region as a whole. For the presentation of exhibits it would be important to set changes, innovations, new, untried things against a

sentation der Exponate wichtig, Wandlungen, Innovationen, Unerprobtes immer auch vor einem Hintergrund des Beständigen zu stellen. Demzufolge haben wir eine Anlage vorgeschlagen, die als städtische Enklave in der Grünzone liegt. In ihrem Kern sind sämtliche geforderten Einrichtungen konzentriert. Ein ringsumlaufender Arkadengang im Erdgeschoß erschließt die Ausstellungshallen, Bankfilialen, das Postamt und eine Reihe von Läden und bildet zugleich den Übergang ins Grüngelände. Befahrbare Rampen führen zum platzartigen großen Foyer im Obergeschoß und dem ebenfalls ringsum-

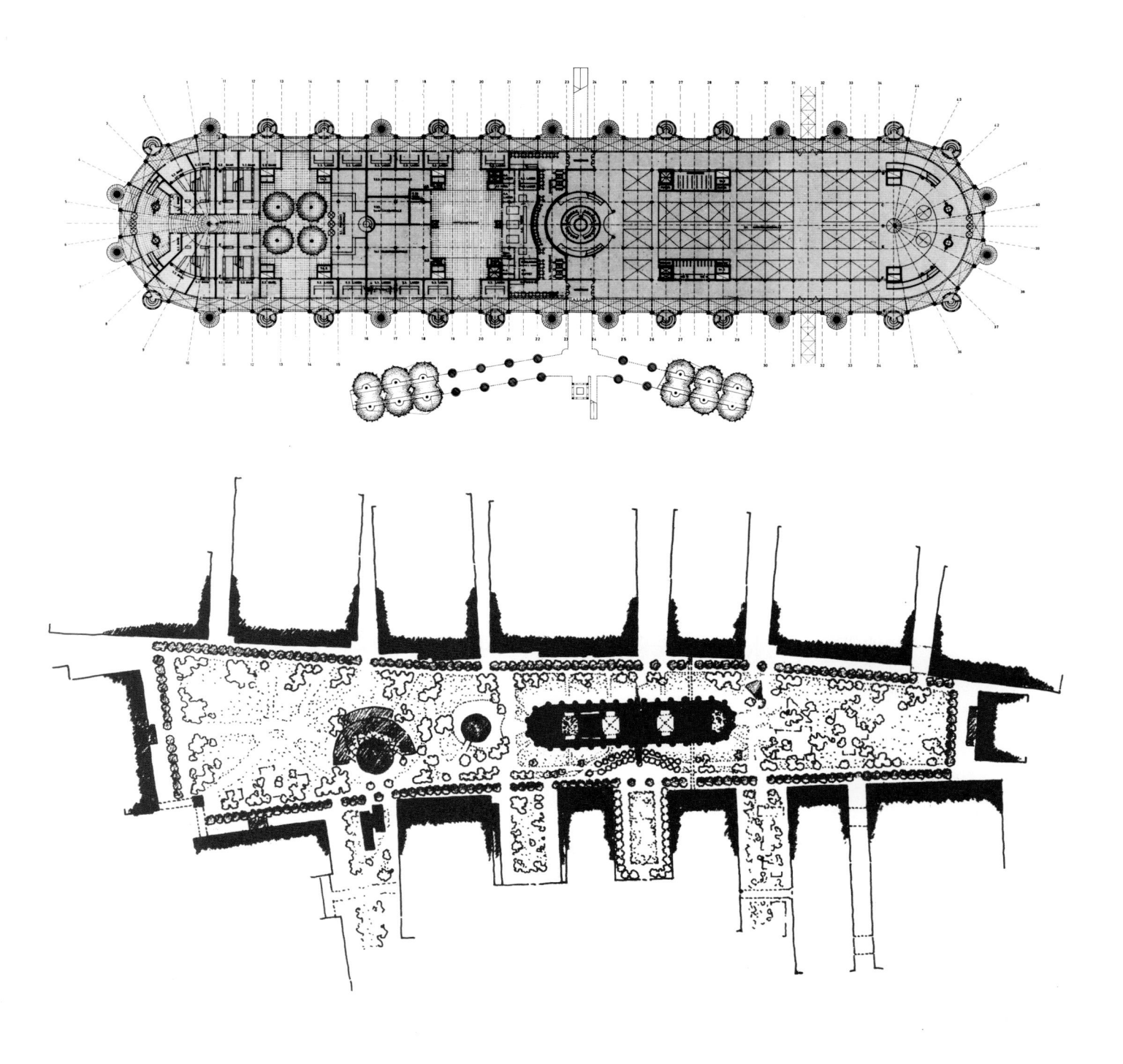

background of permanence. We accordingly proposed a development that would have the character of an urban enclave set in this green, landscaped zone. Concentrated at its heart would be all the facilities required in such a situation. A ground floor arcade about the circumference provides access to the exhibition halls, to the branches of the various banks, to the post office and a number of shops. At the same time it also forms a transition to the surrounding landscaped area. Vehicular ramps lead up to a large foyer in the nature of a public square on the upper floor and to the promenade, which also runs round the perimeter of the building. From here one enjoys changing views into the exhibition areas, restaurants and shops,

laufenden Promenadenweg. Von diesem aus hat man immer wieder neue Einblicke und Durchblicke in Ausstellungsräume, Restaurants und Läden, Höfe und Treppenhäuser und natürlich auch nach außen ins Grüngelände mit den Ausstellungshallen. Dadurch kann der Aufenthalt im Foyer zum abwechslungsreichen Flanieren werden, wie man es in einer Stadtstraße gewöhnt ist.

Nach außen hin wird der Promenadenweg von einzelnen Baukörpern begleitet. Ihre massive Bauweise in Ziegelstein bildet einen Kontrast zur Transparenz der Zwischenräume und -höfe mit ihrer leichten Stahlkonstruktion. Dadurch stehen die

courtyards and staircases, and of course to the green planted area outside and the other exhibition halls beyond. The foyer therewith provides the occasion to take an enjoyable stroll, much as one might do in a street in town.

On the outside the promenade is flanked by a series of individual buildings. The permanent form of their construction – in brickwork – is contrasted with the light steel construction and transparency of the intermediate spaces and courtyards. As a result, the technical building components do not assume such prominence. Nowadays one often finds that public buildings are given a highly technical appearance. In many ways this is the converse of the phenomenon of former times, when

technischen Bauteile nicht so sehr im Vordergrund. Es ist ja üblicherweise heute so, daß man repräsentative Gebäude technifiziert, im Gegensatz zu früheren Zeiten, als man technische Bauten, wie Fabriken und dergleichen, palastartig ummantelt hat.

Wir haben das Technische der Bauteile dort gezeigt, wo es sinnvoll und notwendig war. Wir haben aber auch, wo es möglich war, schlichte einfache Konstruktionen und Materialien gewählt, die, wie schon erwähnt, den Charakter des Vertrauten und Bleibenden ebenfalls als wichtiges Element in die Kernanlage der Messestadt bringen.

technical buildings such as factories and the like would be disguised and given the outward appearance of palaces.
We allowed the technical nature of the building elements to remain visible at those points where it was justified and necessary. Wherever possible we chose simple, straightforward materials and forms of construction. As has already been remarked, this lends the facilities a quality of permanence and familiarity, a tried and trusted look that is an important component of the trade fair.

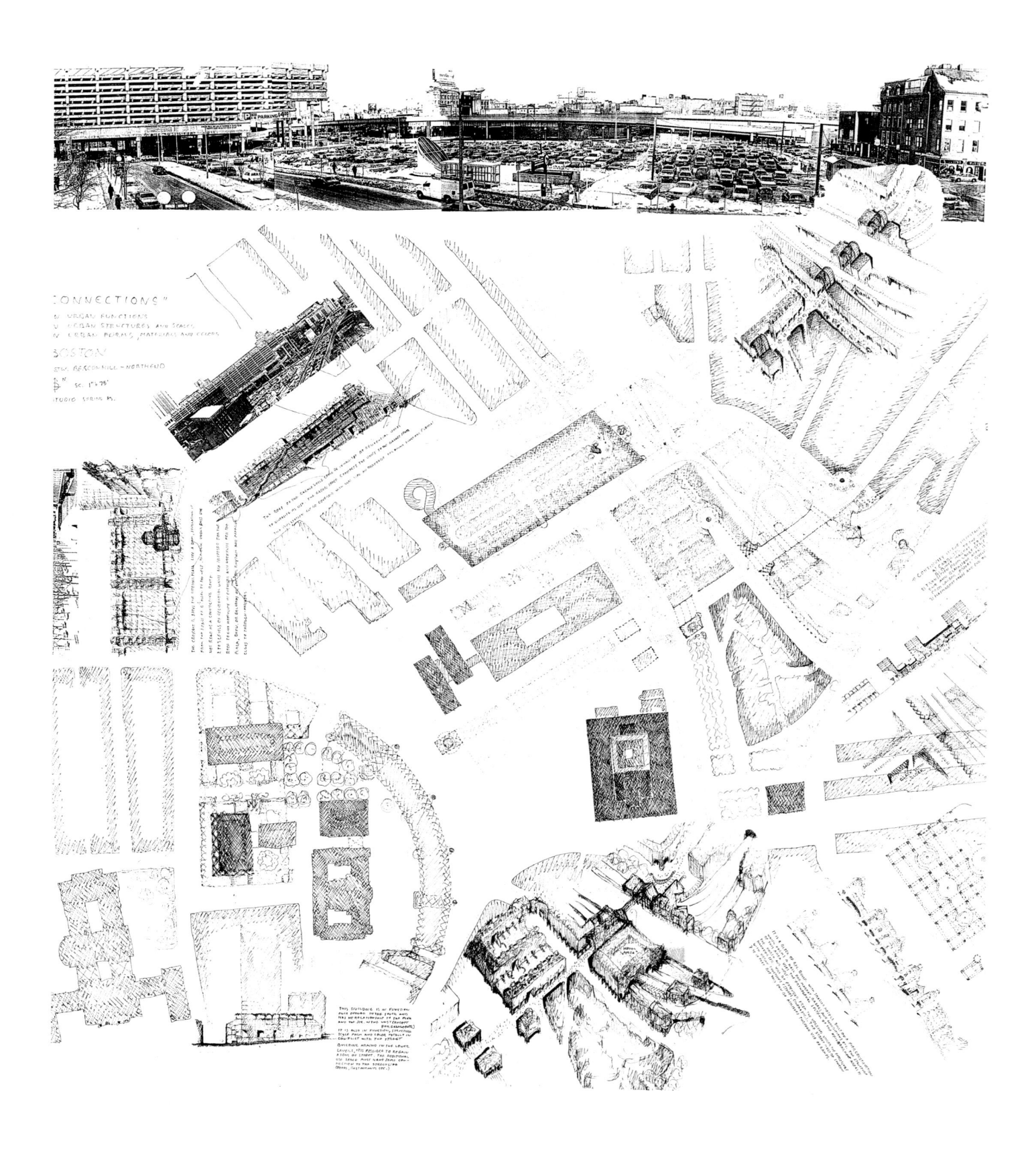

Boston, Stadtzentrum — Seminararbeit am Massachusetts Institute of Technology, Cambridge, 1983

Boston, city centre — Seminar project at M. I. T., Cambridge, Mass., 1983

Philadelphia, Zwischenbereich Stadtzentrum-Universitätscampus   Seminararbeit an der University of Pennsylvania, 1985

Philadelphia, transitional realm; city centre—university campus   Seminar project at University of Pennsylvania, 1985

Starnberg, Seeufersanierung. Starnberg ist eine kleine Stadt am schönen oberbayerischen Starnberger See. Aber sie liegt dennoch nicht an ihrem See. Eine breite, etwas erhöhte Bahntrasse versperrt von der Stadt her den Ausblick, und auch der Zugang zum Seeufer ist nur durch niedrige Fußgängerunterführungen möglich.

Eine Untertunnelung der Bahn wäre sehr kostspielig, und mit ihrem Verschwinden ginge für den Ort etwas sehr Typisches verloren. Aber auch das Stehen und Warten am Bahnsteig der Station, das jetzt mit einem schönen Ausblick auf Stadt und See verbunden ist, würde durch den unerfreulichen Aufenthalt in einer U-Bahnstation ersetzt werden. Eine Untertunnelung der Bahn wäre auch für die Reisenden von Nachteil, denn hier ist die einzige Möglichkeit, vom Zug aus den See zu erblicken, was immer wieder als überraschendes und schönes Erlebnis empfunden wird. Die von uns vorgeschlagene brückenar-

Lake-Shore Rehabilitation, Starnberg. Starnberg is a small town on the beautiful Upper Bavarian lake of the same name south of Munich. Starnberg does not lie directly on its lake, however. A wide, somewhat elevated railway strip blocks the view from the town, and the only access to the shore of the lake is via low pedestrian underpasses. Lowering the railway line into a tunnel would be an extremely expensive operation; and the removal of the station from the surface would mean the loss of something very characteristic of the place. Waiting on the platform for a train, which is now combined with attractive views of the lake and the town, would be replaced by a not particularly pleasant wait in an underground station. Laying the railway in a tunnel would also have the disadvantage for passengers that they would lose the only opportunity of seeing the lake from such close quarters from the train, – a most attractive event and an experience that always comes as something of a surprise. Our suggestion to elevate the railway line on a viaduct-like structure would retain the advantages of the

tige Hochlegung der Bahn erhält die gegenwärtigen Vorteile, zudem stellt sie in breiter Front eine Öffnung der Stadt zum Ufer her und läßt Starnberg zur Stadt am See werden.
Der See könnte in das Innere des Ortes ausgedehnt werden, so daß das Leben und Treiben eines Bootshafens auch zum städtischen Ereignis wird. Eine Schiffswerft an der Ecke zum Hafen würde in der Uferzone als Handwerksbetrieb für normales Stadtleben sorgen. Wir schlagen vor, einige Brückenbogen mit Restaurants, Cafés, Läden und eventuell mit einem kleinen Schiffahrtsmuseum auszubauen. Diese Attraktionen bringen natürlich auch während der Winterzeit eine Belebung. Als Schallschutz ist entlang der Bahn zur Stadt hin eine verglaste Wand geplant. Dadurch bekommt die Bahnbrücke mehr den Charakter eines transparenten Gebäudes, das den Rand der Stadt zum See hin markiert.

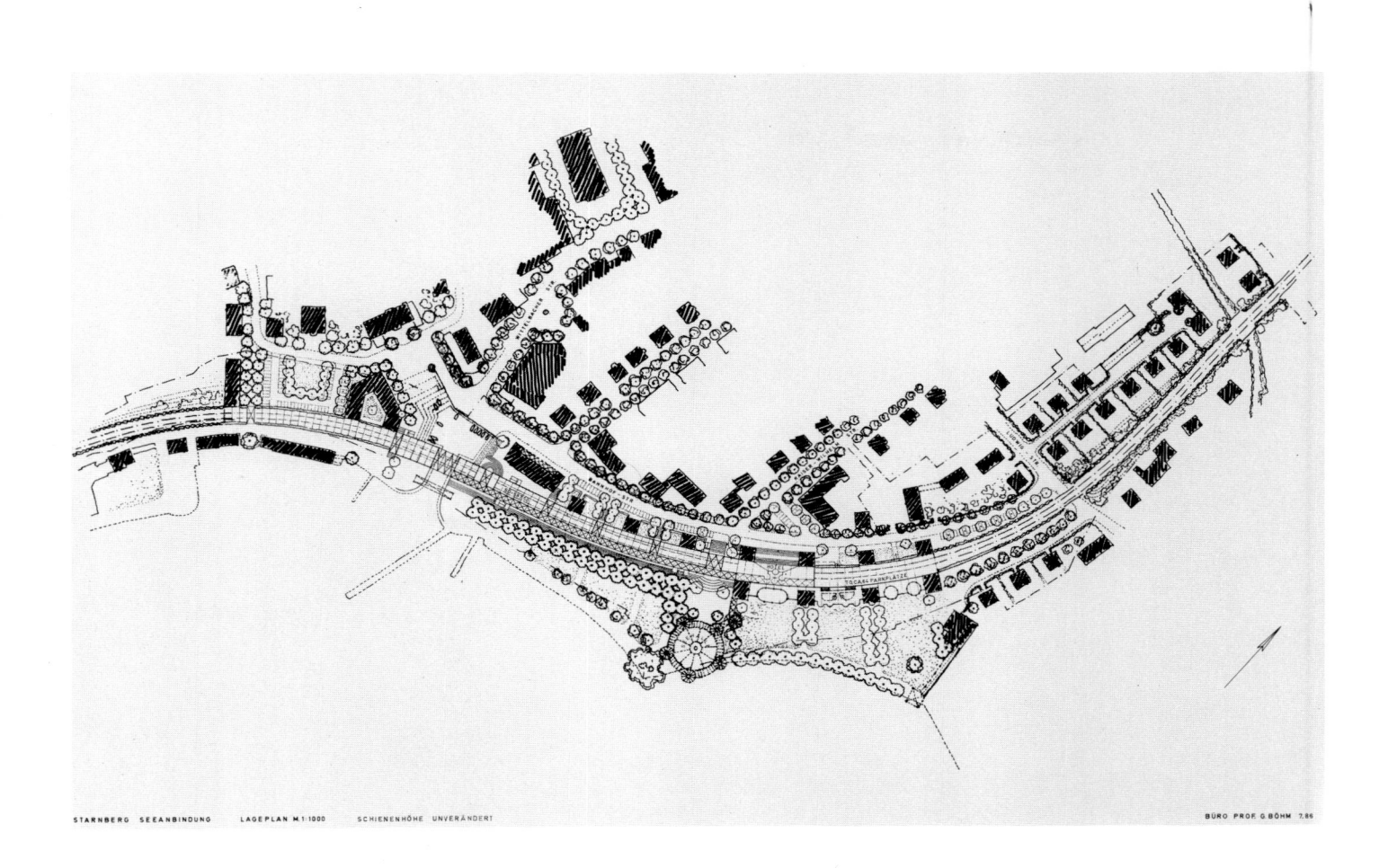

present situation and would at the same time create an opening on a broad front from the town to the lake shore, thus permitting Starnberg to become a town truly on the lake.
The lake could also be drawn into the interior of the town, so that the bustle and activity of a harbour would become an urban event. A shipyard at the corner of the harbour would bring normal urban life and a skilled trade to the lakeside area. We propose housing restaurants, cafés, shops and possibly a small shipping museum in a series of arches under the viaduct. These attractions would of course also ensure a vertain amount of activity in winter.
A glass wall is planned along the railway line on the side facing the town as an acoustic barrier. The viaduct will then have something of the character of a transparent building, defining the edge of the town towards the lake.

Starnberg   Seeufersanie

Starnberg   Lake-Shore Rehabilit

Eisenbahnbrücke

Railway viaduct

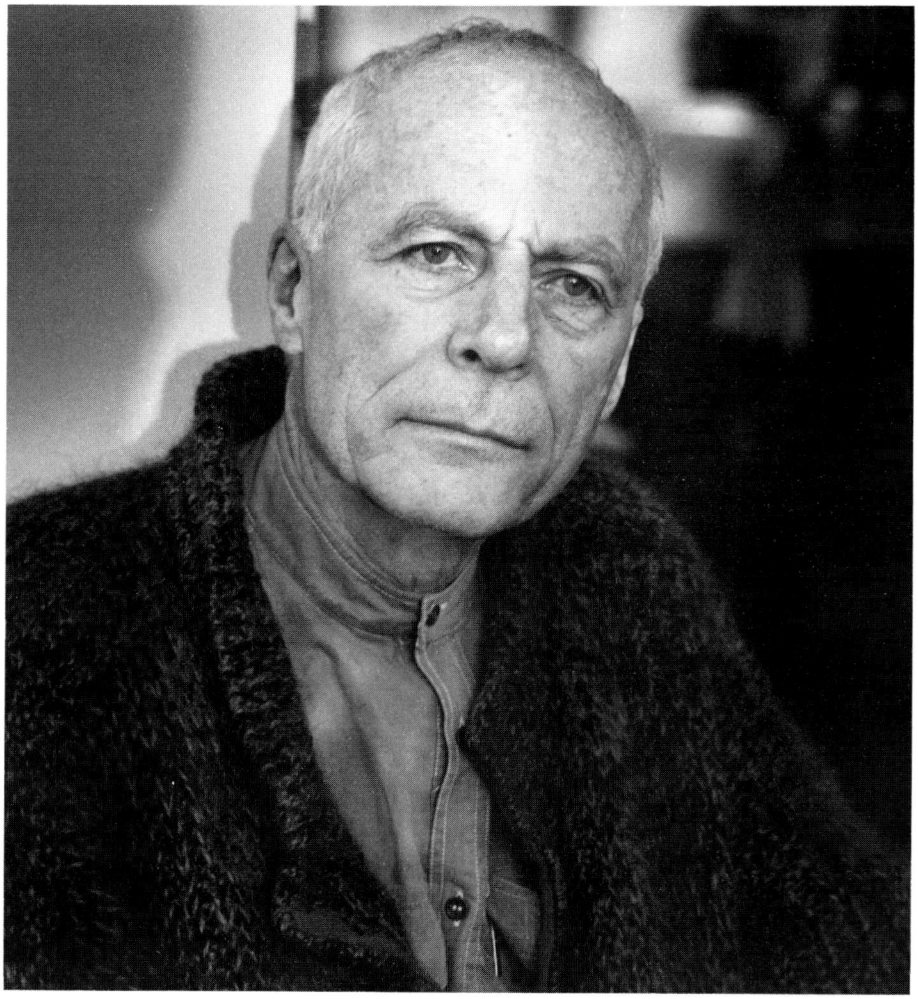

	1920	Born in Offenbach, Germany, the son of Prof. Dominikus Böhm and Maria Böhm, née Scheiber
	1939	Matriculation examinations at Aposteln Gymnasium, Cologne
	1942 –1947	Studied architecture and sculpture at Technical University, and Academy of Arts, Munich
	1948	Married Dipl.-Ing. Elisabeth Haggenmüller
	1948	Collaboration with father, Dominikus Böhm, on projects in Cologne
	1950	Worked with Rudolph Schwartz (City of Cologne Reconstruction Corporation)
	1951	Worked in office of C. Baumann, architect, New York
	1952	Collaboration with his father until the latter's death in 1955
	1955	Took over direction of his father's architect's office
	1963	Professor at the Technical University of Rhineland-Westphalia in Aachen (Chair for Urban Planning and Materials)
	1968	Member of Academy of Arts, Berlin
	1976	Member of German Academy for Urban and Regional Planning, Berlin
	1983	Member of Academy of Architecture, Paris
	1983 + 1986	Conducted a seminar at M. I. T., Cambridge, Mass.
	1985	Conducted a seminar at University of Pennsylvania, Philadelphia
	1986	Member of Academia Pontificia ad Pantheon, Rome
	1988	Conducted a seminar at Washington University, St. Louis

Various prizes and awards at home and abroad, including:

Pritzker Architecture Prize 1986
Cret Chair 1985/86, University of Pennsylvania
Fritz Schumacher Prize for Architecture, Hamburg, 1985
Honorary doctor of Technical University, Munich, 1985
Grande Médaille d'or of the Academy of Architecture, Paris, 1982
Honorary Fellow of AIA, USA, 1982
Honorary professor of National University »F. Villarreal«, Lima, 1977
BDA »Großer Preis«, Bonn, 1975
Eduard von der Haydt Prize
Gebhard Fugel Prize

Ortsregister

Amsterdam
  Rathaus, Wettbewerbsentwurf 1973, S. 126
Bad Kreuznach
  Ausbau einer Burgruine als Restaurant, 1969–76, S. 218
Bensberg
  Rathaus, 1962–64, S. 124
Bensberg-Refrath
  Kinderdorf, 1963–65, S. 30
Bergisch-Gladbach
  Bürgerhaus, 1977–80, S. 158
Berlin
  Fasanenplatz, Wohnbaukomplex, 1984, S. 50
  Hasenheide, Wohnbebauung, Projekt 1980, S. 44
  Prager Platz, Projekt 1977–80, S. 54
  Prager Platz, Schwimmbad, Projekt 1977, S. 216
Blumenau, Brasilien
  Kirche 1954, S. 81
Bocholt
  Rathaus und Kulturzentrum 1973–77, S. 128, 153
Bonn
  Theater, Wettbewerbsentwurf 1959, S. 148
  Bundestag-Bundesrat, Entwurf 1974, S. 191
  Zwischenbereich Bonn/Bad Godesberg mit dem Regierungsviertel, Gesamtprojekt 1977, S. 188
Boston
  Stadtzentrum, Seminararbeit 1983, S. 302
Brusque, Brasilien
  Kirche 1955, S. 81
Bremerhaven
  Hochschule, 1. Bauabschnitt 1985, S. 290
Dudweiler, Saar
  Stadtmitte 1979, S. 286
  Bürgerhaus mit Theater 1979, S. 154
Düsseldorf-Garath
  Gemeindezentrum mit Altenheim, Kindergarten, Läden und Wohnungen, 1962–64, S. 40
Essen-Werden
  Theater- und Konzertsaal, 1986, S. 182
Formosa (Taiwan)
  Missionsstation, 1960, S. 86
Frankfurt a. M.
  Messehallen und Verwaltung, Wettbewerbsentwurf, 1985, S. 248
Hamburg
  Museumserweiterung, Wettbewerbsentwurf 1986, S. 208
Hannover
  Das neue Steintor, Wettbewerbsentwurf 1984, S. 265
  Messe, Wettbewerbsentwurf 1986, S. 298
Kalscheuren
  Kirche, 1958, S. 80
Itzehoe
  Stadttheater, Projekt 1984, S. 147, 164
Kassel
  Friedrichplatz, Wettbewerbsentwurf 1978, S. 258
Kassel-Wilhelmshöhe
  Pfarrkirche, 1958–59, S. 90
Kettwig
  Gemeindezentrum, 1. Bauabschnitt 1977, 2. Bauabschnitt 1983, S. 110
Köln
  Bürgerzentrum »Feuerwache«, Wohnungen und Gewerbe, Projekt 1980, S. 214
  Museumsneubau, Wettbewerbsentwurf 1979, S. 278
  Dom-Bereich, Sanierungsvorschlag 1984, S. 284
  Pfarrzentrum, Krefelder Straße, 1961, S. 92
  Platz Heumarkt, Sanierungsvorschlag 1980, S. 270
  Platz Heumarkt, Hotel Maritim, Projekt 1987, S. 274
  Rathaus, Wettbewerbsentwurf 1960, S. 123
  St. Columba, 1949–50, S. 76
  St. Columba, 1. Wiederaufbau-Projekt 1948, S. 79
  St. Columba, Erweiterungsprojekt 1957, S. 78
  Technisches Rathaus, Wettbewerbsentwurf 1975, S. 134
Köln-Chorweiler
  Sozialer Wohnungsbau, 1967, S. 34
Köln-Kalk
  Rathaus, Projekt 1986, S. 136
Köln-Melaten
  Kirche, 1. Entwurf 1963, S. 105
  Kirche mit Jugendheim und Bibliothek, 1968–70, S. 104
Köln-Weiss
  Wohnhaus, 1955, S. 20
Mannheim
  Universitätsbibliothek, 1987, S. 220
München
  Wohnhaus, 1967, S. 24
  Residenztheater, Wettbewerbsentwurf, 1984, S. 180
Neulussheim
  Brücke, 1986, S. 222
Neviges
  Wallfahrtskirche, 1962–64, S. 96
Oldenburg
  Pfarrkirche, 1958, S. 88
Paderborn
  Diözesanmuseum und Wohnungen, 1969–71, S. 204
Philadelphia
  Zwischenbereich Stadtzentrum-Universitätscampus, Seminararbeit 1985, S. 303
Peking
  Lufthansa German Center, Wettbewerbsentwurf 1986, S. 294
Porz-Zündorf
  Sanierung, Projekt 1973–80, S. 26
  Einfamilien-Reihenhäuser, 1980 und 1986, S. 27, 28
Rheinberg
  Stadthaus, 1977–80, S. 130
Saarbrücken
  Baukomplex, Talstraße, 1978, S. 46
  St. Albert, 1951, S. 80
  Schloßbereich-Sanierung, Wettbewerbsvorschlag 1978, S. 196
  Schloßrestaurierung, Projekt 1979, S. 201
  Schloß-Mittelrisalit-Neubau, 1987, S. 202
Salzburg-Aigen
  Altenwohnheim mit Krankenhaus, Wettbewerb 1986, S. 66
Seeger, Allgäu
  Seeger Haus, 1948, S. 18
Schildgen bei Köln
  Pfarrkirche, 1958, S. 84
Starnberg
  Seeanbindung, Städtebauliches Gutachten 1986, S. 304
Stuttgart
  Umgestaltung des Opernhauses, Wettbewerb 1981, S. 168
  Pavillon-Anbau, 1984, S. 172
  Züblin-Haus, Verwaltung, 1984, S. 228
  Daimler-Benz AG, Verwaltung, Wettbewerb 1982, S. 254
Trier
  Theater, Wettbewerbsentwurf, 1959, S. 150
  Dom-Restaurierung, 1969–75, S. 116
Tubarao, Brasilien
  Kathedrale, Projekt 1957, S. 82
Turin-Lingotto
  FIAT-Werke, Vorschlag 1983, S. 60
Wesseling
  Rathaus für eine Industriestadt, Wettbewerbsentwurf 1969, S. 138
Wigratzbad
  Wallfahrtskirche, 1972–76, S. 114

Index of place names

Amsterdam
  City Hall, competition design, 1973, p. 126
Bad Kreuznach
  conversion of castle ruins into restaurant, 1969–76, p. 218
Bensberg
  Town Hall, 1962–64, p. 124
Bensberg-Refrath
  children's village, 1963–65, p. 30
Bergisch-Gladbach
  civic hall, 1977–80, p. 158
Berlin
  Fasanenplatz, housing complex, 1984, p. 50
  Hasenheide, housing scheme, 1980, p. 44
  Prager Platz project 1977–80, p. 54
  Prager Platz, swimming baths project, 1977, p. 216
Blumenau, Brazil
  church, 1954, p. 81
Bocholt
  town hall and civic centre, 1973–77, pp. 128, 153
Bonn
  theatre, competition design, 1959, p. 148
  Bundestag-Bundesrat scheme, 1974, p. 191
  area between Bonn and Bad Godesberg, including governmental district; overall scheme, 1977, p. 188
Boston
  city centre scheme; university project, 1983, p. 302
Bremerhaven
  university, phase 1, 1985, p. 290
Brusque, Brazil
  church, 1955, p. 81
Cologne
  "Feuerwache" civic centre, housing and commercial uses; project 1980, p. 214
  new museum development, competition design, 1979, p. 278
  cathedral precinct, rehabilitation proposals, 1984, p. 284
  parish centre, Krefelder Strasse, 1961, p. 92
  Heumarkt, rehabilitation proposals, 1980, p. 270
  Heumarkt, Hotel Maritim project, 1987, p. 274
  City Hall, competition design, 1960, p. 123
  St. Columban's Church, 1949–50, p. 76
  St. Columban's Church, 1st reconstruction project, 1948, p. 79
  St. Columban's Church, extension project, 1957, p. 78
  Technical City Hall, competition design, 1975, p. 134
Cologne-Chorweiler
  public authority housing, 1967, p. 34
Cologne-Kalk
  town hall project, 1986, p. 136
Cologne-Melaten
  church, 1st design, 1963, p. 105
  church with youth club and library, 1968–70, p. 104
Cologne-Weiss
  housing, 1955, p. 20
Dudweiler, Saar
  town centre development, 1979, p. 286
  civic hall with theatre, 1979, p. 154
Düsseldorf-Garath
  community centre with old people's home, kindergarten, shops and housing, 1962–64, p. 40
Essen-Werden
  theatre and concert hall, 1986, p. 182
Formosa (Taiwan)
  missionary station, 1960, p. 86
Frankfurt-on-Main
  trade fair halls and administration buildings; competition design, 1985, p. 248
Hamburg
  gallery extension; competition design, 1986, p. 208

Hanover
  new "Steintor" development; competition design, 1984, p. 265
  trade fair, competition design, 1986, p. 298
Itzehoe
  civic theatre project, 1984, pp. 147, 164
Kalscheuren
  church, 1958, p. 80
Kassel
  Friedrichplatz, competition design, 1978, p. 258
Kassel-Wilhelmshöhe
  parish church, 1958–59, p. 90
Kettwig
  community centre phase 1, 1977; phase 2, 1983; p. 110
Mannheim
  university library, 1987, p. 220
Munich
  house, 1967, p. 24
  Residenztheater, competition design, 1984, p. 180
Neulussheim
  bridge, 1986, p. 222
Neviges
  pilgrimage church, 1962–64, p. 96
Oldenburg
  parish church, 1958, p. 88
Paderborn
  diocesan museum and housing, 1969–71, p. 204
Peking
  Lufthansa German Center; competition design, 1986, p. 294
Philadelphia
  area between city centre and university campus; university project, 1983, p. 303
Porz-Zündorf
  rehabilitation scheme, 1973–80, p. 26
  single-family terraced housing, 1980, 1986, pp. 27, 28
Rheinberg
  town hall, 1977–80, p. 130
Saarbrücken
  Talstrasse complex, 1978, p. 46
  St. Albert's, 1951, p. 80
  palace precinct rehabilitation; competition proposals, 1978, p. 196
  palace restoration project, 1979, p. 201
  palace: central tract, 1987, p. 202
Salzburg-Aigen
  old people's home with hospital; competition, 1986, p. 66
Schildgen, near Cologne
  parish church, 1958, p. 84
Seeger, Allgäu
  Seeger House, 1948, p. 18
Starnberg
  lake-shore link; urban planning study, 1986, p. 304
Stuttgart
  opera house redesign; competition, 1981, p. 168
  opera house; pavilion extension, 1984, p. 172
  Züblin Administration Building, 1984, p. 228
  Daimler-Benz Administration; competition, 1982, p. 254
Trier
  theatre; competition design, 1959, p. 150
  cathedral restoration, 1969–75, p. 116
Tubarao, Brazil
  cathedral project, 1957, p. 82
Turin-Lingotto
  Fiat works proposals, 1983, p. 60
Wesseling
  town hall for an industrial community; competition design, 1969, p. 138
Wigratzbad
  pilgrimage church, 1972–76, p. 114

Fotographenverzeichnis / Index of Photographers

Inge Bartholomé, Aachen: 21, 31, 112–113 oben
Klaus Beckmannshagen, Wuppertal: 27, 41, 48, 49, 109, 132, 133
Beton-Verlag, Düsseldorf: 100, 223
Manfred Hanisch, Essen-Rüttenscheid: 32, 97
Peter Kleinert, Köln: 125
Foto Kops, Köln: 30
Bruno Krupp, Freiburg: 152
Ingrid von Kruse, Wuppertal: 308
Dieter Leistner, Dortmund: 43, 159, 160–161, 182, 183, 207, 222, 288, 291, 293
Isolde Luckert, Köln: 153
Marie-Luise Manthei, Aachen: 22, 23
Ivan Nemec, Frankfurt a.M.: 158
Artur Pfau, Mannheim: 85, 91
Inge von der Ropp, Köln: 124
Inge + Arved von der Ropp, Köln: 39, 42, 69, 101, 106–107, 162–163, 205, 219
Hugo Schmölz, Köln: 77, 93
Karl Hugo Schmölz, Köln: 176, 177, 178, 229, 231, 239, 240–241
Schmölz-Huth, Köln: 95
Thorbecke, Postkartenverlag W. Koessler, Lindenberg, Allgäu: 114
Züblin-Bildstelle, Stuttgart: 226, 234, 236, 238